BEASTS BEYOND BELIEF

SNEAKY WEREWOLVES, FLYING CATS, AND ACCIDENTAL APES

Michael D. Winkle

illustrated by Mel. White

UNCLE BEAR
PUBLISHING®

Beasts Beyond Belief
Sneaky Werewolves, Flying Cats, and Accidental Apes

Copyright © 2026 by Michael D. Winkle

This publication is a creative work fully protected by all applicable copyright laws, as well as by misappropriation, trade secret, unfair competition, and other applicable laws.

No part of this book may be reproduced in any form without permission in writing from the publisher, except by a reviewer who wishes to quote brief passages in connection with a review written for inclusion in a magazine, newspaper, or website.

All rights to this publication will be vigorously defended. For reviewers who wish to obtain copies of this book or to obtain author interviews or other information, please contact the publisher at (760) 902-5960 or email contact@unclebearpublishing.com. You may also write to:

Uncle Bear Publishing, LLC
68089 Risueno Rd.
Cathedral City, CA 92234-3690

Uncle Bear Publishing® is a registered trademark of Uncle Bear Publishing, LLC.

Cover and interior illustrations: Mel. White

ISBN: 979-8-9922415-0-1
Library of Congress Control Number: 2025942531

Printed in the United States of America.

Please visit us at www.unclebearpublishing.com

BEASTS BEYOND BELIEF

SNEAKY WEREWOLVES, FLYING CATS, AND ACCIDENTAL APES

Michael D. Winkle

illustrated by Mel. White

UNCLE BEAR PUBLISHING

All text and images in this publication have been created
by human authors, artists, and photographers.
Uncle Bear Publishing pledges to never use
AI-generated content in its books.

No computers were harmed in the creation of this publication,
but some trees were. Sorry about that.
Our office is solar powered, so we think that may help, don't you?
Why are you still reading this silly notice?

ABOUT THE AUTHOR

Michael Dayne Winkle was born in Tulsa, Oklahoma, many long years ago. He marks important life events mainly by the books he has encountered. The high point of Hoover Elementary School, for instance, was discovering the works of Jules Verne and H. G. Wells. High school in the small town of Bixby coincided with his discovery of science fiction literature, H. P. Lovecraft, Andre Norton, P. J. Farmer's pulp-hero meta-fiction, Marvel Comics, astronomy, true crime and Charles Fort. Then came Oklahoma State University with its library of two million volumes.

After receiving a B.A. in English, Mike worked as a library assistant, bookkeeper, intern in a mortgage foreclosure office (bound to make one popular), and in the usual array of "writer experience" jobs, from car washer to postal worker. He is the author of 30 or so professionally published stories and articles, including: "Wolfhead" (*Tales of the Witch World 3*, edited by Andre Norton); "A Wondrous Portal Opened Wide," (*Illumen*. Vol. 13, no. 2, Winter 2017); and "After the Matilda Briggs Went Down" (*Orson Scott Card's Intergalactic Medicine Show*, June 2017).

In 2018, he published two nonfiction books of his own: *The Eyrie: A Book of Gryphons* and *I Heard of That Somewhere*.

Mike can be reached at the creaky old email address sakria@aol.com or at the slightly newer sakria@outlook.com.

His website, the Fantasy World Project, can be found at (predictably): http://www.fantasyworldproject.com/index.html.

ABOUT THE ILLUSTRATOR

Mel. White is a multifaceted creator and scholar. She co-wrote (with the late Robert Asprin) and illustrated the *Duncan and Mallory* graphic novels and contributed short stories to a number of anthologies, including the Mercedes Lackey collection *Sword of Ice*.

CONTENTS

Before We Begin i
Introduction iii

Aharoni's Hamsters 1
The Aura of an Ape 5
Batsquatch and Friends 9
Behind The Birds 15
Bigfoot Kidnappings 17
The Bird of Lincoln's Inn 23
The Brentford Griffin 27
The Bunny-Man Cometh 29
The Carbuncle 37
The Cheshire Beasts 43
The Choccolocco Monster 49
Colorado Raptors 53
The Dark Woods Bogey-Man 57
The Elusive Coelacanth! 59
Feline Phantoms 63
Flabbit the Flying Rabbit 77
Flying Felines and the Chalk Outline Man 85
Hairy Hands of Dartmoor 91
The Hexham Heads 99
Hollywood Dogmen 111
Imitate the Action of the Tiger 115
Invasion of the Doggy Snatchers 119

The Land Between Night and Day 123
Lemmings from Heaven 137
Mammal 411...141
My Name Is Su..153
Out of Africa 161
The Pacing White Mustang 173
The Pennsylvania Ouroboros 177
The Rat-King..181
The Red Dragon Stamps 185
Return of the Megafauna 187
Rex of Sunnybank.. 203
Sneaky Werewolves 207
The Steeds of Poseidon................................213
Tales to Make Your Skin Crawl......................217
The Texas Dragon 223
Twice Told Tales...227
Victory through Were-Power 231
What Color Is Your Yeti? 241
Who Are You Calling Imaginary? 247
Wisconsin Werewolf—And Odd
  Things about Elks 251

Epilogue: The Unclassified Residuum 255

BEFORE WE BEGIN

These stories are about real animals. Almost all meet a tragic end, for this is nature's law concerning wild things. But in each is the stamp of greatness.

—Ernest Thompson Seton,
Wild Animals I Have Known

Throughout history, Earth's many life forms have met sad and painful fates at the hands of Man. This is true for paranormal or supernatural animals as well as those of more mundane varieties. As for ghostly animals, the way an animal became a ghost in the first place is often a heart-wrenching tale.

This volume contains accounts of human beings attacking various creatures, creatures attacking humans and even of humans attacking other humans while disguised as animals. In the name of accuracy for the hundreds of authors and witnesses referred to in the text, I could not bring myself to censor or bowdlerize these sometimes disturbing accounts. I myself found some of these stories difficult to write up. So if you do not think you would enjoy the emotional rollercoaster ride of flying bunnies, followed by dogs dragged off by UFOs, followed by imaginary playmates, followed by cannibalistic cults, I certainly understand. In the realm of family friendly, animal-themed literature, let me recommend the works of James Herriot, a favorite author of mine for nearly half a century.

INTRODUCTION

This is not a book about cryptozoology—not exactly. Certainly, we touch upon the subject of the search for hidden animals because this volume is about animals and the unknown. In addition to animal species as yet unrecognized by science, however, we will be looking at ghostly animals, animals of myth and folklore, animals with seemingly supernormal powers, and bizarre beasts that are not only of no known species but are not ordinary life forms in any way a zoologist—crypto- or otherwise—would define them.

There are also stories about the effects of the paranormal on animals, whether they are frightened by spirits or abducted by UFOs. We will look at stories of lycanthropy and shapeshifting in which the lines between human and animal blur. We will even look at people who affect the appearance of animals, perhaps trying to channel the spirit and abilities of other animate beings as much as any ancient cave-dwelling shaman.

In fact, we will touch upon almost every aspect of the unusual, the unknown, and the Other because any kind of paraphysical event that has ever bedeviled humanity has affected our furry, feathered, and scaly friends as well. Since they cannot narrate their own misadventures to us, however, we can only know of the relationship between animals and the unknown second hand.

THE OTHER

Human beings, for the most part, have given a human mask to the Other, whether the unknown was called ghost, specter, devil, angel, fairy, pagan god, or extraterrestrial visitor. Most of these entities are envisioned as being superior to mortal men, or at least more powerful and more frightful. Humanity also has a habit of anthropomorphizing all quantities over time. Lightning becomes a giant magic spear hurled by a giant magic man. The earth from which all life springs becomes a mother-figure, who gives birth to crops and domestic beasts every year. Totemic animals became the animal-headed gods of Egypt, which were the predecessors of the more-or-less human gods of Greece, Rome, and other lands. The Hindu bird-god Garuda, as Peter Costello points out in *The Magic Zoo*, "naturally evolved, becoming in time partly human."

"It seems that the Garuda was an older god than Vishnu, perhaps one of the aboriginal animistic gods which were taken over by the invading Hindus," continues Costello [p. 81]. Humans being what they are, Garuda became less important than Vishnu and ended up as little more than a flying mount.

Despite this, animal imagery always returns to humanity's thoughts, imagination, art, and literature. Over the centuries, Cerberus and Garm became the Black Dogs of medieval Britain and the Dogmen of the Internet and podcast era.

Why does the guise of the animal return time after time? Perhaps it is programmed into our very genes, into the collective unconscious, as Carl Jung might say. Perhaps it lies in an even older biological imperative, as Carl Sagan suggested in *The Dragons of Eden*—in a pre-human primate's eternal vigilance against hawks, bears, terror birds, saber-tooth cats, and other predators.

Perhaps each generation learns anew to appreciate the beauty, the strength, the passion and the wonderfully interconnected world of non-human creation, even in this ever-more technology-dependent, polluted, and desensitized existence.

And occasionally, perhaps, the image of the animal arises because something outside humanity, unaffected by our expectations or desires, not caring about our ideas of what should and should not exist, bears that form.

Cryptozoological writers Janet and Colin Bord looked over a vast array of unknown animal reports and divided the majority into five broad categories:

Introduction

1. Lake monsters, sea-monsters, and sea-serpents: the unknown beasts found in both fresh and salt water, of which the best known is the Loch Ness Monster. Centuries ago, such creatures were described as "serpents," but after naturalists discovered fossils of prehistoric life forms the descriptions tended toward plesiosaur- and mosasaur-type reptiles.

2. Yeti, Bigfoot, Sasquatch, Yowie, Woodwose, and other hair-covered humanoids. Specific descriptions range from the almost completely human (if hairy) to the utterly bestial, apelike, or even monkey-like, the lattermost sometimes being called "Devil Monkeys." The Bords created the acronym BHM (Big Hairy Monsters) to describe the entire spectrum of hominids and semi-hominids. Size can vary from a mere three or four feet tall, like the Agogwe of West Africa, to the truly immense Sasquatch of Canada, some individuals of which reputedly reach ten feet tall or more. Footprints often resemble the tracks of barefoot humans (which is why the beasts were dubbed Bigfoot to begin with). However, four-toed and three-toed prints, and even handlike prints like those of anthropoid apes, have been found.

3. Feline animals that resemble mountain lions, African lions, and black panthers, but are found in environments where such animals are unknown. Here we have a cryptid that is often explained away as a known animal that has escaped from a circus, zoo, or exotic pet owner—or, in the case of a puma-like beast, one that has wandered away from its usual territory. These uncatchable cats are called ABCs (Alien Big Cats) in the British Isles and Phantom Panthers in North America.

Cryptid hunters like the Bords and Loren Coleman formerly pointed to Phantom Panthers' strange behaviors when suggesting they were something beyond ordinary wild animals. They are known for attacking humans unprovoked, attacking or crashing into vehicles, killing farm animals without eating any flesh, and wandering through towns and suburbs in broad daylight. These days, encroaching urban construction has put environmental pressures on all wildlife, so I no longer think behavioral oddities are trustworthy indicators of paranormal panthers. Certainly, the number of attacks on *Homo sapiens* by *Puma concolor* has risen over the past 30 years.

A detail that remains constant is the high percentage of phantom big cats reported as being "black panthers." "Black panther" is not a species but an occasional melanistic mutation that occurs among leopards and jaguars. Such beasts are rare, and if unexplained felines were all escapees, spotted cats should vastly outnumber black ones, but the opposite is the case.

4. Black Dogs, Hellhounds, Barguests, and giant wolves. In recent times, this archetype has expanded to include huge semi- or completely bipedal canids (Dogmen, Manwolves, or "Werewolves"). It is hard to accept either the old or new permutations as being normal flesh-and-blood critters. Black dogs are usually described as being huge (calf- or sheep-sized), having long, shaggy fur, and possessing enormous fiery-red or yellow eyes that are "as wide as saucers," as one common descriptive phrase goes. They often appear mysteriously on quiet country lanes, frightening and even attacking humans and animals. They then disappear in an even more spectacular fashion: a burst of flame or a lightning-like blast.

As for Dogmen, as journalist Linda Godfrey commented after years of studying the subject, there is simply no evolutionary mechanism by which a canine species would be goaded into bipedal locomotion.

5. Giant birds, "Thunderbirds," pterosaur-like reptiles, and inhuman winged humanoids *à la* West Virginia's infamous Mothman. In recent decades, more gargoyle-like entities have been reported. This category covers basically any unknown winged creature. It is very difficult to pass these off as simple undiscovered life forms because many are simply too massive to leave the ground, according to the laws of physics. The more esoteric fliers like Mothman are supposed to reach velocities exceeding 100 miles per hour without so much as flapping their wings.

Some writers ponder deeply upon the mythological, psychological, and sociological meanings of these five cryptid classes, suggesting that they might be Jungian archetypes lurking within the subconscious mind of every human: the feline and canine beasts that lurk beyond the fire; the deadly unknown waiting beneath dark waters; the inhuman, cannibalistic ogres of our fairy tales; and the aerial hunters dreaded by our apelike ancestors.

If I read George Eberhart's bibliography *Monsters* correctly, however, the next largest group of seemingly paranormal animals is Phantom Kangaroos. It is hard to take these marsupial hoppers seriously as meaningful psychological archetypes. Perhaps Charles Fort was right in thinking that a Cosmic Clown has fun pranking humanity when life gets too grim and analytical. Or perhaps unknown animals do as they do without regard for human motives or expectations.

Introduction
WHAT ARE THEY? WHERE DO THEY COME FROM? WHY ARE THEY HERE?

One of my favorite fortean books is John Keel's *Strange Creatures from Time and Space*. One of many amazing ideas I took from this volume is known as the Window Theory. Essentially, ghosts, UFOs, monsters and assorted paranormal phenomena appear and disappear in the same distinct areas year after year, even century after century. Keel dubbed these areas "Windows," and in these places it is as if openings sometimes appear between our Earth and some other universe.

This was my favorite fortean idea as a boy. It certainly gave one an easy out if an unlikely creature was reported. Where did it come from? Another dimension. Why can't the search parties find it? It went back.

Unbelievable? Well, if monsters and phantoms weren't popping in from other spacetime continua, what did that leave? Were all creature reports hoaxes, hallucinations, or mistakes? I found that difficult to believe as well.

If parallel worlds exist, and if objects, vehicles, people and creatures can pass from one to the other, then maybe some of the world's more bizarre monster sightings are of temporary visitors from beyond. This seems especially likely if specters, creatures, and UFOs of different types appear in the same limited area—a "Window Area."

There are, of course, theories lying between the extremes of dimensional crossovers and all-hoaxes-or-mistakes. Some odd life-forms may be cryptids in the classical sense, animals that simply have not yet been captured and examined by biologists. Some may be visions of creatures that once existed but don't anymore, their images somehow embedded in the local environment, a phenomenon known as retrocognition (see "Return of the Megafauna"). Nessie, for instance, may be the visual recording of a long-deceased plesiosaur, and the huge thunderbirds of the American Midwest the recordings of teratorns or pterodactyls.

These and other theories will be discussed in the following pages, but at the end of the day we must admit that unknown animals remain mysterious.

As for myself, I admit that after half a century of clipping weird newspaper stories, digging through 200-year-old back issues of scientific journals, and shelling out money for rare paranormal publications, I'm afraid I have started backsliding. I have lost faith in the various theories and possibilities I have formed over the years, and I am not as interested in other researchers' hypotheses and explanations as I once was. I no longer stress over how a huge beast could appear in a crowded urban neighborhood or where it could go afterwards where it can't be found. I don't worry about how absurd a talking cartoonish penguin seems or why hairy humanoids, UFOs, poltergeists, and other anomalies tend to appear in the same areas at the same time. I let the reports and stories speak for themselves.

I do note correlations between events, of course, and I will mention theories as just that—hypotheses that may or may not have some bearing on the rules governing psychic or UFO or fortean phenomena. I have to consider also that some secrets may never be revealed and some events in this universe may never be explained.

The stories are entertaining, however, and the journey is fascinating; perhaps by the end of this volume we'll understand the fellow inhabitants of Earth a little better.

A NOTE ON SOURCES

The present author belongs to the old-fashioned, bookwormish sort of researcher who burrows through dusty, hardbound journals and squeaks through reels of yellowing microfilm. My distrust of internet sources—from Creepypasta and Reddit stories masquerading as reality to badly proofed entries on Project Gutenberg—reflects my prejudices. When I do refer to online sites, the reader can assume that they are maintained by researchers I trust, or else they are the only available sources for certain reports, updates, or authors.

Of all the nightmarish cryptids and specters haunting Earth, with which should we begin? What monstrosity will lead off this procession of the damned? The Beast of Gevaudan? The Hairy Hands of Dartmoor? The Black Dogs of British lore, the Waheela of the northern wastes? After long nights of pondering, I decided we will start with golden hamsters.

SOURCES:

Bord, Janet and Colin. *Alien Animals* (Harrisburg, PA: Stackpole Books, 1981).

Costello, Peter. *Magic Zoo* (New York: St. Martin's Press, 1979).

Eberhart, George M. *Monsters: A Guide to Information on Unaccounted for Creatures* (New York: Garland Publishing, 1983).

Keel, John A. *Strange Creatures from Time and Space* (Greenwich, CT: Fawcett Publications, 1970).

Sagan, Carl. *Dragons of Eden* (New York: Ballantine Books, 1977).

AHARONI'S HAMSTERS

As a child, like many children, I kept a variety of pets: goldfish, kittens, a box turtle, a dog. I also tried terrariums with crickets, praying mantises, and lizards, with varying levels of success.

I read about all sorts of animals, wanting to raise them all, but a passage in one of Carroll B. Colby's books for young readers made me stop and think.

> "All the golden hamsters we keep as pets today are descended from one family—an adult female and her litter of twelve which were captured alive in a burrow near Aleppo in Syria in 1930. Strangely enough, there is no record of any wild hamsters being captured since then."
> [Colby, p. 63]

The story of this small, unassuming, long-furred rodent struck me as very strange, even at age nine. It sounded like the discoverer, a zoologist named Israel Aharoni, had either come across a species on the verge of extinction and brought it back, or a pregnant representative of a species not of this earth had popped out of thin air in the arid hills of Syria.

Of course there was more to the story. Chris Henwood, an expert in small rodent husbandry, looked into the matter for the British Hamster

Beasts Beyond Belief

Association. The golden hamster did not pop out of nowhere. It was first mentioned by Alexander Russell in his 1797 book, *The Natural History of Aleppo*. It was described in greater detail in 1839 by George Robert Waterhouse, the young (age 29 at the time) curator of the London Zoological Society, based on "a single rather elderly female specimen" caught in Aleppo. (Henwood asks, "Isn't it strange how Aleppo appears at every stage in the history of this species?")

Aharoni's 1930 specimens were housed in a wooden box, which they promptly chewed through. Nine were recaptured; then five more escaped. Not to worry, though: The four that remained produced scores of pups within a year.

Despite their prolific rate of reproduction, golden hamsters proved exceedingly hard to find in the wild. None are known to have been captured between 1930 and May 1971, when 13 were caught near Aleppo. A rodent control officer found two in 1980 that had eaten rat poison, and the same officer caught two alive in 1982. It is probable that all of these were descendants of the 1930 escapees.

Golden hamsters may not be dimensional visitors, but they are so rare in the wild they might as well be. Forty-one years without an appearance of a species—especially one that seems to lurk exclusively near a city as large as Aleppo—is suggestive of extinction. Its reappearance puts one in mind of John Michell and Robert J. M. Rickard's "theory of revivals," outlined in their book *Living Wonders* (1983), based loosely in turn on the works of biologist Rupert Sheldrake and Austrian zoologist Paul Kammerer. Essentially, living creatures—all the members of a single species—leave a sort of echo—a "field"—in spacetime. Under certain circumstances these "species-fields" might act as templates, causing the chromosomes of a similar species to develop into those of the first, "even though it may have been extinct for millions of years."

"We note that among all the hidden beasts whose existence is hinted at by the cryptozoologists—the giant reptiles, pterodactyls, mammoths, hairy bipeds and the great unknowns of seas and lakes—there is nothing new." [Michell and Rickard, p. 36]. This is an odd theory, but a useful one. It might be that animals far more spectacular than hamsters could return one day.

On second thought, compared to the "theory of revivals," perhaps it is not too outlandish to suggest that golden hamsters infest a world parallel to ours and that every few decades a portal somewhere near Aleppo opens, allowing a few specimens of the blond-brown rodents to scamper though.

SOURCES:

Colby, Carroll B. *Pets* (New York: Duell, Sloan and Pearce, 1960).

"Golden Hamster": Wikipedia: https://en.wikipedia.org/wiki/Golden_hamster (accessed April 26, 2020).

Henwood, Chris, "Discovery of the Syrian (Golden) Hamster, *Mesocricetus Auratus*." Originally printed in the *Journal of the British Hamster Association*, Spring 1992. Reprinted online: https://www.britishhamsterassociation.org.uk/get_article.php?fname=journal/discover_syrian.html

Michell, John, and Robert J. M. Rickard. *Living Wonders* (New York: Thame and Hudson, 1982).

THE AURA OF AN APE

On August 4, 1913, "Miss M. B." (the name on file with the Society for Psychical Research) invited her friend Mr. L. C. Powles and his wife, Isabel G. Powles, over to meet James W. Sharpe, who had some reputation for seeing visions or "auras." The Powles lived in Rye, East Sussex, United Kingdom, and Miss B. lived about three miles away. That day, unfortunately, Mrs. Powles felt too ill to travel, so Mr. Powles rode off alone.

Mr. Powles himself had only recently recovered from pneumonia, and the wind that day was unusually strong and cold for August. Isabel worried about him, so she started reading the latest issue of *The Strand Magazine* to occupy her mind. She became engrossed in what she described as "a very horrible story of a man disguised as a gorilla who came behind his enemy and broke his neck with his powerful hands."

"I have always had a great horror of gorillas from childhood, and far-fetched as it was, I was made very nervous and oppressed by the story," Mrs. Powles continued.

At Miss B.'s house, meanwhile, tea-time arrived, and the conversation touched upon psychical matters. Mr. Powles asked Sharpe about the "auras" he saw around people and whether he saw one around him (Powles). At first, Sharpe claimed to see nothing, but later he said ominously, "You asked me to tell you; I do now see something." Sharpe saw two images lurking near Powles. One was a young woman whose description fit Mrs. Powles'. The other, however, was a "dark, non-human, creature behind me with his knotted hands on my shoulder[s]." [Sidgwick, p. 53]. The woman was trying to "avert this monster's apparently evil intent."

Sharpe believed the creature to be a "health-warning," a symbol of approaching illness. Mr. Powles returned home that afternoon to hear his wife speak of the strange story she had read and of the "nervous state" it left her in. Their conclusion was that Mr. Sharpe had not only "picked up" Mrs. Powles' appearance but that of the fictional murderer she had become fixated on.

It is rather creepy that Sharpe did not say the woman *thought* about a hairy creature, but that he *saw* it with its paws on Mr. Powles' shoulders, as killer and victim were described in the story.

Mr. Powles did not fall ill at any time before writing his account for the Society for Psychical Research three years later. Rather than a symbolic health-warning, the "gorilla strangler" was a personification of what preyed on Mrs. Powles' imagination.

Mr. Sharpe, from what little is mentioned of him, did not normally have such odd visions, nor did the Powles ordinarily undergo psychic readings. The implication is that the juxtaposition of the psychic reading with Mrs. Powles' story reading created a unique telepathic entity.

This might have been a forgettable incident of parlor magic had Mrs. Powles' thoughts not been objectified in a form visible to Mr. Sharpe. The concept of a "tulpa"—an entity formed of pure thought—became popularized by the lady explorer Alexandra David-Neel in her 1932 book, *Magic and Mystery in Tibet*. A "tulpa," however, supposedly takes months to create and shape, while the "gorilla strangler" sprang whole from a single psychic observation.

Janet and Colin Bord list hundreds of reports of unknown creatures in *Alien Animals*. After concluding that many such creatures seemed too fantastic to be physical animals, they tackle the problem of what they *could* be. One possibility "is the idea that the human mind is, by its power of 'image making,' capable of creating a physical being which can then exist as an independent creature." [Bord, p. 191]

People might expect to see, or hope to see, or imagine they see a monster, like the hair-covered semi-humans the Bords call BHMs. "So are they solely hallucinatory, taking shape from the archetypal monster image?" they continued. "They might sometimes originate in this way, but then take on an independent existence, feeding by vampirism on whatever energy source is available." [Bord p. 192]

I am fascinated by the part chance played in this account. No one expected to see a "monster." No one tried to create a "tulpa." The gorilla image came about only because: 1) Mrs. Powles happened to read that

The Aura of an Ape

specific story in that specific magazine on that specific day; 2) it had an exceptionally upsetting effect on her; and 3) Mr. Sharpe happened at that time to examine Mr. Powles' "aura." It was truly an accidental ape. It is doubly ironic that it took on a visible existence, since even in Mrs. Powles' work of fiction there was no real ape.

Perhaps if the Powles had told and retold the story, and others dwelt on the idea of the phantasmal gorilla, it might have taken on a life of its own . . . and perhaps something like this has happened elsewhere, because there are legends in Britain of such things as the Hairy Hands of Dartmoor, the Man-Monkey of Staffordshire, and the Big Grey Man of Ben MacDhui.

SOURCES:

Bord, Janet and Colin. *Alien Animals* (Harrisburg, PA: Stackpole Books, 1981).

Sidgwick, Eleanor Mildred, *et. al. Phantasms of the Living* (New Hyde Park, NY: University Books, 1962 [1886]).

BATSQUATCH AND FRIENDS

Mount Rainier National Park is an area of multiple strange events. It was the setting of the Kenneth Arnold UFO encounter of June 24, 1947, which marked the beginning of the modern UFO era and which also gave us the term "flying saucer."

Arnold spent much of his subsequent life investigating UFO sightings and other strange phenomena, many in the same area. "I remember one particular case that was related to me," he explained in a speech at the First International UFO Congress in 1977. "It happened to a young family in Tacoma, Washington. Their twelve-year-old boy turned up missing, and after a very extensive search they found him in Lusk, Wyoming. They didn't have relatives there and the boy, when he was found, didn't know how he got there." [Fuller, p. 26]

David Paulides is a name that appears occasionally in this book. As will be explained elsewhere, he has charted hundreds of cases of mysterious disappearances of human beings and discovered that many occur in small areas he calls "clusters.." "Mount Rainier has been classified as a cluster zone of missing people who fit the profile we've established," he writes in his book about hunters. [Paulides, p. 233]

Beasts Beyond Belief

One particularly puzzling case was that of Joe Blackburn, a trapper, hunter, and forest guide who lived with his wife and five-month-old baby in Goose Prairie, east of Mount Rainier. He was one of the most knowledgeable people in Washington when it came to the countryside around the mountain. He rented and sold equipment to hunters and other outdoorsmen, and in late October 1946 the 34-year-old mountain man rented a horse to a hunter named Blake Lowry.

On the ominous date of October 31, Lowry did not return with the horse as agreed. Blackburn surmised that the hunter had gotten lost, so he rode out in search of him. Lowry had traveled into an area west of the Blackburn home, an expanse of forest Joe knew as well as his own yard. Joe took only a Thermos of coffee with him, expecting to be gone just a few hours.

Blackburn did not return. In the morning, his wife called the authorities. The sheriff's department and the Naches Ranger District started searching immediately.

On November 3, Joe's horse returned to the Blackburn property alone, riderless, and with a limp. On November 4, searchers located the horse's saddle and bridle, as well as some of Joe's personal belongings. Soon after this, the original missing man, Blake Lowry, stumbled out of the woods onto a road and found his way back to civilization.

Joe Blackburn was never seen again.

Bigfoot hunter John Green recorded several sightings of hairy hominids in the Mount Rainier area and found himself on the trail of—something—outside the nearby city of Puyallup.

"If there is one fact in this whole strange business that has been established beyond a shadow of a doubt it is that something screams at Puyallup." [Green, p. 393]

The saga of the Screamer began in the early 1970s in and around a new housing project southeast of Puyallup called Forest Green. Marlin Ayres, a resident of the subdivision, wrote to the Tacoma *News Tribune* in July 1972 about a creature that screamed at night in the woods behind his home. Whatever it was, it greatly upset the neighborhood dogs, which would bark wildly. He made several recordings of the Screamer by simply hanging a microphone out a window. His neighbors made their own recordings. Although dogs carry on in almost every recording, the unidentified cries are much louder. Green describes them as a long "whooOooOooOoo" or "woopwoopwoop.."

Batsquatch and Friends

No one ever saw the Screamer, so there is no proof it was a Sasquatch, though there were reports of the hairy giants in the same general area. John Green himself tramped around Puyallup but heard the screaming only once. However, as he writes, "When I have been there the frantic barking of dogs has been almost a nightly occurrence."

Skeptics dismissed the sounds as coyote calls, but the addition of coyotes to the mix simply made things stranger. Some recordings sounded like the canids, but the volume was just too loud. Other tapes carried what seemed to be coyote howls—with an extra voice that sounded similar but was *not* coyote.

It appeared that the Screamer could imitate coyotes, an ability attributed to both Bigfeet and Dogmen. One night Washington State trooper Mark Pittenger recorded a particularly strange exchange: From one area echoed genuine coyote calls; from another direction came not-quite coyote calls. The two sets of vocalizations drew closer and closer to each other until there was a sudden outburst of violent noise, then silence.

The next day, Pittenger hiked through the area and found two dead coyotes. They had been "smashed" rather than bitten or slashed.

"I find it absolutely fascinating that it goes on year after year without anyone being able to prove what is doing it," writes John Green. [p. 395] The Screamer seemed to patrol a sizeable territory around Forest Green. It had to pass across rural and neighborhood roads every half mile or so. In 1976, veteran Sasquatch chaser Green organized a project for volunteers to track it by its cries and the barking of dogs and intercept it as it crossed one of the roads.

By this time, however, there had been much more development southeast of Puyallup, and as more trees fell, more houses rose, and more land vanished under pavement, the Screamer roamed less often and finally moved on completely.

That's one way to get rid of a monster—and all other inhabitants of nature, for that matter.

On Saturday night, April 16, 1994, Brian Canfield, 18, was driving his Toyota pickup from his girlfriend's house in Buckley, Washington, to the small rural community of Camp One in the foothills of Mount Rainier. At about 9:30 P.M. his engine died, and he rolled to a stop in the middle of a gravel road. His headlights still burned. After a moment, something dropped into view about 30 feet ahead, landing with a *thud* that raised dust on the road.

"It" was a muscular humanoid creature with vast batlike wings as well as arms, a wolfish head, and pointed ears with lynx-like tufts. It stood about nine feet tall and was covered with blue fur. A local newspaper described the color as a conservative gray-blue, but Canfield insisted that it was a quite striking shade "like the bright blue in the NBC-TV peacock logo." [Benjamin, p. 30]

"Its eyes were yellow and shaped like a piece of pie with pupils like a half-moon. The mouth was pretty big. White teeth. No fangs. The face was like a wolf." [Roberts, p. 1] The creature fixed Canfield with a penetrating stare, but it gave off an air of puzzlement as well, as if it were trying to get its bearings. It stood there for several minutes then spread its wings. It turned, giving Canfield a final look over one shoulder before flapping off toward Mt. Rainier. The backwash shook the small pickup.

After a moment, the pickup started again (it is unclear from the articles whether Brian started it, or if it came to life by itself *à la Close Encounters of the Third Kind*). The boy rocketed home and roused his parents. The youth convinced his father and a neighbor to gather gun and camera and accompany him back to the site. There was, unfortunately, nothing to be found on the gravel road five miles from the Canfield house.

Canfield couldn't resist talking about his encounter at school. Some of his fellow students laughed, but others came up with the name "Batsquatch." Dave Kiele, a student of an artistic bent, took Brian's rough sketches and fleshed them out for the local newspaper.

Journalist C. R. Roberts interviewed Canfield, his family, and his neighbors and came to the conclusion that Brian was an average high school senior "who wasn't into drugs, heavy metal music, nor Dungeons & Dragons." A year later, in an article for *The INFO Journal*, Phyllis Benjamin evaluated C. R. Roberts as well as Canfield: The newspaperman impressed her as "committed, decent and thoughtful," and Brian seemed to be down-to-earth and truthful. When told that fortean writer John Keel doubted the creature's size, Brian responded that he was sure the Batsquatch was nine feet tall because it was standing next to a tree that served as a local landmark. He added that he was rushing home to get ready for a date, not coming back from one as reported.

"In an interesting aside, Brian mentioned that the Camp One townspeople heard peculiar high-pitched cries several days before and after the sighting." [Benjamin, p. 31]

In recent years, reports of "Dogmen" have grown more and more frequent: huge, upright canine creatures with wolflike heads. Some match Batsquatch in height, and, curiously, many witnesses mention tufted ears like those of a bobcat or lynx. The bright-blue fur and the wings seem to be Batsquatch's alone.

SOURCES:

Benjamin, Phyllis. "Batsquatch, Flap, Flap," *INFO Journal* no. 73 (Summer 1995), pp. 29–31.

Fuller, Curtis G., *et al.*, eds. *Proceeding of the First International UFO Congress* (New York: Warner Books, 1980).

Green, John. *Sasquatch: The Apes Among Us* (Seattle: Hancock House Publishing, 1978).

Paulides, David. *Missing 411: Hunters* (North Charleston, SC: CreateSpace, 2016).

Roberts, C. R. "Mount Rainier-Area Youth Has Close Encounter," *Tacoma News Tribune*, May 1, 1994.

Webster, Kerry. "'Bigfoot' Prowling County?" *Tacoma News Tribune*, January 27, 1975.

BEHIND *THE BIRDS*

Alfred Hitchcock's 1963 thriller, *The Birds,* was loosely based on the novella of the same name by English suspense author Daphne du Maurier. Certain events in the early 1960s spurred Hitchcock to translate it to the screen despite the technical difficulties he faced in the special effects area. These bird-related events make rather creepy reading.

Birds started acting strangely beginning on or about April 26, 1960, in La Jolla, California, "where a thousand birds flew down a chimney and ravaged the inside of a house." [Paglia, p. 10] Soon thereafter, "Residents in a quiet Midwestern town—the quintessential American Hitchcock setting—suddenly found themselves under invasion by a covey of barn swallows, who seemed to delight in dive-bombing newsboys . . . [S]ea gulls were reported to be terrorizing fishing ports along Germany's North Sea coast, pilfering piles of fresh fish and attacking fishermen and chimneysweeps." [Counts and Rubin, p. 26]

Several characters in the restaurant scene in *The Birds* discuss an event that occurred on the night of August 17–18, 1961. The August 18 *Santa Cruz Sentinel* headlined the story as "Seabird Invasion Hits Coastal Homes." At about 3:00 A.M., gulls known as sooty shearwaters, numbering supposedly in the millions, "crashed into cars and buildings, broke television aerials and streetlamps, and tried to enter houses when the residents ran out to investigate the noise." [Paglia, pp. 10–11] The birds "pecked people, smashed into houses and cars, knocked out car headlights, broke windows, chased people around the streets and staggered around vomiting pieces of anchovy." ["Deranged," p. 10] Alfred Hitchcock jumped on the story so quickly, the *Sentinel* mentions him calling the paper for information that very morning.

Hitchcock officially began work on his film on March 22, 1962, and even this was shadowed by eerie synchronicities. On that day, a red-tailed hawk started attacking children in Victoria Park and had to be shot. *Cinefantastique* magazine mentions that "a Bodega Bay farmer approached Hitchcock during filming to report that he was having trouble with birds pecking out the eyes of his young lambs." [Counts and Rubin, p. 26]

There are probably complicated natural explanations for the pre-Hitchcock "attacks." The Santa Cruz invasion has been blamed on domoic acid in the fish eaten by birds in Monterey Bay. An alga called *Pseudo-nitzschia australis* produces domoic acid when it is starved of certain nutrients, and this toxin builds up in fish and crustaceans—and anything that eats them. It can cause erratic behavior, aggressiveness, and, eventually, death. ["Deranged"]

The brains of birds are constructed differently than those of mammals. Some biologists consider them to be much more intelligent than previously assumed. Even so, they could not plot and carry out large-scale assaults—or could they?

Always be kind to your fine feathered friends just in case. Toss peanuts to the ducks in the park and spread birdseed around the yard. Maybe they won't peck the hand that feeds them.

SOURCES:

Counts, Kyle B., and Steve Rubin. "The Making of Alfred Hitchcock's *The Birds*." *Cinefantastique* Vol. 10, no. 2 (Fall 1980).

"Deranged by Dodgy Anchovies." *Fortean Times* no. 83 (Oct.–Nov. 1995), p. 10.

Paglia, Camille. *BFI Film Classics: The Birds* (London: British Film Institute, 1998).

BIGFOOT KIDNAPPINGS

I Was Bigfoot's Love Slave
Lumberjack's story of forbidden love will amaze you!

Weekly World News lead headline, October 30, 2001

It's a story as old as time: A hairy man-beast seizes an innocent human woman and drags her off into the wilderness to a fate worse than death.

There are many stories about Bigfoot, Yeti, and other hairy monsters carrying off humans, possibly as food, possibly as mates. They range from ludicrous tabloid tales to frightening modern reports of people vanishing in wilderness areas. Curiously, some of the most famous concern men rather than women being carried off.

There was Muchalat Harry, a member of the Nootka Indian tribe of Vancouver Island, British Columbia. Most of the Nootka people shied away from the deep wilderness of Vancouver Island, fearing the hairy giants who dwelt there. Muchalat Harry, however, was a trapper who often wandered the forest for weeks at a time.

In the autumn of 1928, Harry gathered supplies and traps and paddled a canoe to the mouth of the Conuma River in Tlupana Inlet. He then hiked about 12 miles upriver and built a lean-to. At night, he slept only in his underwear, wrapped in his blankets. One night, a Sasquatch caught him up and carried him two or three miles into the hills before dumping him again.

In the morning, Muchalat Harry found himself up against the base of a cliff, surrounded by 20 or so Bigfeet of all sizes. Mostly they just stood and stared at him, but Harry noticed piles of bones around the clearing and decided they were going to eat him.

The shaggy humanoids never harmed him, however, and by that afternoon they seemed to grow bored. Several of the creatures left the area, and when the remaining man-beasts turned their attention to other pursuits, he jumped up and ran.

Harry did not stop until he reached the river. Following it, he even located his campsite, but he shot past without stopping. He didn't slow down until he reached his canoe; then, despite being clad only in his underwear, cold and exhausted, he paddled 45 miles back to the settlement of Nootka.

A local priest, Father Anthony Terhaar, nursed Muchalat Harry back to health. As the clergyman explained to Bigfoot hunter Peter Byrne, Harry never went back for his rifle and traps, which were valuable items to a Nootka hunter. In fact, he never ventured into the woods again. [Byrne, pp. 1–6]

The longest and most detailed story of a Sasquatch kidnapping is probably the account written by Albert Ostman. Although the event supposedly took place in 1924, Ostman kept quiet until the 1950s, when the first stories of northern California's "Bigfoot" appeared in the papers. He surrounded himself with the supplies and materials he used on prospecting trips 30 years earlier to bring back memories. Then he started writing.

In that year of 1924, Ostman took time off from logging and construction work to look for gold in British Columbia. He hired a native guide to take him to Toba Inlet, and, ironically, he pooh-poohed the Indian's story of hairy giants in the wilderness.

He left the guide at the head of the inlet and worked his way inland for six days. He found the perfect place for a permanent camp beside a cliff face and a spring, but each night thereafter something entered his camp while he was asleep and took food items. On the third night, he lay in his sleeping bag fully clothed, with his boots and rifle, hoping to surprise the unwelcome visitor.

It was Ostman who was surprised. Something picked him up, sleeping bag and all, and carried him away. The prospector could not move to reach his knife; the hobnails of his boots poked him, and he could feel the cans and tools of his backpack bump against him—whatever had grabbed him had taken his pack as well.

After an estimated three hours of being carried (and dragged), his captor dumped him on the ground. Ostman crawled weakly out to find four large forms surrounding him in the morning mist. They wore no clothes but were covered with hair.

"They look like a family, old man, old lady, and two young ones, a boy and a girl," Ostman wrote. "The boy and the girl seemed to be scared of me. The old lady did not seem too pleased about what the old man dragged home." [Green 1973, p. 25]

The creatures all chattered over him, then, oddly, they wandered away. Ostman saw that he was in a basin several acres in size, surrounded by mountains. A V-shaped fissure eight feet wide was the only exit, and the "old man" sat prominently beside that.

The prospector had several cans of food, coffee, a few tools, and six shells in his rifle. He found a spring and made himself at home as he pondered the problem of escape.

The younger Sasquatches (young but still about seven feet tall) found the human fascinating. Ostman gave the boy an empty snuff box with a hinged lid that opened and closed; both youngsters played with it for hours. After a day in the basin, the prospector decided he would run out of food if he didn't leave soon. He packed up and headed for the exit. The "old man" had other ideas.

"I pointed to the opening, I wanted to go out," Ostman recalled. "But he stood there pushing towards me—and said something that sounded like 'Soka, soka.'"

After a few more moments of this, Ostman gave up on the straight approach.

The "old lady" gathered grass and twigs and nuts. The young male brought Ostman some of the grassroots, which were edible. In return he handed the creature a small amount of snuff. The youth shared it with the old man, who seemed to like its taste.

After a couple more days, Ostman built a fire and boiled coffee in a can. Both male Bigfeet approached him. The prospector pulled out a can of snuff and took a pinch. The "old man" grabbed the can and swallowed the contents whole. After a minute or two, he started groaning. He grabbed Ostman's coffee and swallowed it, grounds and all. Then he ran for the spring.

Ostman knew this was his chance. He grabbed his belongings and ran for the exit. The "old lady" blocked the way, but he fired a shot at the rocks over her head and she turned back.

Ostman hiked and hiked. From a ridge top he spotted Mount Baker, and he knew which direction to go. By the time he stumbled out into a logging camp, he was bedraggled and ill. The loggers gave him food, new clothes (and a bath), and in a few days he was on a boat back to Vancouver. He never went prospecting again.

While Albert Ostman's account makes the hairy giants seem like a sitcom family, one Bigfoot kidnapping story for which I searched for years is downright chilling.

O. R. "Red" Edwards and his hunting partner Bill Cole discussed the event with no one, not even each other, for nearly 20 years. When sightings of "Bigfoot" started appearing in the newspapers, Edwards, who lived in Fresno, California, wrote to Cole, who had moved to Nebraska. They compared notes, and Edwards committed the entire story to paper.

In October 1943, the two men went on a hunting trip south of Mount Ashland, Oregon, probably just across the border into California. One morning, they decided to investigate patches of brush on the side of a steep hill. The hunters split up to go around an oval patch of tangled growth, Cole to the left and Edwards to the right. Edwards thought he saw an apelike head bob up above the bushes and vanish again.

"Then I hear the 'pad pad pad' of running feet, heard the 'whump' and a grunt as your bodies came together," Edwards wrote.

Edwards ran back around the wild patch in time to see a seven-foot-tall manlike creature that was covered with brown hair and loping down the slope. It appeared to be carrying a man in its arms; the hunter could only see legs and boots. After a few seconds, it disappeared behind more underbrush.

Mr. Edwards could not wrap his mind around what he had seen. He found trampled leaves and grass where man and creature had collided, but he did not know what tracking signs to look for. He climbed to the top of the ridge, where he could see the valley below, and smoked a couple of cigarettes.

After half an hour, he started working his way around the valley by following the ridge; he was frightened of what might lurk lower on the slopes. It took him all day to reach the mouth of the valley, and once there he picked his way down. He realized he was following a beaten path of some sort.

From a tangle of bushes and saplings came a "Shhht!" Edwards made out a dark shape within the tangle, and he yelled that he was armed. The shape turned out to be two figures; one ran to the right and hid behind a large tree, while the other ran to the left and plunged into brush.

He aimed his rifle at the bush-diver, but then he heard "the damnedest whistling scream" from the tree. He spun as something huge withdrew behind the tree. He kept the tree covered for several minutes, moving only to edge a few feet closer to the valley entrance.

"Then I noticed a knot on the side of the tree about six feet from the ground and to my right as I looked there seemed to be an eye in the middle of this knot . . . I shut my eyes real tight for a minute to clear out the tears, and when I looked again the knot was gone." [Green 1978, p. 415]

Edwards had enough. Lost friend or no, he was going to go back to the car (which happened to be Cole's) and flee. As he marched away the thing behind the tree leapt powerfully back into the first patch of brush.

He reached the car several minutes later, and in it sat Bill Cole, waiting. Neither would admit to having heard or seen anything unusual, and that's how things stood for two decades.

Bill Cole's version of the tale was short and to the point. After colliding with the hairy giant, he had fallen down, but he did not lose consciousness nor did the beast pick him up. He had simply made his way back to his vehicle.

I've come across a simple version of this Bigfoot tale in more than one book: basically, Cole and the Sasquatch bump each other; the hairy humanoid picks the hunter up and carries him a few feet; then it dumps him. This is one of the rare stories that grew eerier as I came closer to the source. The longest account (from *Sasquatch: The Apes Among Us*), with its multiple creatures (two? three?) and "tree knot with an eye" creeped me out.

And if the first creature did not scoop up Bill Cole, whose legs and shoes did Edwards see?

SOURCES:

Byrne, Peter. *Search for Bigfoot* (New York: Pocket Books, 1975).

Green, John. *On the Track of the Sasquatch* (New York: Ballantine Books, 1973).

Ibid. Sasquatch: *The Apes Among Us* (Saanichton, BC: Hancock House, 1978).

THE BIRD OF LINCOLN'S INN

Remarkable stories filtered into the office of a nameless Terror which haunted a set of barristers' chambers in Lincoln's Inn.

J. Wentworth Day, *Here Are Ghosts and Witches*

Lincoln's Inn, London, is not an inn but a court lined by several Georgian houses. In the late 19th and early 20th centuries, rumors flew concerning one particular building. Supposedly, one man had committed suicide there; another had gone insane. Other people had moved out, too frightened to describe the things they had experienced. Eventually, the newspapers got wind of the stories.

Ralph D. Blumenfeld, news editor of the London *Daily Mail*, and Sir Max Pemberton, no less than owner of the same newspaper, decided to spend a night in the haunted rooms. The main chamber was completely empty of furniture, fixtures, and carpeting outside of bare electric lights. The journalists provided two chairs and a card table. On Saturday, May 11, 1901, the two men entered the house, closed and shuttered the windows, spread chalk dust all over the floors in case pranksters somehow got in, broke out sandwiches, a pack of cards, whiskies, and sodas, and waited. "Even a black beetle could not have escaped unobserved," Blumenfeld said later.

Doors at either end of the chamber led into smaller secondary rooms. At 12:43 A.M., one of the doors unlatched quite audibly and swung open.

At 12:56, the door to the second room also unlatched and opened. The two men shut the doors and sat back at their card game.

Just before 2:00 A.M., the first door opened again, then the second door opened. Pemberton and Blumenfeld closed them again. At 2:07 AM, both doors banged open. The journalists jumped up and investigated the adjoining rooms. "The men found, clearly defined about the middle of each floor, footprints of a bird, three in the room to the left and five in that to the right. Both thought these imprints were such as a bird the size of a turkey might have made." [Haining, p. 4] More specifically, they were two inches long, having three toes in front and a spur behind. [Murdie 2017, p. 16] The men decided to leave.

Earlier that same night, Margaret Verrall of Cambridge University was experimenting with automatic writing, which is the process of clearing the conscious mind and allowing an outside intelligence (some would say merely the subconscious) to write with one's hand. At about 11:10 P.M., she found herself writing in Latin and ancient Greek.

"This is what I have wanted at last. Justice and joy speak a word to the wise. A. W. V. and perhaps someone else. Chalk sticking to the feet has got over the difficulty." [Murdie 2008, p. 16] More followed, much of it unintelligible, but Mrs. Verrall (or whoever controlled her hand) also scribbled a cartoonish drawing of some sort of bird with a "leering" expression. She and her husband took it all in stride, calling the creature the "cockyoly bird." After they read the newspaper story about Lincoln's Inn, they could not help but think the two events were related.

That's no wonder, especially since Mrs. Verrall mentioned chalk sticking to feet and drew her "cockyoly bird" two or three hours before the final manifestation at the Lincoln's Inn house!

What was the Lincoln's Inn entity? J. Wentworth Day, editor of *The Field* and *Country Life*, suggested it was a "bird elemental," whatever that may be. Most people, I'm sure, would call it a demon. As archeologists Jeremy Black and Anthony Green write about the ancient Mesopotamian underworld, "In almost all cases these hellish demons are said to have been winged and to have had the talons of birds." [Black and Green, p. 43] Beneficent spirits were also depicted with such attributes, but demons with bird talons is a trope that has lasted into the modern era, as seen in movies like *Paranormal Activity*.

Perhaps the bird thing was not necessarily hellish. Jim Brandon seemed to think that an energy/ force/ intelligence ("Pan") wells out of our planet on occasion, creating fortean phenomena wherever the earth is disturbed. For example, the surprisingly violent Bigfoot encounters near the Enrico Fermi Power Plant near Monroe, Michigan, in the 1960s might have been a "sort of semifocused protest by the unconscious biosphere at humanity's increasing disruptions of the harmonious life of all," as he wrote in *Weird America* [Brandon 1978, p. 114].

All of which has nothing to do with giant bird tracks. However, Brandon's diggings through ancient lore, myth, and legend led him to suggest that there are extraterrestrial influences on our world as well. For example, a malevolent force seems to be associated with the constellation Orion in several mythologies.

"Richard Hinkley Allen, the star lore expert, notes that Orion was often known in earlier times as 'the Cock's Foot' or the 'Foot Turning Wanderer.' The cock's foot, or 'turkey track,' is practically a universal glyph in American rock art." [Brandon 1983 p. 233]

Whatever the Lincoln's Inn Bird was, I doubt I'd ever say, "Who's a pretty boy, then?" to it.

SOURCES:

Black, Jeremy, and Anthony Green. *Gods, Demons and Symbols of Ancient Mesopotamia* (Austin, TX: University of Texas Press, 1992).

Brandon, Jim. *Weird America* (New York: E. P. Dutton, 1978).

———. *Rebirth of Pan* (Dunlap, IL: Firebird Press, 1983).

Day, J. Wentworth. *Here Are Ghosts and Witches* (London: B. T. Batsford, Ltd., 1954).

Haining, Peter. *Mammoth Book of True Hauntings* (London: Morning Press, 2008).

Murdie, Alan, "More Courtroom Ghosts," *Fortean Times* no. 236 (July 2008), p 16.

Ibid. "Avian Manifestations and Messages," *Fortean Times* no. 354 (June 2017), pp. 16-18.

"The Phantom of Lincoln's Inn," London *Daily Mail,* May 13, 1901.

THE BRENTFORD GRIFFIN

In the London district of Brentford (northwest of Wimbledon) one can find the Griffin public house. Fuller's Griffin Brewery, with its griffin trademark, is located in nearby Chiswick. The Brentford Football Club plays at Griffin Park and the coat of arms for Brentford and Chiswick consists of two griffins holding a shield. Is it any wonder, then, that the mysterious flying beast seen in Brentford in the 1980s was called a griffin?

In mid-1984, while walking along Braemar Road, Kevin Chippendale spotted a creature flying near the roof of the Green Dragon apartment building. "He described it as resembling a dog with wings, having a long muzzle [beak?] and four legs with what looked like paws." He saw the thing again in February 1985 on the same street, and he realized it resembled the griffin painted on the sign over the Griffin pub. "Mr. Chippendale then described his sightings to his colleagues, one of whom, Angela Keyhoe, said that she had seen, from a bus, a big, black, bird-like creature, perched on the top of the gasometer next to the Watermans Arts Centre. Other passengers also saw the creature." [McEwan, pp. 153–154] The griffin was even seen by a psychologist, John Olssen, one morning while he was jogging beside the Thames. By March, the griffin was mentioned frequently in the press and featured on London Weekend Television's *The Six O'Clock Show*.

Initially skeptical, writer Andrew Collins interviewed Kevin Chippendale and came to believe in some of the reports. He ended up writing a pamphlet entitled *The Brentford Griffin: The Truth behind the Tales* (Wickford: Earthquest Books, 1985).

There were a few tales containing little truth, however. Novelist Robert Rankin, who "spins weird yarns with tongue placed firmly in cheek," attached himself to the Brentford Griffin and its attendant publicity. In an interview ten years later, Rankin said, "Nearly every sentence in his pamphlet is totally inaccurate—people, locations, times all wrong. I didn't think for a minute that there was a griffin on the island in Brentford, but I thought it was a fine idea and did my best to help it along." According to Rankin, "When the TV crew came down, they brought people with them who didn't live in Brentford. They stood there and talked about the griffin they'd seen. It was priceless!" The locals, too, came up with griffin sightings—when the cameras were pointed their way. [Coolie, p. 28]

Yet the Brentford Griffin was not entirely a joke. Andrew Collins, in a letter to the *Fortean Times*, wrote, "The information and data used in the text was obtained directly from the people concerned and everything was carefully checked before publication." He continued, "Rankin had no problems with *The Brentford Griffin* at the time, so his flippant, dismissive attitude 10 years later is difficult to understand." [Collins, p. 57] "We set up a Griffin Hot Line and people started ringing in," Rankin admitted; "they'd seen it, their parents had seen it, someone had seen it at the end of the War rising like a phoenix. I thought: 'Hang on a minute, even if this thing had no reality at first, it has now.'"

Andrew Collins' explanation for it all was to reference that fortean favorite, the Cosmic Joker, who had "simply re-activated an archetype that had been in Brentford's popular consciousness (such as Fuller's Griffin brewery, the Griffin pub and the Griffin football ground) for centuries."

SOURCES:

Collins, Andrew, "The Brentford Griffin," *Fortean Times* no. 81 (June–July 1995), p. 57.

Coolie, Stuart, "To Brentford and Back," *Fortean Times* no. 80 (Apr.–May 1995), p. 28.

McEwan, Graham J. *Mystery Animals of Britain and Ireland* (London: Robert Hale, 1986).

THE BUNNY-MAN COMETH

MICHIGAN BUNNY MAN

Sometimes a new category of strangeness throws itself at one without any effort on one's own part. After the death of journalist, artist, and cryptozoology author Linda Godfrey on November 27, 2022, I visited her website to see if someone had listed the cause of death. There was as of that time no mention of her death, but there was a strange little anecdote about the "Michigan Bunny Man."

Ms. Godfrey met a woman at a book signing in Iron Mountain, Michigan, who had a story to tell. The tale was actually her mother's. It seemed that this woman had been working at a camp in Michigan's Upper Peninsula in 1958. One day, she came across a rabbit—a bunny about five feet tall, standing upright. Rabbits can stand on their hind legs, of course, from which position they scan the surrounding area for danger. They do not normally walk—or even hop—on their hind legs. The daughter, however, "said it ran away from her mother on two legs" and that "her mother wasn't the type to make things up, and often marveled that she had seen such a thing." This sighting took place in the same area that local spooklights called "The Paulding Lights" or the "Dog Meadow Lights" are seen.

PENNSYLVANIA HOPPER

Curious, certainly, but I had a book to write, so I carried on, searching my piles of books, Xeroxes, and magazines for cryptozoological treasures. Anyone who knows anything about the paranormal landscape of Pennsylvania knows the name of Stan Gordon, a researcher who has investigated phenomena in that state since the 1960s. Starting with *Silent Invasion* in 2010, Gordon published a series of casebooks documenting hundreds of strange incidents. For weeks I had noticed that "Casebook Four" was not to be found, under "G" for Gordon or anywhere else. After days of searching, the book (*Creepy Cryptids and Strange UFO Encounters of Pennsylvania*) turned up at the bottom of a random stack of volumes in the bedroom.

What do I find when I crack open this Prodigal Son of a book? The title "I Swear I Saw a Giant Rabbit." A man Gordon has known for many years insists he had a strange sighting as a boy in the early 1960s. His family took a weekend trip to a small house near Spruce Creek, rural Huntingdon County, Pennsylvania. At one point, some family members, including the witness, took a scenic trip around a mountain. They rode in a Jeep, the boy sitting on the passenger side. As they rattled down a mountain road, the boy spotted something off to the right, 75 to 100 feet away. A "dirty white rabbit" about six feet tall hopped along parallel to the road.

"The witness told me he saw the man-sized lepus hopping on its two back legs with its two front paws dangling down in a curled position." [Gordon, p. 146] He lost sight of it as the Jeep drove on. No one else in the vehicle saw the creature, and whenever he tried to tell people about the giant bunny over the years, they simply laughed at him. Again, rabbits don't normally jump upright on their hind feet only.

The witness did more than sketch the manlike bunny. He memorialized the encounter with a diorama, a photo of which graces Stan Gordon's book. A row of pine trees, like silhouettes painted on thin wood, lines a high shelf. There are also silhouettes of a bear and a leafless deciduous tree. Standing among them is the white cut-out of a rabbit, the same size as the bear, perfectly erect. Its feet look more like a human's than a rabbit's in proportion. It really looks like a person wearing a fursuit (the animal costumes worn by people in the furry fandom).

LINCOLNSHIRE, TOO?

Well, one can't waste too much time on bunnies when there are thun-

The Bunny-Man Cometh

derbirds and dogmen on the loose. I purchased issue 406 of *The Fortean Times* (June 2021) because the cover title, "Mystery Big Cats," looked promising. I opened it to the back, where each issue carries a column called "It Happened to Me" in which readers send in their own experiences. One reader, Andrew Mitchell, delivered an account entitled "Rabbit Man."

Mr. Mitchell grew up in the small Lincolnshire, England, village of Branston Booths, which consisted of "a pub, an old wooden village hall and a chapel" and little else. Children found adventure enough in the local woods, where there were abandoned caravans, an island surrounded by a moat, and "a body of reedy water known locally as the 'Delph,'" which ran through the hamlet and emptied into the River Witham.

One summer evening in 1985, young Master Mitchell and four other youths aged 12 to 14, stopped near the Delph, which was lined with high, dikelike banks. The quintet was about to split up to go home, and the lads were saying their goodbyes. Three had their backs to the stream; Andrew and his friend Darrell stood facing it.

Suddenly something popped up from behind the bank. It was a rabbitish head as large as a man's, sitting atop wide, manlike shoulders. As Andrew and Darrell stared open-mouthed, the anthropomorphic beast ducked down again. Andrew compared it to the animal-masked cultists in *The Wicker Man*, but he insisted it was a living creature.

The two witnesses tried to explain to their three companions what they had seen. They searched the area but found nothing, though "if truth be told—we didn't look very hard. It was a terrifying encounter." [Mitchell, p. 75] The three non-witnesses dismissed the creature as simply an oversized rabbit or hare, as did other people over the years. "I have seen enough rabbits and hares to know that they do not pop up in that way, or have human-like shoulders."

Mr. Mitchell finishes with a question: "Was the entity, perhaps, a cousin of the 'giant rabbits' of the mythical island Hy-Brasil?"

Here is the perfect excuse to drop that legendary island into the mixture. Hy-Brasil (or O'Breasil, Breasail, Brasylle, Berzil, etc.) had nothing to do with the South American country of similar name. It was a mystical island, almost perfectly circular in outline, situated in the Atlantic due west of Ireland. Like Avalon, Tir-na-nOg, and other islands of Faerie, it was visible sometimes, and sometimes it vanished into the Otherworld.

In 1674, Captain John Nisbet, an Irish seafarer, pulled into Killibega Harbor with a strange tale. He had landed at a great, black, rocky island dominated by a lone castle, which he identified as Hy-Breasil. It appeared that an evil wizard dwelled within the castle, who cast spells upon the captain and his men. Nisbet and his crew defeated the wizard by building a huge fire—"for fire, as anyone knows, is the power of light against the power of darkness." Almost as an aside, we are told the island was overrun by giant black rabbits.

Nisbet brought back several Scottish castaways from the island who backed up his story, but no one paid much attention to the brave captain. [MacDougall, p. 294; Ramsey, p. 91]

THE BUNNY MAN OF WASHINGTON

At this point I gave up. Destiny decreed I write something about the silly yet frightening figure known as the Bunny Man of Washington.

The Bunny Man's story, like all good urban legends, is an odd mixture of the amorphous and the specific. He has always been localized in the Maryland/District of Columbia/northern Virginia area, and his favorite haunt, everyone agrees, is a railroad overpass near Fairfax Station, Virginia, locally known as "Bunny Man Bridge."

His legend, however, remained undeveloped compared to old standards like "The Hook" and "The Boyfriend's Death." The Bunny Man carried an ax with which he killed children, mutilated animals, attacked couples parked in Lovers' Lanes, and chopped on people's houses. Kids whispered about him on sleepovers, scoutmasters warned their young charges of him by campfires, and legend trippers dared one another to wander out on "his" railroad bridge. That was as far as the story went.

In the early 1990s, Brian A. Conley, the historian archivist for the Fairfax County Public Library, received a visitor in the library's "Virginia Room." The woman was trying to find out about murders that had supposedly been committed near her home. Children's bodies had been found "hanging from a covered bridge," and the culprit turned out to be an "escaped inmate dressed in a bunny suit." It certainly sounded like the story Conley remembered from his youth, but he was inclined to dismiss it as a tale made up to scare children. As time passed, however, more and more library patrons came in asking about the long-eared boogie-man.

Conley finally took a deep dive into local history to search out the truth about the Bunny Man.

Conley assumed the Bunny Man would be associated with violent crimes, most likely murder. In those pre- (or at least primitive, dial-up)

internet days, this meant digging through decades of old newspaper files. Fortunately, two volunteer workers, Malcolm Richardson and Barbara Welch, had spent ten years creating an index to Fairfax County newspapers. With the volunteers' help, Conley tracked down details of every Fairfax County murder between 1872 and 1973—some 550 cases.

Sadly, none of these crimes seemed to fit the Bunny Man. None involved couples in Lovers' Lanes or attacks on people, animals, or property with an ax. Most telling of all, none mentioned anyone dressed like a rabbit.

Serendipity came to the rescue in 2000. On November 11 of that year, the *Washington Post* ran an article about the Maryland Folklore Archive and mentioned a 1973 paper called "The Bunny Man" by Patricia Johnson. Ms. Johnson, a student at the University of Maryland, concluded that the Bunny Man was an "urban belief tale," but that she had never heard of it before Halloween 1970. Conley checked the *Washington Post* around that era and discovered both his mistake and the Bunny Man. He had assumed the story was a venerable old folklore narrative when it was actually of relatively recent vintage. As for the ax-wielding bogey....

"MAN IN BUNNY SUIT SOUGHT IN FARFAX"

It seems that during the night of Saturday/Sunday, October 10/11, 1970, Robert Bennett, a cadet at the Air Force Academy, was parked with his fiancée in the 5400 block of Guinea Road when someone "dressed in a white [bunny] suit with long bunny ears" popped out of some nearby bushes.

"You're on private property and I have your tag number!" yelled the lepine-guised interloper.

Rather than rely on any implied legal action, the Bunny Man hurled a hatchet right through the driver's closed window. Fortunately, the weapon missed both Bennett and his female companion. The furry assailant "skipped" off into the night.

Aside from the hatchet, the police found no clues. The accusation of trespassing seemed strange, as Bennett was visiting his uncle at the time, and his uncle's house sat right across the street from where the couple had parked.

Rather appropriately, the Halloween edition of the *Post* carried further news...

"THE 'RABBIT' REAPPEARS"

It seems that late Thursday, October 29, 1970, Paul Phillips, the night watchman at a local construction site, spotted someone—or something—on the porch of the newly built house at 5307 Guinea Road. The figure appeared to be a human-sized, upright rabbit. This time, however, the long-eared lunatic carried a full-sized wood ax.

"I started talking to him," Phillips said, "and that's when he started chopping." ["'Rabbit' Reappears," p. B1]

The anthropomorphic apparition vigorously whacked a roof support of the house. "All you people trespass around here," he yelled. "If you don't get out of here, I'm going to bust you on the head."

Phillips ran back to his car to retrieve his handgun, but the Bunny Man fled before he returned. He said the person within the fur sounded like a male in his early twenties.

Six police officers arrived on the scene by 10:00 P.M., but again, there was not much they could do.

A day or so later, a worker at the Kings Park West Subdivision received a call from someone who called himself "the Axe Man."

"Mr. _____, you have been messing up my property, by dumping tree stumps, limbs and brush, and other things on the property." Despite his threatening name and demeanor, the Axe Man suggested they meet that night to "discuss the situation." The police staked out the proposed meeting place, but no one showed up, bunny-suited or otherwise.

This was the last anyone heard from either the Bunny or Axe Man. The authorities were inclined to believe the two were the same person. He was never apprehended; apparently, no one was specifically accused or even rumored to be him/them.

Up until 1970, most of Fairfax County, Virginia, consisted of forests, streams, pastures, and farms. The nation's ever-growing capital, however, required a larger and larger work force, which in turn required more housing. The Kings Park West Subdivision eventually encompassed 1,500 new houses, and it was only one of several subdivisions built in Fairfax County in the early 1970s. Construction crews (an ironic name if ever there was one) tore up hundreds of acres of woods and meadows to make way for this suburban progress. Certainly, many locals were upset at seeing more and more of their wilderness areas being destroyed.

Perhaps the rabbit costume was a sign of something other than cartoonish lunacy. Perhaps it symbolized the denizens of the forest, and the Bunny Man gave voice to the protest the local animals could not express.

The Bunny-Man Cometh

Brian Conley's search for the Bunny Man was long and arduous, and I'm sure final victory tasted sweet, but I could have saved him years of trouble. Starting at age 12, a friend of mine produced a series of fairly sophisticated home movies about cowboys, monsters, spies, and alien invaders. This was in the early 1970s. His main "soundstage" was the family garage. As I helped him with one such 8mm epic, I noticed a pile of *Fate* Magazines on an old cabinet. Nosy kid that I was, I flipped through them.

This publication featuring all things paranormal had brought the District of Columbia bogeyman to national attention in its March 1971 issue. "Here Comes Bunny Man" told of this "ill-tempered, probably dangerous hatchet-wielder" lurking around the suburbs of Virginia and D.C. He smashed the window of a dating couple in a car and told them they were trespassing before "he hopped off into the woods." Two weeks later a security guard probably started reassessing his career goals when he found a man in a bunny suit chopping away at an unfinished house in a new addition.

"You are trespassing," said the white rabbit. "If you come any closer I'll chop off your head!"

The brief *Fate* article ended with the testimony of three schoolchildren from Seat Pleasant, Maryland. They came home from school and reported "this man on the street with this bunny rabbit suit on with a hatchet."

How had Conley missed the news stories (if not the tabloid-esque *Fate*) at the time of their appearances? I believe he erred in assuming the tale took years, even decades, to evolve, passing by word of mouth from generation to generation. His earliest proposed Bunny-inspired crime took place in 1918. In reality, the long-eared bogey sprang fully developed into folklore within a few months of the Guinea Road incidents. One cannot tie a schedule to concepts as fluid as storytelling, wonder, and the fascination with strange events.

SOURCES:

Conley, Brian A., "Bunny Man Unmasked: The Real Life Origins of an Urban Legend." http://www.fairfaxcounty.gov/library/branches/vr/bunny/bunnyprint.htm.

Godfrey, Linda, "Michigan Bunny Man" on "Linda Godfrey's Blog," April 11. 2020. https://lindagodfrey.com/2020/04/11/michigan-bunny-man/

Gordon, Stan. *Creepy Cryptids and Strange UFO Encounters of Pennsylvania* (Greensburg, PA: Bulldog Design, 2022).

"Here Comes Bunny Man," *Fate* Vol. 24, no. 3 (March 1971), p. 77.

MacDougall, Curtis D. *Hoaxes* (New York; Dover Publications, 1968 [1940]).

"Man in Bunny Suit Sought in Fairfax," *Washington Post*, Oct. 22, 1970, p. B2.

Mitchell, Andrew, "Rabbit Man," *Fortean Times* no. 406 (June 2021), pp. 74–75.

Paulding Light: https://en.wikipedia.org/wiki/Paulding_Light (accessed 2/7/2023).

"The 'Rabbit' Reappears." *Washington Post*, Oct. 31, 1970, p. B1.

Ramsey, Raymond H. *No Longer on the Map* (New York: The Viking Press, 1972).

THE CARBUNCLE

DUKE SENIOR: Sweet are the uses of adversity,
Which, like the toad, ugly and venomous,
Wears yet a precious jewel in his head.

—William Shakespeare, *As You Like It*, Act II, Scene I

A carbuncle is the gem form of almandine (an iron-aluminum garnet) when cut in a convex fashion called *cabochon*, according to the *Encylopaedia Britannica*. The word comes from the Latin *carbunculus*, "a little coal," which may explain how a gem *resembling* a little coal became confused with an animal that *carries* a bright, coallike light on its body.

A Spanish priest named Martin Barco del Centenera once spotted the latter (so he claimed) in the highlands of Paraguay. As he wrote in 1602 in a book entitled *Argentina y Conquista del Rio de la Plata*, he saw "a smallish animal, with a shining mirror in its head, like a glowing coal." [Borges, p. 51] Barco got it into his own head that the animal he saw was something called a *carrabuncle* and that the mirror or crystal on its brow possessed magical powers. He pursued it for years through the rain forests and plains of Paraguay with the tenacity of a fortune hunter seeking more mundane treasure, but he never caught it.

One night, a conquistador named Gonzalo Fernandez de Oviedo saw two lights shining out of the darkness as he sailed through the Strait of Magellan. He, too, came to believe these were magical gems set into the heads of the mysterious carbuncles.

This seems like an odd conclusion to jump to, but there is an odd, obscure thread of belief running through history that certain creatures have a supernatural jewel inside their brains or visible on their brows like a prototype unicorn horn.

Isadore of Seville, the archbishop of Seville in the 7th century CE, compiled, like Pliny before him, a series of volumes containing all the knowledge then known of the world—what we now call an encyclopedia. He wrote of the legend in his *Opera Omnia*:

> It is taken from the dragon's brain but does not harden into a gem unless the head is cut off from the living beast; wizards, for this reason, cut the heads from sleeping dragons. Men bold enough to venture into dragons' lairs scatter grain that has been treated to make these beasts sleepy, and when they have fallen asleep their heads are struck off and the gems plucked out. [Costello, p 159]

The attributes of the Asian dragon (*lung* or *long*) are vastly different from its Western counterpart, being as it is a holy beast, a rain-god, and an all-around benevolent spirit as opposed to the European dragon's identification with the Devil. The two share one interesting trait, however: The *lung* has no wings, yet it can fly due to a magic "organ" on its head called the *Chi'ih muh*, which certainly reminds one of the Western dragon stone. [MacKenzie, p. 46]

Conventional anthropology has it that the legends of the European dragon and the Asian *lung* developed independently, as their functions in myth and literature are so different. It would have been a long and difficult trip, but it is possible that the general idea of powerful, serpentine creatures might have followed merchants and adventurers along the series of trade routes known as the Silk Road.

However, how does one explain a very carbuncle-like story from the native people of North America, known long before the first European (and, most likely, the first Asian) explorer set foot in the New World?

The Carbuncle

Anthropologist and ethnologist James Mooney was famous for his works preserving the traditions of Native Americans. His book *Myths of the Cherokee* could not have been produced without the help of A'yun'ini, or "Swimmer," a "genuine aboriginal antiquarian and patriot" from whom nearly three-fourths of the Cherokee folktales were obtained. [Mooney, p. 236]

One Cherokee tradition handed down by A'yun'ini was that of a monster called the Uktena. "Uktena is a great snake, as large around as a tree trunk, with horns on its head, and a bright, blazing crest like a diamond upon its forehead, and scales glittering like sparks of fire."

The resemblance to the carbuncle doesn't stop there. "The blazing diamond is called *Ulunsu'ti*, "Transparent," and he who can win it may become the greatest wonder worker of the tribe." [Mooney p. 297] This is harder than it seems because the light from the *Ulunsu'ti* enthralls one so that "he runs toward the snake instead of trying to escape."

The significance of the story did not escape the notice of compiler James Mooney. "Myths of a jewel in the head of a serpent or of a toad are so common to all Aryan nations as to have become proverbial," as he mentions in an endnote. [p. 459] Several white traders and military officers claimed to have seen a *Ulunsu'ti*, but no amount of money could induce a native medicine worker to part with one.

From a semiprecious stone to a jewel in a dragon's head to a lighthouse-bright creature at the southernmost tip of the New World, the carbuncle legend, as obscure as it is, has seen some strange peregrinations. Yet it has been found in stranger places.

Nathaniel Colgan, an Irish naturalist, gathered folklore about plant and animal life in the southern county of Kerry in the late nineteenth century. To him "carbuncle" meant the dark red gemstone.

A book entitled *The History and Present State of the County of Kerry* by Charles Smith (1756) mentioned that a "carbuncle" was said to lie at the bottom of the Lakes of Killarney, visible only during fair weather. Smith obviously thought the name referred to a valuable gem.

In 1884, Henry Hart published an article, "Plants of Some of the Mountain Ranges of Ireland." It seems a local man accompanied Mr. Hart as he tramped around Brandon Mountain in 1883. This local informed the naturalist that from nearby Lough Veagh people collected "pearl shells." "These come off an enormous animal called the 'Carrabuncle' which is seen glittering like silver in the water at night. The animal has gold and jewels and precious stones and shells hanging onto it." [Colgan, p. 60]

In 1888 Colgan himself visited Mount Brandon and by an amazing stroke of luck met Hart's informant. Naturally, Colgan asked after the Carrabuncle. "He told me that it was a kind of snake that lived in Lough Geal, not L. Veagh, and made the lake shine, and threw off shells with precious stones in them."

Colgan and the local man met for dinner at a pub in the village of Cloghane. The pub owner, Mr. Connor, also spoke of the Carrabuncle. Supposedly, it was seen only once every seven years and looked "like a cashk [cask] rowlin' about on the water." Mrs. Connor "remembered men coming some years before and getting pearls in the lakes and rivers."

Word must have spread about Colgan's quest for knowledge because the following day a postman felt the need to tell the naturalist about the self-same beastie. "It lit up the whole lake, he said, and the pearls found in the river that flowed out from Lough Geal came off the Carrabuncle."

Colgan concluded that this Carrabuncle was a permutation of the wyrms, dragons, and water-horses of the Irish lakes, probably a very local tradition as the name was unknown elsewhere in the British Isles.

Imagine his surprise when, a year or so after his visit to Kerry, he read Alfred Russell Wallace's *A Narrative of Travels on the Amazon and Rio Negro*. Wallace mentioned literal Amazons, the warrior women said to dwell near that vast Brazilian river. Wallace wrote, "I fear the story of the Amazons must be placed with those of the Curipura, or Demon of the Woods, and Carbunculo of the Upper Amazon and Peru."

Carbunculo was obviously the Spanish or Portuguese version of *carrabuncle*, used apparently in the same context, meaning a fantastic creature that dwelt in water. Colgan wrote to Dr. Wallace, but the eminent scientist/explorer replied that he no longer remembered the legend. Wallace suggested contacting fellow explorer Henry Bates. Mr. Bates, by then the secretary of the Geological Society, rather tersely replied that "he knew nothing about the Carbunculo, and had long since ceased, as he told me, to take any interest in such things."

So, the mystery of how this upper Amazonian name/legend/beast reached a small area in southern Ireland remains unsolved.

Peter Costello remarks in *The Magic Zoo* on how the belief in the Carbuncle has spread from Italy to Ireland and into South America, but

The Carbuncle

even he underestimated the legendary beast's hold on the human psyche. At least, he never mentioned the British merchant William Finch, who visited Sierra Leone in West Africa in 1607 and wrote a long description of the land, its people, and its animals and resources. After listing the types of trees, fishes, birds, and mammals found, he mentions a strange creature inhabiting the mountains "which our interpreter called a carbuncle, which is said to be often seen, but only in the night. This animal is said to carry a stone in the forehead, wonderfully luminous, giving him light by which to feed in the night, and on hearing the slightest noise he presently conceals it with a skin or film naturally provided for the purpose." [Beatty p. 141]

Our own globetrotting finishes (for now) with a more recent Carbuncular connection to South America that draws in not toads, snakes or dragons, but a creature even more unexpected.

The black dog tradition is mentioned more than once in this book, with the accompanying information that it is associated with the Celtic and/or British world. The following excerpt from Robert Chambers' *Book of Days* (1888) is typical. Chambers interviewed the witness, a local schoolmaster, personally:

> "I was returning home," said he, "late at night in a gig with the person who was driving. When we came near the spot, where a portion of the gibbet had lately stood, we saw on the bank of the roadside, along which a ditch or narrow brook runs, a flame of fire as large as a man's hat. 'What's that?' I exclaimed. 'Hush!' said my companion, all in a tremble; and suddenly pulling in his horse, made a dead stop. I then saw an immense black dog lying on the road just in front of our horse, which also appeared trembling with fright. The dog was the strangest looking creature I ever beheld. He was as big as a Newfoundland, but very gaunt, shaggy, with long ears and tail, eyes like balls of fire, and large, long teeth, for he opened his mouth and seemed to grin at us ... In a few minutes the dog disappeared, seeming to vanish like a shadow, or to sink into the earth. [Chambers, p. 434]

Having established the very Celtic-ness of Black Dogs, I must sheepishly add that a widespread Black Dog tradition can be found throughout Central and South America. This fact is rather odd; European folktales and legends in the New World came over with explorers and immigrants, but we can't blame the conquistadors for American hellhounds—the black dog tradition is almost unknown in Spain.

At any rate, the Latin American dogs share many characteristics with their Celtic counterparts: long, shaggy black fur, glowing red eyes the size of saucers, enormous size (descriptions include sheep-, mastiff-, pony-, and donkey-sized), a tendency to appear near rivers or on bridges, etc.

The black dog of Columbia and southern Ecuador, however, is known for one particular aspect, far different from the average black dog yet quite familiar. This beast is "a Black Dog with a diamond in its forehead that dwells in rivers and streams and is also strongly linked to the earth as well. It is the owner of all subterranean treasures, such as gold veins and mineral deposits, and also protects the forest against charcoal burners who burn too much wood." [Burchell, p. 17]

And the name of this canine apparition? The Carbunco!

SOURCES:

Beatty, K. J. *Human Leopard Society: Ritual Murder and Cannibalism in Colonial Africa* (London: Notoir Books, 2020 [1915]).

Borges, Jorge Luis, and Norman Thomas di Giovanni. *Book of Imaginary Beings* (New York: Avon, 1967).

Chambers, Robert. *Book of Days*, Vol. 2 (London: W. & R. Chambers, Ltd., 1888).

Costello, Peter. *Magic Zoo* (New York: St. Martin's Press, 1979).

MacKenzie, Donald A. *Myths of China and Japan* (London: Bracken Books, 1985 [1924]).

Mooney, James. *Myths of the Cherokee* (Nashville, TN: Charles and Randy Elder, 1982). Originally published in the *Nineteenth Annual Report of the Bureau of American Ethnology* (1900).

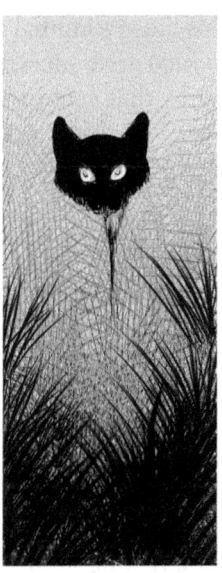

THE CHESHIRE BEASTS

*"In **Land and Water**, March 7, 1874, a correspondent writes that he had heard of depredations by a wolf, in Ireland . . . a killer was running wild, in Cavan, slaying as many as 30 sheep in one night. There is another account, in **Land and Water** . . . This correspondent knew of 42 instances, in three townlands, in which sheep had been similarly killed — throats cut and blood sucked, but no flesh eaten."*

— Charles Fort, *LO!*, Chapter 13

When I first developed the idea of a fantasy world in which I would set epic stories and novels, I knew it would have to be inhabited by many strange and magical creatures. Oh, there were the obvious fantasy tropes of elves, dwarves, unicorns, and dragons, but it was more fun to make up critters of my own. One I had in mind that I never fleshed out I dubbed the Cheshire Beast, a quadruped predator that appeared, struck at deer, sheep or even people, and vanished again, never seen coming or going, impossible to catch. It was named, of course, for the Cheshire Cat. The idea was that these creatures could teleport from their world to ours, attacking, eating, and fleeing with little fear of reprisal, leaving behind only dead animals and frightened farmers. Perhaps a pack, mobbing someone, could carry them bodily back to the Otherworld.

My main inspiration for this elusive animal was Charles Fort's *LO!*, especially chapters 13 and 14, which are concerned with strange attacks on animals and people by creatures that seem to come from nowhere and then disappear without a trace. The major theme of *LO!* was teleportation, so Fort seemed to imply such marauders were, indeed, popping in and out from Elsewhere.

Closer to the present, just days, in fact, after setting up my first Facebook account, the subject of thylacines popped up. Thylacines, *aka* Tasmanian wolves or Tasmanian tigers ("Tassies" for short), were meat-eating marsupials, the Down Under equivalent of big cats, wolves, and jackals. Doglike in form, they bore tigerish stripes on their hindquarters and possessed amazingly long jaws and tapering, kangaroo-like tails. Though they could lope like canines, they could jump like 'roos if need be.

Also, they are officially extinct, the last known specimen having died in the Hobart [Tasmania] Zoo in 1936. I linked a film clip of this sad creature to my Facebook page. All well and good.

I started a little housecleaning, digging through my mass of old magazines and hoping to find a few to delete. Totally at random, I pulled out the *Fortean Times* no. 76 (Aug.–Sept. 1994). Within its pages I found an interview with Australian cryptid hunters Tony Healy and Paul Cropper.

Two Tasmanian wolves (*Thylacinus cynocephalus*) were on exhibit at the Washington Zoo in 1904 (photo: Smithsonian Institution).

The Cheshire Beasts

"There have been more than 400 reported thylacine sightings in Tasmania since the beast's 'extinction' in the 1930s," according to these adventurous gentlemen.

Then I pulled out a *FATE Magazine* at random, Vol. 58 no. 9 (Sept 2005). "Devil Pigs and Dinosaurs" by Dr. Karl Shuker described mythical animals of New Guinea, including the "dobsegna," which sounded suspiciously like a thylacine. "Its head and shoulders are dog-like, but its mouth is huge and strong, and its tail is very long and thin. Villagers claim that from its ribs to its hips it has no intestines (but this merely suggests that it is very thin in this particular body region), and that in this region it is striped." [p. 62]

In an aside, Shuker mentions that "the chronicles of cryptozoology are fairly bulging with unconfirmed post-1936 sightings [of Tassies] both on Tasmania and in mainland Australia," which in itself would be odd, as the marsupial carnivores became extinct on the Australian mainland about 2,000 years ago.

A third magazine (arbitrarily yanked from the pile) was *Fortean Times* no. 298 (Apr. 2013), with the article "The Wild Dog of Ennerdale" by Crispin Andrews, which brings us back to *LO!*

The Ennerdale story has always stuck in my mind. I looked up hundreds of Charles Fort's sources during my college years, but *Chamber's Journal* (the main source of the Ennerdale story) was not available at the Oklahoma State University or University of Tulsa libraries. So, the one incident I really wanted to flesh out the "Cheshire Beasts" was the one I never found. Naturally, I read "The Wild Dog of Ennerdale."

The descriptions of the Ennerdale beast sound amazingly like a thylacine. Even the "vampire" aspect fit: According to conservationist Nick Mooney, "Any carnivore will start at the best parts, blood being the best food. If it's a big prey animal (like a sheep) that's all it can physically eat." Apparently, grown sheep are too large to be torn apart by a single thylacine, so it can only eat a few soft organs and lap the blood.

Crispin Andrews uncovered a witness description that stated the beast had stripes on the back half of its body. *Voila*! A Tasmanian tiger!

How did a Tassie end up near a small village in the Lake Country near the Scottish border? Well, writes Andrews, the Romans, William the Conqueror, King John, and others had coliseums, parks, and menageries. As the centuries passed, there were also circuses, zoos, and private collections of exotic animals. They displayed elephants, giraffes, lions, tigers, and hyenas. Tassies are never mentioned, but "a thylacine could easily have found itself in a British menagerie." I suppose.

At the end of his overview of the Ennerdale affair, Andrews lists some other cases of mysterious ravening beasts that might have been thylacines: 1888, Winslow Arizona—weird striped animal shot; neither the mountain man who shot it nor the local Navajos had ever seen anything like it. 1874, Cavan Ireland (mentioned above). Nov. 1905, Badminton Gloucestershire—blood-sucking beast. 1934, Tennessee—animal kills dogs and leaps like a kangaroo.

Well, continues Andrews, zoos lose animals. I wonder how many zoos or circuses existed near those areas at those time periods. How many such institutions even had thylacines back then? How many zoos/menageries/circuses were near those places, in those eras, and had thylacines, and the thylacines all escaped? Sounds a bit off.

Finally, though, it hit me: *Here were my Cheshire Beasts!* The Tassies obviously saw what happened to the indigenous people of Tasmania and decided to leave in a fashion unavailable to more mundane creatures. They teleported to the mainland of Australia, then to New Guinea, England, Arizona, Tennessee, and I suppose they've been popping around the world ever since.

Maybe now, in a time when everyone regrets the downfall of the marsupial predators, they are venturing back to their island home, loping through the Tasmanian wilds with big Cheshire grins on their muzzles.

ADDENDA: THE ABCS OF UNKNOWN CRITTERS

As mentioned in the Introduction, Janet and Colin Bord divided unknown animals into several general archetypes, including phantom panthers: cougar-like felines that often had black fur.

The most enthusiastic collector of Alien Big Cat (ABC) reports in Britain was probably Di Francis, author of *Cat Country* (1982). After hearing Ms. Francis speak about mystery cats on the radio, Ms. Merrily Harpur became fascinated by the subject and sought out Francis. She accompanied the researcher into the field in Devonshire, and when Ms. Francis moved to Scotland, Harpur inherited stacks of reports and letters concerning Britain's phantom panthers. Harpur became a cryptozoologist whether she wanted to be or not—in fact, becoming "the" expert on Alien Big Cats in Britain. In her "Alien Big Cat Diary" in the *Fortean Times*, she sounded rather irritated that people were reporting a creature that didn't sound like a black panther in any way, "the kind of

ABC which gives headaches to those researchers who would like to pigeonhole Britain's big cats as released or escaped pets."

What is this weird new monster? Martin O'Neill, while cycling in Dorsetshire, described it as "fair in colour—tan—with what I thought were stripes on its back." It had "cat's ears—pointed and quite large—and huge eyes." It was about the size of a German shepherd. It walked across the road in front of him, and O'Neill added, "What struck me was its tail," which had "2 in to 3 in [5-8 cm]-long fur, and [was] tapered." Can't people tell a phantom panther from a thylacine? [*Fortean Times* no. 240, Oct. 2008]

Or perhaps something else is at work here. Southern England was notorious for early phantom panther outbreaks, starting with the "Surry Puma" in 1962 and continuing to the present day. In one panther-haunted area (Branksome, Dorsetshire), Joan Gilbert reported a decidedly non-panther-ish beast on April 7, 1974, at 3:30 in the morning. "It had stripes, a long thin tail, and seemed to be all grey, though it might have had some yellow on it. It was thin and definitely not a fox." It trotted across Western Avenue sweet as you please and wandered back off the map. (Bord, p. 59)

Ms. Gilbert later identified the creature in an illustrated book on animals. It was a thylacine. For all we know, thylacines have some affinity for other cryptids.

SOURCES:

Bord, Janet and Colin. *Alien Animals* (Harrisburg, PA: Stackpole Books, 1981).

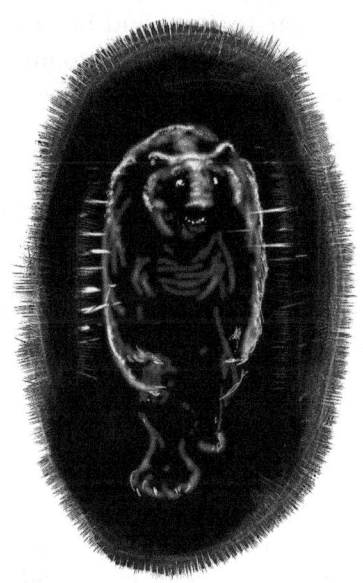

THE CHOCCOLOCCO MONSTER

Starting in mid-May 1969, something began appearing at night in the forests by the Iron City cutoff and Choccolocco Road between Iron City and Choccolocco, east of Anniston in Calhoun County, Alabama. Margaret Teague, who worked at the Cleburne County Hospital, was driving home late on the cutoff when she spotted something she called a "booger" at the edge of the road. It walked on its hind legs and was covered with hair. Its head was huge. "Oh, Lordy, Lordy, what a head," Ms. Teague exclaimed later.

"I turned the car around in the middle of the road to get another look, and it got caught in the ditch," she told a reporter for the *Anniston Star*. "I just knowed the booger had me for sure." [Creamer, p. 3]

A man driving down the Choccolocco Road in late May saw what he described as a "varmint," "a humpbacked combination of bear and panther." [Coleman and Clark, p. 161] The night after this, Johnny Ray Teague and three friends were driving in the same area when their car stalled. After they climbed out to look at the engine, they heard something crashing through the brush beside the road. They saw a beast "the size of a cow, gray to black in color, humped similarly to a camel." It had a huge head and big teeth. The quartet jumped back in their car and locked the doors. The monster, enjoying its captive audience, circled the car a few times before lumbering off into the trees.

Teague finally got his car to start, and he and his three passengers roared away. About half a mile from the encounter site, they claimed to see three or four more of the creatures that were even larger than the first! This is particularly odd, as we will discover.

Other witnesses also described the monster as gray or black with large teeth and a hump. Some added long, stringy head hair that obscured its features. By June 1969, people from all over the state were patrolling the Choccolocco roads with guns or rifles in hand. Several fired at suspicious shadows or forms. There were so many gun-toting fellows about, in fact, that local farmers grew angry. "I'll tell you one thing, if one of our cows or bulls is shot, and we can find out who it is, somebody is going to pay dear," Mrs. Bobby Murphy told a *Star* reporter.

After June, the monster no longer appeared.

In October 2001, a Nances Creek resident named Neal Williamson revealed the truth about the Choccolocco Monster to reporter Matthew Creamer of the *Anniston Star*. "Back then, you didn't have nothing to do, really. You didn't have computers," he explained.

On a boring weekend night in 1969, Williamson, then 15, crept out while his parents were asleep and drove down the country lanes in their 1950 Ford. He realized that an old cow skull he'd found was still in the back seat. Soon thereafter, he donned a long, black coat, took the skull out to a dark stretch of road, and waited. When a car approached, he ran out with the skull held above his head, did a dance of sorts, and ran back into the trees before the driver and/or passengers could get a good look at him. On occasion, he wore a white sheet instead of the coat, thus creating variations in the witnesses' descriptions.

One night in June 1969, as Williamson played monster, he had with him two companions to whom he had revealed the joke. As the teenager pranced out before an approaching truck, the vehicle slowed down and someone in the cab fired a rifle several times in his direction. Williamson and his friends fled through the woods as a spotlight from the truck raked the trees. No one was hit, but Williamson popped out on the far side of the small woods, ran across a pasture, and crashed into a barbed-wire fence.

That was his last performance as the Choccolocco Monster.

The shooter's identity was never revealed, but he was quoted as saying that the monster ran back into the hills after he fired at it, letting out "an almost humanlike cry." [Clark and Coleman, p. 161] No doubt.

One has to wonder about Teague and his companions, who fled in horror from the cow-skull-topped apparition only to spot more of them—bigger and more horrible than the first—farther along Choccolocco Road. Did they feel the need to "improve" their story? Or were they so panic-stricken that cows, or shadows, or bushes stirred by the wind became monsters in their minds? Whether deliberate or not, such exaggerations can make a legend grow.

On the other hand, for once we know there *was* something unusual standing by those Alabama roads, so people weren't imagining things. In fact, the witnesses may even have suppressed one detail to make their stories sound more believable: No one mentioned that the horned, hairy, humpbacked monster *danced* every time he appeared.

SOURCES:

Clark, Jerome, and Loren Coleman. *Creatures of the Outer Edge* (New York: Warner Books, 1978).

Creamer, Matthew, "The Choccolocco Monster: Jokester reveals 32-Year-Old Prank," in *The Anniston Star*, October 31, 2001, pp. 1–5. (Online link is no longer valid.)

COLORADO RAPTORS

It all started innocently enough when Ms. Myrtle Snow of Pagosa Springs, Colorado, sent a letter to the *Denver Post*'s Sunday supplement, *Rocky Mountain Empire Magazine*. The letter was published in its August 22, 1982, edition. Ms. Snow had lived in the Pagosa Springs area all her life, and she had encountered some very intriguing creatures.

In May 1935, when she was three years old, Myrtle claimed she and a friend discovered five "baby dinosaurs" in a "nest" in an outhouse. The friend's mother couldn't identify them; the unnamed friend decided they were "snakes with legs." The girls finally threw them out into a field.

Several months later, a farmer named John Martinez began losing sheep to an unknown predator in a canyon about five miles from his ranch. Eventually, he shot the culprit, and what a culprit it was!

An Apache youth dragged the carcass back to the ranch with a team of mules. Martinez put the corpse in a barn, and the local farmers came to gawk at it. "My grandfather took us to see it the next morning," wrote Ms. Snow. "It was about seven feet tall, was grey, had a head like a snake, short front legs with claws that resembled chicken feet, large stout back legs and a long tail." [Rickard, p. 8] Years after writing her letter, in an interview with Nick Sucik, she added that "its body was covered in fine gray hairs." [Sucik, p. 144] (Could the "hairs" have been downy feathers? Velociraptors and similar dinosaurs are now thought to have been partially covered by feathers.) No one could figure out what it was, but the Apache boy thought it was something his tribal elders called a "Moon Cow"—always rare and hardly ever seen in the modern era.

Two years later, according to Snow, she visited a friend well out in the country and went exploring in the woods by herself. She found a shallow cave, and while examining it she heard a loud snakelike hissing. She froze; then she realized the hissing came from a tree some distance away. There was a dinosaurish creature by the tree that looked like the one she'd seen in the Martinez barn. It stood erect, possibly because it was after something in the tree, and it was green from the waist up and brown from the waist down. The brown areas seemed to be hair-covered. A line of "humps" ran down its back.

The beast snatched something out of the branches and held it for a moment in its foreclaws as if examining it. Then it shoved its catch into its mouth. Myrtle was able to sneak away unseen, or perhaps the creature just ignored her.

One can dismiss recollections from early childhood, when the boundaries between reality and imagination are somewhat plastic, but in her letter Snow mentioned one more encounter as an adult: "On Oct. 23, 1978, as I was returning from Chama, NM, about 7:30 PM, in a driving rain, I saw another one going through the field towards the place where I had seen the one in 1937." (Chama is about 30 miles southeast of Pagosa Springs, just across the New Mexico border).

When Nick Sucik interviewed Snow (*c*. 2000), she told him that she had seen another bipedal saurian on the same stretch of highway a few years after writing her letter. A passenger this time, the driver also saw the creature.

Sucik took it upon himself to locate witnesses to bipedal "dinosaurs" in the Colorado area. Finding witnesses turned out to be nearly as hard as finding dinosaurs. Snow knew of several, but they were all either dead or had moved away, and she didn't know where.

A buddy from Sucik's Marine days recalled an episode of *Sightings* or *Unsolved Mysteries* in which a couple of ranchers on horseback come upon a "dead dinosaur" near Cortez, Colorado. Other people remembered the show, but neither TV series listed such an episode.

Sucik put an ad in the *Cortez Journal* requesting stories or sightings of little "dinosaurs.." He expected a stream of hoaxes and jokes, but he received only one response: A man had seen something like that in California in the 1950s.

An abortive house-to-house survey brought forth no dinosaur witnesses—only a few angry dogs.

Beasts Beyond Belief

The Colorado Raptors

Finally, he scraped together a few sightings, mostly of two-legged creatures dashing across roads in front of cars. Some sounded like collared lizards. Some sightings were due to an escaped emu. One drawing of a creature was obviously a coatimundi, a relative of the raccoon.

He heard a story about "baby dinosaurs" sent to the Cortez Museum in 1963. It turned out to be a box of baby dinosaur *fossils*, which in turn proved to be bones of various mammals mixed together.

Yet there were enough stories to keep Sucik interested. When he worked for the Navajo Nation, there were many rumors of giant reptiles being seen, but the subject was taboo among that First Nations people, so he could dig up no specifics.

On February 17, 1993, two truck drivers in a convoy saw a creature cross the road in front of them somewhere between Snowflake and Heber, Arizona. It stood 10 to 12 feet tall and had small arms like a *Tyrannosaurus rex*.

A man told Sucik about his two aunts—sisters—who traveled with their parents during the Depression to work on farms. A bizarre little creature started eating scraps at their campsite. The sisters caught it and put it in a birdcage. It looked exactly like a *T. rex*, but it was only the size of a kitten. Eventually, their father made them to let it go.

As if to bring things full circle, Sucik started receiving reports of a quadrupedal "dragon"—not a two-legged quasi-Velociraptor—being seen near Pagosa Springs. Former police chief Leonard Gallegos claimed to have seen it back in the 1950s, when he was a schoolboy. It resembled a Komodo Dragon, greenish-gray and "at least the size of an alligator."

"Sightings continue to this day," wrote Sucik.

Meanwhile. . . . In 1993, Texas UFO researcher Jimmy Ward published an article called "The Mountain Boomer," a collection of folktales from the Big Bend National Park area of Texas (almost as far west as Pagosa Springs but much farther south). A "Mountain Boomer" was supposedly a "giant lizard that walked on its hind legs and whose voice sounded like the roll of distant thunder." The creatures were usually greenish or brownish, standing five or six feet tall, their short forelegs held like arms. While hunting down stories, Ward met up with a Connecticut family who spotted such a creature while *en route* to California. They agreed that it was the very image of the nasty Dromaeosaurs of *Jurassic Park* fame. (One should point out that the eastern collared lizard is sometimes called a mountain boomer, and that it can run on its hind legs when threatened.)

Cryptozoologist Chad Arment suggests that some "baby dinosaur" stories might be caused by people seeing species of lizards that can run (momentarily) on their hind legs, like the real mountain boomer or the South American basilisk (the latter presumably escaped pets). How to explain reptiles standing six or even ten feet tall, though?

Although skeptical of the Texas and Colorado stories, Arment mentioned that: "Some friends of mine in the reptile trade had done business a few years ago with an individual who had collected some Colorado species and had offered to catch some 'river dinos' for them." [Arment, p. 39] Arment's friends didn't have the money, but yes, the description given of a Colorado "river dino" was of a bipedal, theropod-dinosaurish reptile. The hunt continues.

When I was a dinosaur-crazed kid, I hoped that remnants of the great reptiles survived somewhere, hidden from men, maybe in Asia, Africa, or South America. Perhaps I don't have to travel so far, after all, to find a "lost world." But I might regret finding it, if I did.

SOURCES:

Arment, Chad, "Dinos in the U.S.A.: A Summary of North American Bipedal 'Lizard' Reports." *North American BioFortean Review* Vol. II, No. 2, (2000), pp. 32–39.

Gerhard, Ken, and Nick Redfern. *Monsters of Texas* (Bideford, North Devon: CFZ Press, 2010).

Rickard, Bob, "A Reprise for 'Living Wonders.'" *Fortean Times* no. 40 (Summer 1983), pp. 4–15.

Sucik, Nick, "'Dinosaur' Sightings in the United States." *Cryptozoology and the Investigation of Lesser-Known Mystery Animals* (Landisville, PA: Coachwhip Publications, 2006), pp. 137–168.

Ward, Jimmy, "Mountain Boomer." *Far Out* Vol. 1, no. 4 (Summer 1993), pp. 45–46.

THE DARK WOODS BOGEY-MAN

In his book *Natural Likeness,* philosopher and fortean John Michell notes that many moths have dull, bark-colored wings that blend in with the brown, gray, and shadowed surroundings of a thick forest. However, these insects flash open their wings when frightened or disturbed, revealing large, round, yellow-ringed spots that resemble staring eyes. These "eyes," combined with the moths' thorax and head, form the illusion of a face, a protective adaptation particularly noticeable in the Eyed Hawkmoth's "nightmare animal's face complete with fur and snout." This "face" frightens off birds that would otherwise snap up the harmless insects.

It is taken for granted that this is a form of natural mimicry, the moths having evolved to resemble the harsh stare of predatory owls. However, when attacked or startled, owls open their eyes to reveal bright-yellow rings as if they are mimicking something even more frightful. Michell writes "it is not necessary to conclude that one of these creatures has been designed

Many moths such as this Dryandra moth have evolved eye-like markings on their wings to frighten away predators.

Beasts Beyond Belief

by natural selection to mimic the other." [p. 53] It is possible that owls as well as moths are mimicking something else, the countenance of some "universal symbol of terror," "the glaring bogey-men" that little children believe lurk in dark woods.

What is this *ur*-creature that insects and owls imitate? Something like West Virginia's "Mothman," with its vast wingspan and burning, hypnotic gaze? Perhaps it is some entirely unknown monster, yet one simultaneously ancient and omnipresent, an occasional unwelcome visitor from some parallel world—an archetypal terror feared instinctively by birds, animals and humans alike—the Dark Woods Bogey-Man!

SOURCES:

Michell, John. *Natural Likeness: Faces and Figures in Nature* (New York: E. P. Dutton, 1979).

THAT ELUSIVE COELACANTH!

Monster hunter F. W. Holiday noted that the lake monsters of Britain seemed to avoid cameras deliberately—their presence even making cameras malfunction. For example, two women photographed a pair of monsters at Fort Augustus (Loch Ness) in 1970. As the tourists were looking for a suitable landscape to snap, "a large long-necked animal came into view round a headland out in the loch. Presently, it was joined by a similar but smaller creature." Naturally, the women forgot landscapes and shot several pictures of Nessie and son. Unfortunately:

> This film turned out a complete blank. The mechanism had failed to wind the film into frame and the shutter had simply been clicking on a piece of static backing-paper. [Holiday, pp. 191–192]

Other Nessie hunters dubbed this phenomenon the "Loch Ness Gremlin," but camera shyness is not confined to the Scottish Highlands. It affects every aspect of the paranormal, from Bigfoot hunting to UFO encounters. In fact, one is tempted to say, like Dana Carvey's Church Lady, "Well! Isn't that con-*veeen*-yent!"

Yet, long before cameras reached the point of being incorporated into cellphones, Charles Fort himself wondered if there wasn't an "occult police force" trying to vacuum up all evidence of paranormal phenomena.

On the other hand, a curse upon cameras has been observed in cases that are only mildly fortean. Take the story of the first Coelacanth.

In the 1930s, the East London Museum in East London, South Africa, was quite modest. The curator, a young woman named Marjorie Courtenay-Latimer, tried to build up its exhibits with little help and virtually no money. She at least assembled a formidable marine exhibit, since the local fishermen saved interesting specimens for her. On December 22, 1938, a trawler called the *Aristea*, under a Captain N. Goosen, presented her with a fish unlike any she had ever seen.

The creature was five feet long and weighed 127 pounds. It had huge eyes, a mouthful of nasty sharp teeth, and silvery-blue, armor-like scales. It had been hauled aboard the ship in a net with hundreds of other fish. Hours after the toughest shark had died, the thing still writhed and snapped on the deck.

It was dead by the time Miss Courtenay-Latimer got to it, however, and after the arduous task of returning with it to the museum (the museum didn't even own a handcart; she had to borrow one), she sketched the fish and wrote a letter to chemist and ichthyologist James L. B. Smith in Knysna, 350 miles away.

When he read the curator's description and saw the sketch, Professor Smith realized she had perfectly described a Coelacanth, a fish that had first evolved in the Devonian Era 300 million years ago and which had died out (supposedly) with the dinosaurs at the end of the Cretaceous. He naturally wished to travel to East London, but no planes were available to a lowly ichthyologist, and African roads in the 1930s left something to be desired. The 350 mile trip would take five or six days. In that environment, a fish would decay beyond recognition.

Smith telegraphed Courtenay-Latimer, instructing her to preserve at least the skeleton. And, of course, take photos. There was a problem, however.

"All along I had been frantic to see a photograph of the fish, but none came," Smith wrote years later. "For some curious reason something always went wrong with the attempts." [Smith, p. 38]

As Miss Courtenay-Latimer wrote in one letter: "Bad luck seems to have dogged this fish—I went down to ask Mr. Kirsten whom I got to

The Elusive Coelacanth

take photographs of the fish in flesh today and he tells me the entire film was spoilt."

In fact, it sounds almost as if knowledge of the Coelacanth was not supposed to have been released to the general public, and somebody or something was trying to take it back. After a 14 year search, a second Coelacanth was caught, thanks mainly to Prof. Smith's friend Captain Eric Hunt, who sailed among the Comoro Islands off the coast of Africa, handing out leaflets and promising monetary rewards to any native fisherman who captured the prehistoric fish. A fisherman named Ahamadi Abdallah caught one, Captain Hunt secured it aboard his schooner, and Smith appealed to Prime Minister Dr. Daniel Malan for help in bringing the fish to South Africa. [Weinberg, p. 76] Dr. Malan, impressed with Smith's persistence and knowledge, arranged for a Dakota cargo plane to ferry him to the Comoros and back.

However: "We heard later that when Dr. Malan tried to make contact with the Minister of Defence, storms had cut the telephone line at several points and eventually a police officer had to go many miles over bad roads to take a message." [Smith, p. 129]

Eventually, Smith reached the Comoros and Hunt's schooner, and the Coelacanth was flown to Durban.

"I looked hard at that schooner," Smith recalled, "not suspecting that I should never see it again: for a bare two weeks later they were caught in a cyclone and the boat was destroyed and sunk. Our plane did not escape by much. Did Coelacanths bring destruction in their train? I remembered that Goosen's trawler *Aristea* that had caught *Latimeria* was wrecked and destroyed not long afterwards." [Smith, p. 148] Maybe some "fortean censors" were a bit late with their disasters.

Nowadays, Coelacanths are well known. More specimens have been caught around the Comoros, and a second species was discovered in Indonesia in 1998. The ancient fish, which lived long before the dinosaurs and still exists today, is like the proverbial bone thrown to the dogs in the realm of cryptozoology, living proof that prehistoric animals could survive the geological ages to the present. If some "fortean censoring department" was trying to keep it from us, let us be thankful it failed.

SOURCES:

Holiday, F. W. *Creatures of the Inner Sphere* (New York: Popular Library, 1973).

Smith, James L. B. *Search Beneath the Sea* (New York: Henry Holt, 1956).

Weinberg, Samantha. *Fish Caught in Time* (London: Fourth Estate, 1999).

FELINE PHANTOMS

True ghost stories of cats are few and far between, so cat-lovers in general... will welcome the description of their after-death returns.

—Maude ffolkes, *True Ghost Stories* (1938)

Despite centuries of association with witches, ancient Egyptian mythology, superstition, and all things scary and Halloween-ish, actual cat *ghosts* are uncommon as specters go. Canine ghosts and hauntings outnumber them vastly, and such things as ghost horses, cattle, and birds have been reported, but not so many feline phantasms.

My own observation would be that what ghost cats lack in quantity they make up for in sheer weirdness.

SOMEWHAT SKEPTICAL—BUT NOT THIS TIME

Technical writer Mark S. Murley's autobiography, *A Slightly Haunted Life,* is an odd duck in the cryptid/UFO/paranormal genre. While an embarrassing number of such books pool at the extremes of the true believer or hard-headed debunker, Murley gives us many accounts of ghosts, strange aerial lights, and Skunk Apes as experienced by himself, his family, and/or his friends—only to shoot down half of them as probable mistakes or hoaxes. Assuming the existence of such phenomena, there undoubtedly would be many "false positives" for each genuine haunting or cryptid event in a person's life, so Murley's suspicions of hoaxers-as-ghosts and car headlights-as-Spook-Lights are probably true.

One event he does not dismiss, however, is the Night Kitty.

As a young boy, Mark Murley suffered from frequent nightmares, sleep paralysis, and hypnagogic hallucinations (see "The Land Between Night and Day" for information on these phenomena). When he was eight, several months after his family moved into a house near Geneva, Florida, young Mark woke to find a black cat sitting in a round-back wicker chair positioned beneath a window and near the bedroom door.

This does not seem very frightening in itself; the cat simply sat there, languidly flopping its tail. Its fur was utterly black, but its eyes, fixed solidly on Mark, were "like iridescent sea-green dimes." The Murleys did not own a cat, nor did Mark know of any feline like that in the neighborhood.

The boy had awakened from a murky dream, and he felt murky for a few more minutes, "as though someone was pouring syrup over my head." Eventually, he became fully conscious. He could not explain his fear of the black animal, but he dared not make for the door or reach for a weapon. He simply drew the covers up over his head.

Soon, though, he had to check on things. He pulled the sheets down slightly to find the Night Kitty still in the chair, staring at him. It apparently grew bored with the tableau because it narrowed its eyes and opened its mouth (making no sound). It turned completely around. The feline gathered its hind legs beneath itself and, as Mark recalls, "sprang over the top of the wicker chair and through the window behind it. Through the window. The closed window. The cat had melted through screen and glass and vanished back into the night from which it presumably came." [Murley, p. 23]

Mark ran screaming to his parents' bedroom as any child would have done. He told them of the matter-phasing feline. And as any parents would do, the elder Murleys checked Mark's room (finding nothing) and told him it was just a dream.

There does not seem to be much to this event, but it convinced Murley that the paranormal did exist, no matter how many hoaxes he uncovered or mistakes people made about haunted houses or unidentified aerial lights. It does stand out slightly among tales of ghostly animals in that most concern pets returning to their old owners or homes. This cat was unknown in the neighborhood, its interest in the Murley house and boy inscrutable, and its appearance was a unique, one-off event.

Much stranger things were to come.

Beasts Beyond Belief

FLAT CATS

In 1999, Chris Halliday of Coventry, West Midlands, wrote to the *Fortean Times* about a strange thing he saw while he and his wife, Jackie, were setting up their belongings in their new house. The couple found an unfamiliar black cat in their hallway. It did not seem to "belong" to its surroundings in a way that was difficult to describe. "The effect was similar to what would be achieved if you cut a picture of a cat out and stuck it over a picture of our hall, taking no regard of lighting and shadows." After staring at the couple for a few moments (and vice-versa), the cat vanished.

In the year 2000, Trevor Oullette of North Bay, Ontario, wrote in to the same publication to describe a similar experience. He, too, had encountered a "flat" black cat, describing it as "looking distinctly two-dimensional and sharply triangular." This cat was even stranger:

"Another arresting feature that I remember noticing were the thing's eyes—cut-out, or almond-shaped, holes through which I could see the scene directly behind the creature." The event was accompanied by a "timeless dissociation" during which the cat vanished—precisely when he could not say, like a mini-memory loss. Curiously enough, a few years later when living at a university he and several other residents often saw a more conventional ghost—a white cat, this time. [Sieveking, pp. 111–112]

CRYING KITTENS

Writer, musician, and podcaster Steve Stockton became interested in folklore, the paranormal, and the just plain weird as a boy growing up in rural Tennessee. As he approached adulthood, he realized his older relatives and their contemporaries were slowly dying off, and their strange experiences and tales were being lost to the world. He started soliciting stories of the unusual from local people, mostly from Tennessee and other southern states. As he presented these tales on various podcasts and radio programs, more people sent him their own supposedly true stories. Some of these accounts, most given anonymously, he published in his book *Strange Things in the Woods*.

One tale in *Strange Things in the Woods* concerns ghostly kittens.

When the anonymous storyteller was young, a stray cat lived in the family barn. It gave birth to a litter of seven kittens and promptly abandoned them. Sadly, by the time the narrator, his brother, and sister discovered them, the kittens had died. Being kids, they decided to hold a funeral for the tiny felines, preparing an old hatbox from the attic as a coffin and burying them in the bank of a nearby creek.

A week or so later, the sister visited the grave to lay some wildflowers on it. She was shocked to hear the mewling of kittens. She alerted her brothers that they had buried the kittens alive, and the children raced back to the creek with a shovel. All three siblings heard the cries of the kittens.

When they dug up the hatbox, however, they found that all seven kits were very dead, rotted, and smelly. They could do nothing but rebury them. "From then on," the narrator finishes, "for many years, we all continued to hear the muffled sounds of tiny kittens near the grave." [Stockton 2013, pp. 6–7]

This story struck close to author Stockton's heart, because as he revealed in his autobiography, *My Strange World*, he also experienced the sounds of kitten ghosts!

When Steve was only a few months old, his father built a new house for his growing family. The ranch-style house had no basement, only a crawlspace that ran the length of the building. There were windows covered with immovable wire screens for heating and cooling purposes, but otherwise there was only one entrance to the crawlspace: a square opening with a plywood door, which the elder Stockton kept locked.

One day when he was about ten, young Steve was playing in his back bedroom. The floor was hardwood, though covered by a large rug. Growing tired, the boy lay his head on the rug "only to be surprised by the sound of several tiny kittens mewling!" [Stockton, 2020, p. 18] The boy grabbed a flashlight and the key to the crawlspace lock and ran outside.

The boy opened the two-by-three-foot door and crawled into the narrow underworld, sometimes on hands and knees, sometimes in the mud, infantryman fashion. He examined the entire area beneath the three-bedroom house and found nothing but spiders.

Steve returned to his room and lay on the rug again. Within minutes he heard the kittens, and once more he delved into the crawlspace. Still no luck. As weeks and months passed, he made at least a dozen trips beneath the house trying to find the source of the noise—a mystery that grew stranger and stranger, since a single litter would have eventually grown up and left—or starved, trapped underground as they would have been.

Neither Stockton parent could hear the mewling, but Steve's friend from next door noted one day, "Hey, I think you have kittens under your house." Steve had never told him about the auditory haunting.

Feline Phantoms

Young Stockton heard the kittens off and on until he was 15 years old, when the family moved away. One hopes the poor tiny feline spirits have finally found peace.

'OW CAN I CUT OFF AN 'EAD IF THERE'S NO BODY TO CUT IT OFF FROM?

(As the Executioner said to the Queen of Hearts regarding the Cheshire Cat.)

The controversial book *Sybil* by Flora Rheta Schreiber recounts the life of "Sybil Dorsett" (a pseudonym given to psychiatric patient Shirley Ardell Mason to protect her privacy). "Sybil" suffered childhood tortures at the hands of her paranoid schizophrenic mother that resulted in the daughter developing dissociative personality disorder, her psyche eventually splitting into 16 distinct personalities.

One well-remembered passage from the book describes a dream in which Sybil finds a box of starving kittens in a warehouse and decides to take them home. She also discovers the mother cat, which is lying dead nearby, decapitated. She throws the body and head in a river, but they float back to shore.

In the 1976 television miniseries *Sybil* starring Sally Field, this dream is recreated with horrific effect. Rather than simply being dead, the mother cat's body and head pursue Sybil separately as the air echoes with angry feline screeches. Horrific, yes, but the dreams of such a troubled mentality lie far beyond the realms of consensus reality—don't they?

In 1987 Keri Sweeney was a teenager, living with her parents in a three-bedroom house in Tempe, Arizona. One warm night that year, just before going to bed, she gazed out her window over the yard, an empty expanse of grass except for a single large oak tree growing several yards away.

The girl noticed movement at the base of the tree. A black cat lay near the gnarled roots, its forelegs out before it Sphinx-fashion, swishing its tail back and forth as cats do. The Sweeneys did not own a cat, nor had Keri ever seen this one around the neighborhood.

And she would have remembered this cat because as her eyes grew accustomed to the moonlit night, she made out some disconcerting details.

The cat had no head, for one thing. It lay there like some ancient broken sculpture, but it was not dead, as it quite obviously swept its tail back and forth. Keri next spotted something floating around the tree about six feet above the ground.

It was the cat's head, drifting about like a balloon, staring in her direction with bright yellow eyes. The partial apparition seemed aware of Keri's presence because as soon as she focused on the disembodied head, it meowed loudly at her. After a moment, it disappeared. The event began and ended so quickly that Keri only felt horrified retroactively, as it were.

The divided cat specter never appeared again to Keri Sweeney's knowledge. She could not be sure because she never looked out her window at night again. [Rainbolt, pp. 34–36]

Dusty Rainbolt collected a second account of a free-floating feline noggin. A few days before Halloween around the year 2000, Marianna Love of Sweet Home, Oregon, went shopping at a local grocery store. Just as she stepped past the automatic doors, two tiny kittens dashed beneath her feet and hid under a row of shopping carts.

Marianna opened a can of Fancy Feast cat food (paying for it later) and coaxed the kittens out. She took them home and kept them; they were not her first rescues. One kitten had long gray fur; the other was a "tuxedo" cat. Both were female. They were christened Squirrel and Tazzy, respectively.

After a happy five years with Marianna and her husband, Tazzy wriggled out under a fence only to be hit by a car. The cat required extensive surgery, and one foreleg had to be amputated. Tazzy seemed to recover fully and dwelt in the Love house another six months.

Unfortunately, Tazzy had suffered brain injuries similar to Shaken Baby Syndrome. She acted more and more aggressive and erratic, attacking both her fellow felines and her owners. As painful as it felt, the Loves took Tazzy to the vet and had her put down.

Two weeks after they buried Tazzy in the flower garden, the Loves lay in bed still commiserating with each other over the loss of their treasured pet. Suddenly, a glowing sphere appeared in a far corner of the bedroom. The sphere or orb floated up casually, bobbing like a balloon caught in unseen crosscurrents.

The light slowly grew bigger and centered itself near the ceiling, directly over the bed. Then: "In the center of the light, they saw their Tazzy-girl; just her head, like a disembodied Cheshire cat from *Alice in Wonderland*. She wasn't grinning; she was just there, her face staring down intently at them." [Rainbolt, p. 31]

The orb and its spectral passenger vanished like a soap bubble, leaving the observers in darkness. Marianna clicked on a lamp.

"Do you think she was mad at us?" Marianna asked.

"I think she came to say good-bye," her husband answered.

Despite these hopeful words, they slept no more that night.

THE CAPITOL CAT

A ghostly cat is said to wander the basement level of the Capitol building in Washington, D.C. This black beast is in fact known as "D.C.," short for Demon Cat. We may be stepping beyond the perimeters of a simple feline ghost with D.C. because the Demon Cat's appearances, like those of some supernatural harbinger, are supposed to precede history-making events: the assassination of a president, for instance, or a declaration of war. A few people have encountered D.C. with no following disasters, however.

A century and a half ago, rats infested the lower levels of the Capitol; thus, D.C. might be the spirit of an ordinary rat-catcher. If so, his postmortem manifestations certainly stand out. Witnesses claim that D.C. first appears as a black cat of ordinary proportions, ambling along the stone corridors. Upon spotting the observer, he snarls and spits. He marches ominously toward the witness, and then he grows! A newspaper report from 1898 reads, "[I]t has the appearance of an ordinary pussy when first seen, and presently swells up to the size of an elephant before the eyes of the terrified observer." ["Some Famous Ghosts of the National Capitol"]

Since most witnesses are armed guards and watchmen, weapons have been discharged at D.C. to no effect. In contrast, some encounters have ended with the unfortunate victims scratched by sharp claws, and on occasion huge pawprints have been found on the damp floors. [Rainbolt, p. 44] This indicates a physical manifestation, however brief, rendering theories of hallucination and unconscious expectation inadequate.

D.C. supposedly has not been seen since just before the John F. Kennedy assassination in 1963. Perhaps even demon felines tire of basement rats and stone hallways after a couple of centuries. D.C., if gone, is not forgotten, however. The female roller derby team of the nation's capital has officially named itself the DC DemonCats.

The lack of specific dates and witness names in the story of the Demon Cat of the Capitol Building smacks of urban legend to the sophisticated reader. Another case involving morphing cat capers—much better documented and possibly even stranger—comes to us from the north of England. The phantom felines there, however, were but window dressing for one of history's most infamous paranormal outbreaks: the ghost and poltergeist phenomena that plagued Willington Mill.

WILLINGTON MILL

The most outrageous of feline phantoms had to be those reported during the haunting of Willington Mill, itself one of Great Britain's premiere paranormal sequences for two centuries—maybe four, as a witch's house supposedly occupied the site long before any mill, and after that dwelling had been demolished the area was still known for odd occurrences.

Willington Quay is a small village situated by the River Tyne in North Tyneside. Around the year 1800, a flour mill complex was constructed there, consisting of several structures four or more stories tall along with a number of cottages and outbuildings. This being the heyday of the Industrial Revolution, the mill was powered by steam, making the production of flour swift and easy.

George Unthank and his family owned the mill, and they lived onsite for some 25 years. In 1829, Mr. Unthank entered into partnership with his cousin Robert Procter, and in 1831 the Unthanks moved out of their house on the mill grounds, while Mr. Procter and his wife, Elizabeth, moved in.

Upon occupancy, a strange sight met the Procters: The door to a room on the third floor (fourth as Americans would reckon it) had been nailed shut. When forced open, it was discovered that the windows had been bricked over and even the chimney had been blocked. It was as if the Unthanks wanted to keep people out of that room at all costs—or perhaps keep something in.

The chamber below the barricaded room became the nursery for the Procter children. Nursemaids and other servants frequently reported

Feline Phantoms

heavy footsteps resounding from upstairs. Eventually, Elizabeth Procter herself heard noises; besides the usual ghostly tread came rattlings as if of someone building a fire in the hearth or the puttering activity of someone cleaning the room (when no maids were up there).

Robert Procter kept a diary of the events besetting Willington Mill. It is one of the most intriguing and valuable documents in the annals of psychic research, despite the fact that Joseph Procter admitted to omitting numerous events of an embarrassing or shocking nature and that the latter half of the diary was found to be missing after the elder Procter's death.

By February 1835, the phenomena began venturing out of what had been named the "disturbed room," and they added more special effects to their repertoire. First came "ten or twelve obtuse wooden beats as of a mallet on a block of wood" within two feet of Mr. and Mrs. Procter's bed. Next came a noise like a length of steel banging the Procters' son's cradle. Eventually, crashes and bangs as of furniture and wooden crates were heard all over the four-story living quarters. Voices were heard, sometimes imitating the voices of family members. The footfalls of a barefoot child and the swish of a woman's skirt on the floor joined the thuds of heavy boots. Next, human apparitions became manifest, among them a "luminous man" nicknamed Old Jeffrey, a frightful old woman with gray hair and dressed entirely in gray, and a figure wearing a "priestly surplice."

In this account, however, we are most interested in the "funny cat."

Robert Proctor's diary for late October/early November 1841 reads, "Edmund, who is under two years old, was frightened a short time before by what he called a 'funny cat', and showed a good deal of timidity the rest of the evening, looking under chairs, etc., lest it should be lurking there." [Sitwell, p. 205]

I doubt young Edmund realized just how funny a cat could get.

Mrs. Hargrave (Elizabeth Procter's sister) certainly observed a funny cat while passing a vegetable garden. It was white, larger than a domestic tabby, and possessed quite a long nose, though not a muzzle that would change its identification to a white fox or lapdog. Authors Michael Hallowell and Darren Ritson write that the animal sounds more like a Malaysian moon rat, a sight as unlikely in North Tyneside as any spook or goblin. The cat ambled through the garden, passed through a closed gate, wandered over to the engine room (the building that housed the actual steam-powered machinery), and walked casually through *its* closed door.

It so happened that Joseph Proctor was in the engine house at the time. He witnessed the long-nosed cat's arrival through the closed door. To his further amazement, the feline phantom padded over to the complex's blazing furnace and marched right into the fire.

A Mr. Wedgwood also saw a cat in the furnace room. It seems the ectoplasmic pussy had to top each preceding performance. This time the cat slid bonelessly along the floor like a snake before vanishing through a wall.

However, the feline phantasmagoria to top them all featured a young man named Thomas Davidson.

Mr. Davidson lived and worked in Willington Quay, but he was courting Mary Young, who was employed by the Procters. He often visited the mill complex at night, waiting for Mary to finish work so that they could walk together in the moonlight. The young man would conceal himself in the nearby woodline and "give her the usual signal," whether that was a whistle, a pebble tossed at a window, or something else we are not told. Mary would then sneak out to join him. Such activities were probably mildly scandalous in the early nineteenth century, but Thomas hid mainly to avoid Joseph Procter, who discouraged visitors lest they spread rumors about the haunting.

One star-filled, cloudless night as he waited, Thomas glanced over the surrounding grounds and noticed "what he supposed was a whitish cat" approaching him from the direction of the mill proper.

"It came walking along in close proximity to his feet. Thinking Miss Puss very cheeky he gave her a kick, but his boot felt nothing, and it quietly continued its march." [Bayless, p. 139] Puzzled, the man followed the animal, which simply vanished before his eyes.

Davidson returned to his spot below the window, and as he scanned the area again, he spotted what appeared to be the same white cat approaching again from the mill. "This time it came hopping like a rabbit, coming quite close to his feet as before."

He kicked harmlessly right through it. Confused more than frightened, Davidson followed the hopping cat again, and again it disappeared.

Determined to have a night out with his lady friend, the young suitor returned to the window, and the cat returned one last time. As his son wrote years later:

Feline Phantoms

> "It made its third appearance, not like unto a cat or a rabbit, but fully as large as a sheep, and quite luminous. On it came and my father was fixed to the spot. All muscular power seemed for the moment paralyzed. It moved on disappearing at the same spot as the preceding apparitions." [Bayless, p. 140]

Mr. Davidson decided he wasn't that anxious to meet with Mary that night, so he abruptly left for home, keeping the knowledge of his encounter a secret for years.

One wonders what further evolutions the "whitish cat" might have undergone had the man stayed longer.

The Willington Mill sequence has sometimes been described as a poltergeist case. It is true that poltergeists specialize in loud noises and physical disturbances, and animal apparitions are often part of their paranormal arsenals, but poltergeists normally focus on single individuals—often female, often just entering into puberty. The Willington Mill phenomena lasted for many years, perhaps centuries.

One must then ask whether the feline apparitions of the mill were ghosts in the commonly held sense—that is, the spirits of once-living animals. Other zooforms were reported on the mill property, including a ghost monkey that vanished under a bed and a small donkey with a "bump" on its nose that, like the funny cat before it, passed right through the closed millworks door. There was even an entity to bridge the animate and the inanimate, a quite lively goblin that astonished an aunt of the adventurous Mr. Davidson. She thought this entity "looked like a white pocket-handkerchief knotted at the four corners, which kept dancing up and down, sometimes rising as high as the first floor window." [Hallowell and Ritson, p. 141] My uncle and grandfather were in the habit of creating such "hanky rabbits" when I was a preschooler.

Hallowell and Ritson suggest the Willington Mill menagerie may have been the machinations of a single being, a "shapeshifter" of some sort, but such an entity is even more difficult to quantify than a ghost. Suffice to say that, as we'll see in the upcoming chapter on flying felines, cats are full of surprises in this world and beyond.

THE VAMPIRE CAT

As a change of pace, let us read about a vampire cat. I came across this story as a child in juvenile/young adult books like Bernhardt J. Hurwood's *Ghosts, Ghouls and Other Horrors*. Once I learned the phrase "urban legend," I dismissed this bloodthirsty moggy as such a migrating tale. Lord Halifax, aka Charles Lindley Wood, Second Viscount Halifax, however, may have found the origin of this tale over a century ago, or rather his nephew Everard Meynell did, as Meynell explained to his uncle in a letter.

Mr. Meynell put pen to paper as soon as he heard the account so he would not forget a single detail. In the most Edwardian fashion imaginable, Meynell began: "I was sitting in my club after dinner, smoking a cigarette and drinking my coffee, when a friend of mine, whom I had not seen for some time, came up and began to talk to me on various subjects."

The friend remains unnamed, which is sadly a common convention in most writings of the nineteenth and early twentieth centuries. He had been suffering from insomnia, and the previous Saturday he had visited some acquaintances in Eastbourne, hoping the change of scenery would help him. A number of jovial guests had already arrived at the house, and Meynell's friend felt better immediately.

A large black cat in the house quickly singled out the newest visitor, rubbing against his legs and attempting to climb right up to his shoulder. Every time the visitor ascended to his bed chamber, the feline tried to enter with him, but he succeeded in keeping it out. The rest of the household found the cat's attachment amusing, but Meynell's friend was not impressed, holding as he did "an irrational repugnance" for cats. (He might have gotten along well, then, with Mr. Davidson of Willington Mill.)

The cat shadowed the visitor all day Sunday as well, and the man was happy to shut the door upon it as he retired for his last night.

At least the sea air and quiet scenery worked their magic: He soon drifted into restful slumber.

Sometime during the night, Meynell's acquaintance woke to an unpleasant sensation. In his own words, it was as if he were "breathing only on one side of his body." (Could this have been what we now call a stroke?)

There was more to this episode than a stroke, however. He found the overly attentive black cat pressed against him, its head buried under his arm. His nightshirt was soaked in blood.

The visitor launched himself out of bed while the gore-splattered intruder hissed and spat. The visitor opened the door, and the beast fled.

The tiny vampire had climbed onto its sleeping victim, torn through his nightshirt, and licked with its rough feline tongue until the blood flowed freely. "All the skin on the left side of my friend's body was furrowed up and down, leaving exact marks of the animal's tongue," wrote Meynell. [Halifax, p. 209] All this was accomplished without waking the victim.

A footman had mistakenly opened the visitor's door early that morning, allowing the vampire cat in. We are never told what happened to the animal or whether it was part of the Eastbourne family's household or some opportunistic predator. Meynell's friend consulted doctors in London but suffered no further ill effects from his misadventure.

It appears cats are quite strange across the breadth of the paranormal. After all, how many vampire dogs or horses or bunnies (besides Bunnicula) have you heard of?

SOURCES:

Alexander, John. *Ghosts: Washington's Most Famous Ghost Stories* (Washington, DC: Washingtonian Books, 1975).

Bayless, Raymond. *Animal Ghosts* (New York: University Books, Inc., 1970).

Davidson, Robert. *True Story of the Willington Ghost* (self-published, c. 1886).

DC Rollergirls: https://dcrollergirls.com/teams/legacy-home-teams/dc-demoncats/

Hallowell, Michael J., and Darren R. Ritson. *Haunting of Willington Mill* (Stroud, Gloucestershire: The History Press, 2011).

Krepp, Tom. *Capitol Hill Haunts* (Charleston, SC: The History Press, 2012).

Murley, Mark S. *Slightly Haunted Life: One Somewhat Skeptical Florida Man's Brushes with Spooks, Skunk Apes, UFOs and Night Terrors* (Geneva, FL: Barefoot Tadpole Press, 2022).

Rainbolt, Dusty. *Ghost Cats: Human Encounters with Feline Spirits* (Guilford, CT: The Lyons Press, 2007).

Schreiber, Flora Rheta. *Sybil* (New York: Grand Central Publishing, 2009 [1973]).

Sieveking, Paul. *It Happened to Me!* Vol. 2 (London: Dennis Publishing, 2009).

Sitwell, Sacheverell. *Poltergeists* (New York: University Books, 1959).

"Some Famous Ghosts of the National Capitol," Philadelphia [PA] *Press*, October 2, 1898.

Stockton, Steve. *Strange Things in the Woods* (Beyond the Fray Publishing, 2013).

——. *My Strange World* (Beyond the Fray Publishing, 2020).

Wood, Charles Lindley, 2nd Viscount Halifax. *Lord Halifax's Ghost Book* (Secaucus, NJ: Castle Publishing, 1986 [1936]).

FLABBIT THE FLYING RABBIT

Many strange events that occurred before or during World War II have been blamed on wartime or pre-wartime jitters. Orson Welles' infamous radio adaptation of *War of the Worlds* would not have fooled many people if the majority of the population was not actively listening for bad news on the airwaves that night in October 1938. In November and December of that year, the folk of Halifax, West Yorkshire (then the West Riding of Yorkshire) walked in fear of the Halifax Slasher, a razor-wielding psychopath who celebrated the fiftieth anniversary of the Jack the Ripper murders by attacking lone women (and a few men) walking at night.

Except the Slasher did not exist.

> "Magically and absolutely the Halifax Slasher—the elusive, razor-bearing criminal maniac who placed an entire town under nocturnal curfew—had gone. And now it not only appeared that there **was** no Slasher, it was authoritatively stated that there never **had** been a Slasher." [Goss, p. 4]

Throughout the war aircrews on both sides reported flying balls of light that seemed to be intelligently controlled playing tag with fighters and bombers of all sizes. Dubbed "Foo Fighters," these proto-UFOs were thought by both the Allies and Axis powers to be secret weapons of the other side.

By July 20, 1945, most people realized the war was winding down. Hitler shot himself in his bunker on April 30, and Germany surrendered unconditionally on May 7. Japan's forces were spread thinly over Southeast Asia and the Pacific, and the apocalyptic capstones to the Pacific war would be dropped on Hiroshima and Nagasaki less than three weeks later.

Perhaps it was fitting that one of the last mysteries of the fading war did not involve alien invaders or blade-wielding bogey-men but a creature cute, Disney-esque, and utterly absurd.

July 20, 1945, promised to be a hot, humid day in Tulsa, Oklahoma, climbing into the nineties Fahrenheit even at 5:00 AM. At that early hour, police captain Glenn Elliott received a call that jolted him out of his summer doldrums.

"Lordamighty, I'm sober but you won't believe it," a man yelled hysterically. "There's the goldarnest animal you ever saw jumping down Lewis Avenue.

"It's a jackrabbit, but it's got something like wings, which are about a foot long, and when it jumps it flies!"

The man calmed down enough to give his name as J. K. Wilson, who lived on the 2900 block of East 23rd Street. Captain Elliott suggested that the man "merely had one too many under his belt."

Still, Elliott felt it his duty to investigate, or at least he felt that someone should investigate. He turned to Tulsa Police detectives Jimmy Lang and Harold Haus.

"Would you mind driving out on South Lewis Avenue and see if you run into a flying jackrabbit?" [Bulloch 1945, p. 15]

The two detectives hesitated, probably waiting for a punchline.

"I just got such a report and I mean it!" Elliott snapped.

The two detectives left, "muttering something about a psychiatrist."

That seemed to be the end of the matter, but about 7:30 AM, before Capt. Elliott could go off duty (and get off the hook for a while), a woman "too hysterical to give her name" called to say that a jackrabbit "has just flown over my head at Harvard and Fifteenth."

Elliott ordered dispatcher Bob Thomas to contact Lang and Haus.

Thomas did so, only to have Haus's voice burst from the radio: "Will you tell Capt. Elliott that the damn thing is only about two blocks ahead of us and is about to wreck traffic!"

Traffic sergeant Don McGuire, overhearing, asked what "damn thing" they were talking about. Detective Haus was happy to explain:

> He said the first real trace of it had come when they found a bus stopped on the side of the street with the passengers and the driver in a state of near fright. "We were going along 21st and Lewis when a rabbit flew right through the bus," said the driver. [Bulloch 1970]

Then McGuire found himself fielding calls about the airborne wonder. He finally contacted Earl Daugherty, head of the city Dog Pound.

"Earl, you better get the boys out. We've got a flying jackrabbit loose on the southeast side." Daugherty's reaction to this news was not recorded.

Meanwhile, Haus and Lang reported that the winged bunny was spotted by various witnesses over some garages on 15th Street. Sightings of the lapine aeronaut faded around noon; perhaps the 100-degree temperatures forced it into the shade. This did not keep the majority of the Tulsa Police Department's intrepid patrolmen from joining in the hunt, however. They spent the rest of their shifts driving around in search of the creature. It was better than working.

The air is alive with tales of monsters.

— *New York World Telegram,* July 27, 1945

Within 24 hours, "Flabbit," as Tulsa's aerial wonder was named, became international news. Back in America's heartland, sightings multiplied so quickly that both witnesses and journalists decided there had to be more than one anomalous fur-bearing critter on the loose. "The United Press today . . . quoted witnesses as saying the animals even have lit on roofs of buildings and on windowsills, awakening sleepers by flapping their wings." ["That Jackrabbit Story," p. 1] Local farmers complained that "something" was nibbling the tops off ears high on cornstalks, implying that the culprit was an animal that could hover several feet above the ground. One man reportedly lost a quarter acre of corn to the unknown marauders, suggesting there was more than one crop raider.

A reporter from the London *Daily Mail* called Tulsa police chief Roy Hyatt about the sky rabbits and mentioned that England was particularly interested because "London was having trouble at the time with flying cats." The police in Sheffield, England, actually captured one of these phenomenal felines. They said that "the cat had wings about six inches long near the shoulders, and that they finally turned it over to the Society for Prevention of Cruelty to Animals."

"Could you imagine any connection between a flying jackrabbit and a flying cat?" asked the journalist from across the pond. Chief Hyatt had no reply. [Bulloch 1970]

While the rabbit sightings faded by noon Friday, by noon Saturday they were just revving up. Sergeant McGuire was flooded with calls because most of the reports involved motorists in their vehicles. "I just nearly wrecked my car," complained one caller. "I threw on my brakes to keep from hitting the rabbit and it took off in front of me like a helicopter." Haus and Lang became "the rabbit detail," which I'm sure they proudly added to their resumes. Perhaps Flabbit got wind of this fact, for he staged a Close Encounter of the Bunny Kind for the officers. They were driving along the 3600 block of 22nd Street when the rabbit jumped out of a field.

> Haus slammed on the brakes, but "the rabbit went straight up in a helicopter take-off," Haus said, "and remained aloft until the car had skidded by. It then landed in the same spot, sort of pink-eyed us and leaped back into the field." ["That Jackrabbit Story"]

These helicopter lift-offs put one in mind of West Virginia's own flyboy, Mothman, who not only shot up in this fashion but rarely if ever flapped his wings.

FUNNY BUNNIES

In the past, more so than today, strange events and unknown creatures became the butt of jokes and the subjects of hoaxes. Something as ridiculous as a flying jackrabbit proved irresistible to local humorists.

Flabbit the Flying Rabbit

In his syndicated column "The Rambler," Roger V. Devlin printed a letter supposedly written by an E. C. Moon. It seemed a cocker spaniel down the street from Mr. Moon also learned the secret of flight: "The spaniel has discovered that by flapping his ears he could gain speed."

The dog almost caught Flabbit, but suddenly the bunny's ears began to revolve. They spun propeller-like, and Flabbit left the cocker far behind.

"Only thing I can figure," said Moon, "is that the rabbit has studied the helicopters which passed over the city recently, and had been practicing in private." [Devlin, 1945]

The *Tribune* announced on July 24, 1945, that Hugh Blaine Davis, the three-and-a-half-year-old son of Mohawk Park Zoo superintendent Hugh Davis, caught the rabbit in a net after spreading out "a mixture of grated carrot and loco weed" to lure it to earth. Unfortunately, the young child could not keep the winged wonder from escaping the trap. An accompanying photo of Flabbit snapped by the elder Davis is pretty blurry even by cryptozoological standards. ["Child and Camera"]

On that same Tuesday evening, Flabbit supposedly overflew a garden party on 22nd Place. The aerial critter made a buzzing noise as it passed overhead.

"I think the Flabbit was vibrating its tongue between its lips. You know, like people make rude noises." ["Flabbit and P-38 Tangle"]

SIGNS AND WONDERS

At the other end of the paranormal spectrum, modern forteans and parapsychologists have come to notice that anomalous events seem to cluster in time and space. When a Sasquatch is seen, quite often witnesses will report odd, spherical "spook lights" of various colors floating around roads and fields. Or a family will witness a UFO while out driving and arrive home only to find that a poltergeist has invaded their house, moving furniture and creating loud bumps and bangs.

I did not deliberately seek out other strange reports while scanning for Flabbit tales, but two odd newspaper anecdotes caught my eye.

The *Tribune*'s rival paper, the Tulsa *World*, ran the headline "Tulsans Report Mysterious Gas" in the July 24 edition. On Monday the 23rd, at about 2:00 A.M., a "colorless sulfur-smelling gas settled down over the western part of the city," waking many sleepers with coughing fits. One citizen who called the police said "I'm choking. Please do something in a hurry or you'll have a casualty on your hands."

The gas seemed most concentrated near the 1800 block of West Easton. Strangely, it seemed to skip every other house, "for residents of some houses reported they were affected while next-door neighbors said they had not noticed the gas." ["Tulsans Report Mysterious Gas"] The gas dissipated by dawn.

Charles Fort himself recorded numerous accounts of unknown gases drifting down over wide areas of city and countryside, sometimes with great loss of life. Such stories slide into accounts of "mad gassers," wherein unknown assailants target innocent people with bizarre chemical-spraying devices.

Back at the *Tribune*, we are told in the issue for July 25 that "Mannford Residents See 'Ball of Fire' in Sky." It seems that several inhabitants of this small town west of Tulsa spotted a strange object overhead early on the evening of Tuesday, July 24. "One woman who reported the incident said her son called to her as she was picking peaches, and as she turned about, she saw a trail of smoke and 'something that looked like a baseball falling.'" Curiously, there was no dismissing of the object as a meteor, and it was noted that no planes had suffered mishaps in the area. ["Mannford Residents"]

Strange balls of fire or light, of course, run riot through fortean reports of all kinds. They are identified, depending on the circumstances, as UFO spy probes, ball lightning, graveyard orbs, "spook lights," or will-o'-wisps—the last being either some natural phenomenon or actual fairy trickery.

THE CROWDED SKY

John Keel wrote extensively about the Year of the Garuda, the baker's dozen of months between the first major sighting of West Virginia's Mothman on November 15, 1966, and the collapse of Silver Bridge over the Ohio River on December 15, 1967, a disaster seemingly heralded by the aerial apparition. The Week of the Flabbit ended with similar distressing news: The Tulsa *Tribune's* banner headline for Saturday, July 28, 1945, reads "Army Plane Strikes 102-Story Empire State Building; 15 Dead."

Truthfully, it was not an Oklahoma-centric disaster, but for several days, as Arthur Weingarten put it in his definitive book on the subject, "the catastrophe shunted aside news of the war still raging in the Pacific, all but relegating Japan's death throes to the inside pages." [Weingarten, p. xi] On that Saturday morning in 1945, Lieutenant Colonel William Franklin Smith Jr. took off from Bedford Army Air Field in Bedford,

Massachusetts, in a B-25 "Billy Mitchell" bomber. His destination was Newark Metropolitan Air Field, New Jersey. In a thick fog covering New York City, he apparently mistook Welfare Island in the East River for Manhattan itself and turned on a heading that took the aircraft straight into the northwest face of the Empire State Building at the 79th floor. Smith, his co-pilot Staff Sergeant Christopher Domitrovich, and 19-year-old military "hitchhiker," Navy Aviation Machinist's Mate Second-Class Albert Perna died instantly. Perna, tragically, was on his way home on emergency leave to be with his family because his brother Anthony had died in the Pacific only two weeks earlier.

Eleven people in the ESB died as well, and floors 78 through 80 caught fire. Pieces of the landing gear and one engine passed entirely through the skyscraper and dropped onto the 12-story Waldorf Building on 33rd Street. The debris set the penthouses of the Waldorf ablaze. Fortunately, fire crews contained all the fires. The whole event was like an eerie precursor to the 9/11 attacks 56 years later.

MY WORK HERE IS DONE

On the morning of July 29, 1945, "the pilot of a commercial plane reported that what he thought was the Flying Jackrabbit had attacked his ship and was destroyed!" [Bulloch 1970] This was apparently the end of Flabbit, for he was seen no more. Perhaps he *was* a harbinger of the aerial disaster in New York, in which case his work on this earth was done.

If the reports of his death were greatly exaggerated, however, then he—and his winged relatives, if any, and the flying cats of England for that matter—must have soared back to whatever aerial Wonderland flying critters hail from.

SOURCES:

"Army Plane Strikes 102-Story Empire State Building; 15 Dead," Tulsa [OK] *Tribune*, Saturday, July 28, 1945, p. 1.

Bulloch, Nolen, "'It Looked Like a Regular Jackrabbit—Except for Wings!'" Tulsa [OK] *Tribune*, Monday, July 20, 1970, p. B-1.

———, "When Jackrabbits 'Take Off' It's Really Oklahoma Weather," Tulsa [OK] *Tribune*, Friday, July 20, 1945, Sect. 2 p. 15.

"Child and Camera Snag onto 'Flabbit' in Blur of Action," Tulsa *Tribune*, Tuesday, July 24, 1945, p. 2.

Devlin, Roger V., "Rambler" [Column], Tulsa *Tribune*, Monday, July 23, 1945, Sect. 2, p. 9.

"Flabbit and P-38 Tangle; Pink Fuzz!" Tulsa *Tribune*, Wednesday, July 25, 1945, p. 10.

Goss, Michael. *Fortean Times Occasional Paper no. 3: The Halifax Slasher* (London: Fortean Times, 1987).

"Mannford Residents See 'Ball of Fire' in Sky," Tulsa *Tribune*, Wednesday, July 25, 1945, p. 4.

"Midsummer Night's Tales," Tulsa *Tribune*, Friday, July 27, 1945, p. 26.

"Nineteen Forty-Five Empire State Building B-25 Crash," Wikipedia entry accessed 2/19/2023, found at: https://en.wikipedia.org/wiki/1945_Empire_State_Building_B-25_crash

"That Jackrabbit Story Multiplies," Tulsa *Tribune*, Saturday, July 21, 1945, p. 1.

"Tulsans Report Mysterious Gas," Tulsa *World*, Tuesday, July 24, 1945.

Weingarten, Arthur. *Sky is Falling* (New York: Grosset & Dunlap, 1977).

FLYING FELINES AND THE CHALK OUTLINE MAN

Robert Lee Eskridge (1891–1975) was an American artist whose work can be found in the Honolulu Museum of Art and even the Smithsonian. In his youth, he traveled extensively, and he visited Tahiti in 1927. During an audience with Queen Marau of Tahiti, the Polynesian ruler suggested he visit the Gambier Islands, 1,000 miles to the southeast, and in particular Manga Reva, "the most interesting, the island for you." Eskridge took her advice and sailed to Manga Reva, where he lived for eight months.

"The natives are always talking about *tu pa paus* (ghosts), and each group of islands has its own eery [*sic*] tales of the supernatural," Erskine observed. Manga Reva proved to be no exception. Eskridge encountered several apparitions and chose to study them rather than fear them. In fact, the Polynesians took to calling him *fetii te tu pa pau*, "ghost cousin," and informed him that the island spirits liked him.

While living on the island, Eskridge became friends with a man he refers to as "Tom," a farmer from Missouri who had tried unsuccessfully to set up a plantation in the South Pacific. Although Tom had married into a Manga Revan family, he continually denied the existence of the supernatural. He had gone native in every other way, he explained; if he believed in the spirits and superstitions of the islands, he feared he would lose his identity as a logical, modern American.

But stuff happened to Tom whether he liked it or not, as he admitted to his fellow American. During his first Christmas on the island five years before Eskridge arrived, he lingered behind while his Polynesian wife and her family attended Mass. Feeling homesick, the farmer simply lay on the grass and listened to the sound of the waves.

Suddenly, a black object flew by only three feet above his supine form. Before he could even flinch, it flew back: "Again it passed me, so close I could almost have touched it. Like a cat curled up asleep it seemed, and it moved through the air just as a fish moves through water." [Eskridge, pp. 200–201] It flew up to the top of a tree by what would eventually become Eskridge's bungalow; then he lost sight of it. "I am absolutely convinced that it was not a bird. It had no wings," Tom finished.

Tom finally experienced a paranormal epiphany while Eskridge, ironically, grew more disconcerted. One night, the artist found himself tossing and turning in bed. He imagined hearing the voices and footsteps of passing people. Eventually, he rose and stepped out on the porch. Ragged clouds slipped across the moon.

"Suddenly beside me, close beside me, flashed a gray cat, apparently fast asleep," Eskridge reported. "It lay curled up, suspended in midair. I jumped. It flew with an abrupt movement beside me, so close that it touched me. I felt it distinctly." [p. 228] The surreal sleeping feline circled Eskridge and whipped out across his garden, Frisbee fashion, until it was lost in the darkness. Robert Eskridge, the "ghost cousin" American that the local spirits liked and approved of, jumped back inside, locked the door, and hid under the covers.

The next morning, Tom wandered over, and Eskridge told him of the sleep-flying cat. To his surprise, the Missourian was eager to see it himself, while the artist found himself reluctant. "This restless flitting about of sleeping cats, without obedience to the laws of gravity, is getting on my nerves."

Nevertheless, after supper that evening, Eskridge and his friend stood out on the back porch, smoking cigarettes in the dusk. As they discussed an upcoming trip to a neighboring island, something totally unexpected happened. The men noticed movement in the open door of the cookhouse, which was pitch black inside.[1] It was a human shape "The figure was a line drawing, such a sight as a child might crudely sketch in white chalk on a blackboard, a child's conception of what a man might be," recalled Eskridge.

---

[1] The kitchen/pantry of many jungle or island residents is located in a building separate from the living quarters, thus it is the "cook house."

Flying Felines and the Chalk Outline Man

The thing left the cookhouse and dashed at them with alarming speed. Its outline did not glow, but it was solid white, like the cliché chalk outline of a body on the sidewalk. At the last moment, it darted across the garden and vanished into the night.

Tom was finally convinced of the existence of the supernatural. He seemed relieved, almost happy, but from then on, his nightly walks became few and far between.

> *A nondescript animal, said to be a flying cat, and called by the Bhells* **pauca billee**, *has just been shot by Mr. Alexander Gibson, in the Punch Mehali [India] . . . Mr. Gibson, who is well known as a member of the Asiatic Society and a contributor to its journal, believes the animal to be really a cat, and not a bat or a flying fox, as some contend.*
>
> The Naturalist's Note Book [journal], 1868

"Winged cats" have been spotted off and on throughout history, like the vampiric version that reputedly haunted Alfred, Ontario, Canada, in 1966. A rare few have supposedly been able to fly like Mr. Gibson's beast, but most of the time cat "wings" are attributable to feline cutaneous asthenia (FCA), a genetic disorder that causes a cat's skin to become elastic and fragile. Grooming, rubbing against objects, and other normal wear and tear causes the fur-covered skin to be stretched out into long folds that look like wings. The skin is easily torn, and the false flight limbs often slough away completely, leaving an ordinary-looking feline behind. Curiously, the torn skin rarely bleeds or gets infected.

FCA can't explain the Manga Reva cats, though, which flew without wings!

If something were flitting back and forth past one, and it had the appearance of a small furry animal with pointed ears, I'd suggest it was a bat. And if it looked curled up as if asleep? Maybe one glimpsed a baby bat, clinging to its mother, curled up against her chest.

Of course, such an explanation makes Eskridge and friend Tom look like complete morons. Bats are usually the first mammals to reach oceanic islands, since the winds carry them there. It's difficult to imagine two men living on Pacific islands for years without knowing what bats look and act like. And if you mistake a bat for something else, why assume it to be something as bizarre as what they claimed? A floating ghost- or witch-cat, maybe. But a levitating, curled-up-as-if-asleep moggy?

I would suggest that Tom's story of the flying feline "caused" Eskridge's sighting, and the fact the two were waiting for something to happen "caused" the chalk-man sighting. Whether in a psychological or paranormal sense, however, I can't say.

Or a family pet napping somewhere, dreaming it could fly. Maybe the levitating felines were astral projections of cats, visible as their sleeping selves were positioned at the time, curled up before a family hearth.

The Chalk Outline Man? You got me there.

PAWPRINTS ON THE SANDS OF TIME

Robert Eskridge became entangled in another strange event that at least implied the existence of a supernatural canine. One evening as he put away his brushes, he heard voices shouting. The native schoolmaster, Hauhine, ran up his steps and yelled, "Come to the beach—black footprints!" Eskridge followed him to a wharf behind a church. A large crowd, including Tom, had gathered on the sand. Tom told the artist that it was the "footprints of the *Tu pa pau* of the Sea."

"There before me was a phenomenon so strange that I hesitate to describe it," wrote Eskridge. [p. 218] Two lines of footprints led up out of the ocean, past the tide line, then turned toward the west end of the island. One set was human; the other belonged to some kind of large dog. Yet they were impossible. "For the prints were black, as black as though they had been printed with ink. Moreover, not by a hair's breadth did they go below the surface of the sand."

Eskridge studied the prints closely. It was as if they had been painted lightly on the loose white sand without shifting one tiny quartz grain. All around them, people's feet sank into the beach as normal.

Hauhine exclaimed, "Someone die tonight!" Tom, to Eskridge's surprise, concurred. "Something will happen tonight," he said.

That evening, the two Americans discussed the strange events haunting the Gambier Islands, and the subject came back to the black footprints. "There are two places in the islands where the footprints have been seen," said Tom. "One of them is near the end of your path . . . The other is on the beach of Aga-kaouitai, that sinister island where the cannibal kings lie buried."

The next morning, Tom reported that a local family's young son died in the night. "I guess the *tu pa pau* and his dog got what they were after."

When Eskridge returned to Tahiti, he was granted another audience with Queen Marau. To his surprise, one of the first questions she asked was, "And the strange footprints on the sand—have you seen them?" The story of the black footprints, it seemed, was known far and wide—at least among Polynesians.

SOURCES:

Eskridge, Robert Lee. *Manga Reva: The Forgotten Islands* (Honolulu: Mutual Publishing, 1986 [1931]).

Shuker, Karl. *Cats of Magic, Mythology, and Mystery* (Bideford, North Devon, UK: CFZ Press, 2012).

HAIRY HANDS OF DARTMOOR

"As far as I have been able to ascertain," wrote Ruth E. St. Leger-Gordon in her book *Witchcraft and Folklore of Dartmoor*, "there is no mention or hint of the Hairy Hands before the second decade of the present [20th] century." There were an unusual number of cases, however, of horses throwing their riders, wagons overturning, and motorcars crashing near a village called Postbridge as far back as 1908.

In June 1921, Dr. E. H. Helby, the medical officer of Provincetown Prison, was riding his motorcycle along the B3212, formerly Carter's Road, between Princetown and Postbridge. He was heading for Postbridge to attend an inquest. In his sidecar rode two young girls, daughters of the deputy governor. Just as they were rolling down a hill into Postbridge, the doctor yelled for the two girls to jump out. They obeyed just as the medical man was flung from his vehicle. He broke his neck, but the girls were relatively unharmed. There seemed to be nothing wrong with the motorcycle.

A few weeks later, a motor coach driving up the same hill swerved unexpectedly into the ditch, though no one was injured. On August 26, 1921, a "Captain M." of the British Army—"a very experienced rider"—crashed his motorcycle outside Postbridge, but he survived. Indeed, he had something very interesting to tell journalist T. Gifford, who published his statement in the London *Daily Mail* of October 17:

> A pair of hairy hands closed over mine. I felt them as plainly as ever I felt anything in my life—large, muscular, hairy hands. I fought them for all I was worth, but they were too strong for me. They forced the machine into the turf at the edge of the road, and I knew no more till I came to myself, lying a few feet away on the face of the turf.

Devonshire folklorist Theo Brown received a letter from Mrs. E. M. Battiscombe (the wife of the doctor who replaced Medical Officer Helby) in which she mentioned a young man visiting people in Postbridge. He, too, went on an errand on a motorbike, but he returned in less than an hour, "very white and shaken." "He said he had felt his hands gripped by two rough and hairy hands and [they made] every effort to throw him off the machine. He had never got much beyond the clapper bridge." [Brown, p. 97]

The authorities blamed the Postbridge accidents on reckless driving, high speeds, and a poor camber on the curves in that section of the road. Repairs were implemented, but if roadwork drove the Hands from the B3212, they made a spectacular reappearance at the abandoned Powder Mills about half a mile north.

Theo Brown and her parents pulled a caravan out of mothballs for one month each summer, hauling it into the country and setting up camp in some rural area. In 1924, as a change of pace from the usual holiday spots, Mr. Brown decided they should camp at the deserted gunpowder factory. (I'm sure it seemed like a good idea at the time.)

Mrs. Brown, having an artistic bent, produced several sketches of the countryside. Young Theo played with the local farm children. One night while her family slept, Theo's mother encountered something horrible. She did not tell her daughter what happened until many years later. In 1950, the young Ms. Brown convinced her mother to write an account of her frightening vision.

"It was a cold moonlit night and I was in my bunk in a caravan on a very lonely part of Dartmoor," Mrs. Brown began. She woke up confused, feeling that something menacing and powerful lurked nearby. She looked around, and her gaze fell upon Mr. Brown, whose bed lay at the end of the caravan under a small window.

"I saw something moving, and as I stared, my heart beating fast, I saw it was the fingers and palm of a very large hand with many hairs on the joints and back of it, clawing up and up to the top of the window which was a little open." [Brown, p. 98]

Hairy Hands of Dartmoor

Mrs. Brown felt instinctively that the hand hated them and wanted to do harm to her husband. She also felt that no weapon would stop it. So, being a good Christian, she made the sign of the Cross and prayed. The hand withdrew.

The family remained at the powder works for several weeks, but the hand or hands did not return. However, Mrs. Brown finished, "I did not feel happy in some places not far off and would not for anything have walked alone on the Moor at night."

The prolific fortean writer Nick Redfern uncovered a Hairy Hands encounter—an outright assault, in fact—as recently as 2008. Michael Anthony, a salesman for a large photocopying firm, was in Postbridge on January 16 of that year closing a deal with the proprietor of a new business, who wanted to rent several copiers. It was about 11:00 PM by the time the papers were all signed, and Anthony felt pleased as he started back home to Bristol and his family.

Just outside Postbridge, the atmosphere in Anthony's car became oppressive. He felt cold, clammy, and afraid. He thought he was having a stroke. Instead, to his horror, a disembodied set of hairy hands or paws clamped over his own hands and tried to steer his vehicle off the road. He fought them off only to have them leap back on the steering wheel and try again. He fought them off a second time, yet they whipped back like a pair of evil bats and grabbed the wheel a third time.

As Anthony struggled against this last assault, a flash of light filled the car, followed by a sulfurous stink. The hands vanished. The salesman roared off and did not stop until he reached a gas station miles away. [Redfern, pp. 54-55]

Michael Williams, author of *Supernatural Dartmoor*, was enjoying a drink with Rufus Endle, a "thoroughly professional journalist," at a Devonshire men's club. When Williams said he was researching the above-mentioned book, Endle told him of a frightening event that befell him one night as he drove from Chagford to Princetown, a route that took him through Postbridge.

"Suddenly, as I approached the bridge, a pair of hands gripped the driving wheel and I had to fight for control. It was a very scary minute or so. God knows how I didn't crash at the bridge, and the hands went as inexplicably as they came. I never wrote about it in the newspapers, or even told anybody else for fear of ridicule."

Even after this confession Mr. Endle worried about admitting to an experience this strange; he made Williams promise not to print it until after Endle's death.

Sometimes, Williams points out, the Hands are seen; sometimes they aren't. Sally Jones, collecting material for her own book on Devonshire, told him of a Somerset doctor who drove through Postbridge in 1977. Although he saw nothing, "he was aware of some powerful force inside his car: 'something quite out of my control...' In his case 'the steering wheel seemed to go wild.'"

Williams may have even uncovered an account of the Hands almost but not quite materializing. In June 1955, a man named Maurice Dart traveled to North Bovey and attended the Fair. "I was cycling home across Dartmoor on the lovely warm sunny Sunday morning, really enjoying the experience," Dart told Williams.

Dart passed through Postbridge and entered a section of road hemmed in by trees and brush. Even a touch of claustrophobia, however, wouldn't explain the feeling of panic that hit him. He continued: "I looked back and upwards over my left shoulder and saw what appeared to be a swirling cloudy mass in the otherwise clear blue sky descending rapidly towards me."

Mr. Dart pedaled for all he was worth, reaching the village of Two Bridges and shooting right through, not stopping until he topped a hill beyond. There the panic left him. He looked back again "and just glimpsed the fuzzy mass disappearing up into the sky, way behind me." [Williams, p. 20]

Another correspondent wrote to Williams about a "furry paw" causing car accidents but that he had not heard any reports of it since World War II. Ruth St. Leger-Gordon and Theo Brown make similar observations in their books of Dartmoor folktales. However, it seems that, whether you see them or not, the Hairy Hands have not gone away.

THE HAIRY HANDS RETURN?

The Pontefract, Yorkshire, poltergeist case is one of the wildest "noisy spirit" events on record. It was a newspaper sensation in the 1960s, but it faded from history until Colin Wilson (*The Outsider, The Occult*) devoted 40 pages of his book *Poltergeist: A Study in Destructive Haunting* to it in 1981. In 2012, a film based on the haunting (*When the Lights Went Out*, directed by Pat Holden) was released to lukewarm reviews.

Nicknamed "Fred," the entity tormented the Pritchard family of 30 East Drive from August 1966 to May 1969, producing virtually every phenomenon ever associated with poltergeists and several that weren't. The series of events began when the family went on holiday to Devon, leaving Mrs. Jean Pritchard's mother, Sarah Scholes, and the Pritchard son, Phillip, behind. Within hours, violent bursts of wind seemed to buffet the house, but the air was still whenever anyone checked outside. A bizarre white powder, apparently chalk dust, started sifting down in the living room. Even if the dust was, for instance, due to paint on the ceiling crumbling, it still acted unnaturally: "The top half of the room was perfectly clear; the falling powder started on a level below his head. And when Mrs. Scholes stood up, her own head rose above the top of the falling powder like an airplane above the clouds." [Wilson, p. 143]

Once the events began, each seemed determined to outdo the one before. Lights turned on and off. Perfectly circular pools of water appeared on the floor (a plumber found nothing wrong). After a loud bang, a potted plant was found halfway up the stairs *sans* pot. The container sat on the landing above.

Creepy things occurred at night, often just out of view. Wardrobes wandered around "tottering and swaying like a drunken man." One night when Jean Pritchard couldn't sleep, she stepped down the hall and saw in the half-light something slithering and rustling along. "It was a long strip of wallpaper, which had been lying in a roll against the wall. Now it was standing on end, and swaying like a cobra." [Wilson, p. 150]

Where ghosts and poltergeists of history might yank the sheets off sleeping people, Fred would lift the whole mattress up like a flying carpet. "Ordinary" spirits might flip over a chair; Fred would pointedly turn over every object and piece of furniture in a room—sometimes two or three rooms. Move a candle? The Pontefract entity would tear the house's electric heater out of the wall despite the screws and plaster holding it in.

One thing that Fred did that *was* common in poltergeist cases was that he slowly seemed to run out of energy and never manifested again after May 1969.

As spectacular as the Pontefract case was, I mention it in this chapter only due to the "guest appearance"—sort of—by the Hairy Hands.

Rather late in the haunting, family matriarch Maude Peerce, Mr. Joe Pritchard's sister, came to stay. She did not believe in ghosts, and she found the notoriety focused on the family unseemly. She was determined to find a logical explanation.

Aunt Maude was certain the children, Phillip and Diane, were behind the supernatural antics. She had no sooner made herself comfortable beside the fire—she had not even taken off her hat and coat—when the refrigerator door opened and a pint of milk floated out and poured itself over her.

Somehow this was the children's fault. The Pritchards suggested she spend the night and see if things didn't happen that would convince even her of Diane and Phillip's innocence.

Aunt Maude agreed and removed her hat and coat. She discovered that her furry gloves were missing. They turned up, though, when the family assigned a bedroom to Maude.

"One enormous hand appeared over the top of the door, while the other was near the bottom of the door, about six inches from the floor. A closer look showed that they were Aunt Maude's fur gloves. Whatever—or whoever—was wearing them must have had enormous arms, since there was a stretch of well over six feet between the top glove and the lower one." [p. 161]

Maude yelled "Get away! You're evil!" and threw a boot at the gloves. They withdrew.

In an ordinary haunting, this would have been enough to convince Aunt Maude that the uncanny goings on were unnatural. Not in the Pontefract case, though. The furry gloves floated out into the middle of the bedroom in front of God and all the world. One beckoned as if to get everyone to follow. When that failed, the same glove clenched into a fist and shook itself at Aunt Maude.

Maude started singing "Onward Christian Soldiers." The gloves conducted her singing, then they vanished.

Aunt Maude left. Jean Pritchard later found the furry gloves in a cupboard and returned them to Maude. "She carried them into the garden with coal tongs and burned them with paraffin on the rubbish heap." [p. 162]

If these weren't the actual Hairy Hands of Dartmoor, they were good stand-ins, and their brief appearance was terrifying and funny as the same time.

SOURCES:

Brown, Theo. *Devon Ghosts* (Norwich: Jarrold & Sons Ltd., 1982).

Fort, Charles. *Complete Books* (NY: Dover Books, 1974 [1941]).

Murdie, Alan, "When the Lights Went Out," *Fortean Times* no. 293 (November 2012), pp. 28-37.

Redfern, Nick. *Wildman! The Monstrous and Mysterious Saga of the "British Bigfoot"* (Bideford, North Devon: CFZ Press, 2012).

St. Leger-Gordon, Ruth E. *Witchcraft and Folklore of Dartmoor* (New York: Bell Publishing, 1965).

Williams, Michael. *Supernatural Dartmoor* (Launceton, Cornwall: Bossiney Books, 2003).

Wilson, Colin. *Poltergeist: A Study in Destructive Haunting* (New York: Putnam, 1981).

THE HEXHAM HEADS

"I'VE FOUND A HEAD!"

In late May or early June 1971, 11-year-old Colin Robson was digging in the garden of the family home at No. 3 Rede Avenue in Hexham, Northumberland, in the northeast of England. The date can be pinpointed because the eldest Robson daughter, Wendy, was on her honeymoon at the time. Colin's spade hit a solid lump, which he quickly unearthed. It proved to be a hard, round object slightly smaller than a tennis ball that felt unusually heavy for its size. A bit of scraping revealed carved features like eyes and a mouth. The object was a small representation of a human head.

Colin's brother Leslie (9) had been watching idly from an upstairs window. Colin called to Leslie "I've found a head!" Leslie, naturally, decided he needed a head too. He trotted down and began digging. Lo and behold, he soon uncovered a second head.

The boys, believing they had made a great archeological discovery, carried the heads into the house. They showed them off to family, friends, and neighbors.

The heads were not identical. One had a skull-like appearance with lines running up and back over the brow and cranium that in Celtic sculpture represented hair. For some reason, it struck people as male, and it was dubbed "the boy." The second possessed prominent eyes, a beaked nose, and a hairstyle resembling a bun or tight-fitting bonnet. It seemed to be female and old; it was nicknamed "the girl" or "the hag." (Years later, Colin recalled that he discovered "the boy" and Leslie found "the girl.") Partial necks protruded from both heads to allow them to be inserted into bases *a la* candleholders. Both artifacts were grayish-green and covered with quartz crystals.

A weird coincidence—if that is all it was—already enters the tale of the Hexham Heads: Six weeks before the discovery, Colin Robson entered an art competition at school. He molded a disembodied head from clay, which was not only the same size as the yet-to-be-found Heads but looked, if anything, even more grotesque with its glaring eyes and froglike mouth. Its present owner, author Paul Screeton, wrote: "It is downright repulsive-looking, almost scary. Painted black, brown, red and blue, and with two broken fangs, it was, however, judged second best in the school competition." [Screeton 2012, p. 15] Well, art is subjective. Photos of this object have often been misidentified as pictures of one of the original Heads.

The Heads were placed on a shelf in the Robson home. Besides the two boys, the household consisted of parents Albert and Jenny Robson; an older son, Philip; the aforementioned Wendy (23), and younger daughter, Judith (18).

Soon after the Heads took up residence, poltergeist activity began. No matter how the Heads were placed on a shelf, they would eventually turn to face the place of their discovery. Wendy recalled this phenomenon nearly 40 years later: "To ensure no one had tampered with them through the night I decided I would place them under my bed where no one could access them, but the next morning they had moved from the top right of the bed to the bottom left—as near as possible to the spot where they had been discovered." ["WendyD" 2011]

Bottles and other small items would fly across the rooms, sometimes shattering against the walls. A "whiplash" sound resounded occasionally from behind the TV. Mirrors and picture frames fell. These psychokinetic events happened mainly around 2:30 A.M.

WEREWOLF FLOWER? EW!

There was one event the present writer always dismissed as pure folklore: that at the very spot where the heads were dug up, "a strange flower bloomed at Christmas and an eerie light glowed." [Screeton 1992, p. 460] I assumed this was a tabloid-born detail half-remembered from Elliott O'Donnell:

> In the mountainous regions of Austria-Hungary and the Balkan Peninsula are certain flowers credited with the property of converting into werwolves [sic] whoever plucks and wears them. [O'Donnell, p. 174]

Yet Colin Robson vividly recalled the flower when interviewed in April 2012:

> Not long after we dug the heads up this flower appeared, and it would be almost luminous. It was almost as if there was a spotlight on it. When you went out—there was no light there, you couldn't see the flower. When you went back indoors, when you looked outdoors, it looked like this flower was glowing. [Screeton 2012, p. 231]

Fortunately (or not, depending on your point of view), no one plucked the flower and turned into a werewolf.

A WEREWOLF IN WERESHEEP'S CLOTHING?

Speaking of our shaggy friends, if you have ever heard of the Hexham Heads, you've probably heard of the lycanthropic apparition that invaded the home of archeologist Anne Ross. Before that, however, something even stranger appeared at No. 1 Rede Avenue, next door to the Robsons (the families shared a back wall).

The Robsons' neighbors were Isaac Dodd; his wife, Ellen (she preferred Nellie); and their two sons and four daughters. Nellie and two of her children were apparently the only people in the neighborhood besides the Robsons to hold the Heads in their bare hands. Perhaps that had some influence on upcoming events. They also witnessed objects moving in No. 3 and heard the whiplash sound from the television.

Anyway, shortly after the Robson boys dug up the Heads, the Dodd girls heard noises like birds nesting or soot falling in the grate. One night, the youngest daughter, Marie (7), lay in bed with an ear infection. It became so painful that Nellie decided to sleep with her and comfort her as best she could. Both sons slept on bunk beds in the same room.

Sometime after midnight, the family dog, Pip, started howling downstairs. Brian Dodd, ten years old at the time, went out on the landing to see why. Almost gale-force winds hit Hexham that night, rattling the windows and shutters. The front door was open. Brian decided his father must have opened it, but the boy felt a sudden, inexplicable terror and ran back to bed. He pulled the covers over his head only to have something grab his hair and pull "hard enough to lift my head off the pillow." He pushed back at whatever it was. [Ferrol, December 2012, p. 46]

Brian's panicky return woke Nellie Dodd. Mrs. Dodd told her son to stop messing about, but then she saw that something huge had joined the four family members in the small bedroom.

Newspaper, tabloid, and magazine accounts over the years have described the intruder as a "man-beast" or outright werewolf. Even Paul Screeton, who studied the case for decades, tried to steer the description of the bedroom invader toward wolfishness. Son Brian and daughter Sylvia, interviewed 40 years later, would have none of it:

> **Brian**: She said it was half-man, half-sheep.
>
> **Sylvia**: And she was adamant . . . Definitely, definitely, half man, half sheep, is what she always said it looked like. Up on two legs, with the cloved—you know, the cloved feet. We said, "Aw, get away," but she said it was definitely half-man, half-sheep. But she thought she was dreaming. But then it appeared to trip or stumble.
>
> **Stu [Ferrol]**: Probably after you pushed it back.
>
> **Brian**: Yeah. [Screeton 2012, p. 34]

The easiest way to explain Nellie Dodd's sighting is to say she was still half asleep, dreaming or suffering a hypnopompic hallucination. That was Mrs. Dodd's own idea for a few seconds.

The "weresheep" had been shambling along near the foot of the bed, apparently headed for the door. When it stumbled, however, it put out an appendage to catch itself (Mrs. Dodd described it as a hand with clawed fingers rather than a hoof). The hand came down right on Ellie's leg. It was solid and had quite a bit of weight behind it. Ellie screamed at this familiarity. The seemingly clumsy creature shifted into overdrive, bolting out of the room. "It was running and on hind legs . . . It had a human-type bottom half and a sheep's head."

Isaac Dodd, alone for the night in the master bedroom, heard his wife's outcry. He jumped out of bed and popped out onto the landing. He saw and heard nothing.

The Hexham Heads

There is something archetypal and awesome about werewolves, but the Hexham "weresheep" was just an embarrassment. If not downplayed or ignored, it was torturously explained away. One popular explanation ran as follows:

A slaughterhouse operated right across the street from No. 1 Rede Avenue until the 1990s. On the night of the weresheep, a drunken ne'er-do-well broke into the abattoir to steal a sheep carcass. He hauled it over the wall; then, in order to carry the large, limp corpse, he draped the sheep over his back like a cape with its head flopped over his own like a hat. As he passed the Dodds' flat—crossing a gap in the hedge a few meters wide, the only point where the road was visible—Mrs. Dodd happened to look out the window and see this fleece-covered apparition. She incorporated it into a dream, and so it became the oddball ovine chimera.

Stuart Ferrol, a writer, actor, and media company director, lived much of his life in Hexham and was quite familiar with the slaughterhouse in question. "I had never heard of any break-ins at the slaughterhouse and remembered how high the wall surrounding it was." [Ferrol, December 2012, p. 46] He pointed out that a butchered sheep rarely retains the head, hooves, or fleece. Also, "When we gained access to the Dodds' house . . . very little of the road was visible without having to lean right into the window cavity." Was Ellie Dodd a sleepwalker as well?

We are not finished with the weresheep, but for now we must move on.

WEREWOLF? WHERE WOLF?

Back at No. 3 Rede Avenue, a wall's width from No. 1, the Robson family heard the commotion elicited by the sheep-thing. They assumed it to be some sort of domestic squabble.

Not long after this Colin and Leslie Robson carried the Heads to Hexham Abbey to get the opinions of the learned clergymen. The Heads were returned a few days later with the suggestion they were of Roman origin, perhaps carved around 200 B.C.E. The Robsons next conveyed the Heads to the Museum of Antiquities in Newcastle upon Tyne, England, where the little carvings were treated like hot potatoes. They were accepted by a Dr. David Bailey, and, according to Newcastle University Museum keeper Lindsay Allason-Jones, "we were satisfied that Bailey passed them to yet another intermediary, Barbara Harbottle . . . who in turn passed them to the then assistant keeper, Roger Miket, who organized drawings of the Heads and sent these with photographs to Dr. Anne Ross. Phew!" [Screeton 2012, p. 90]

No one at the museum seemed to know what to do with the Heads. They ended up in a box in a cupboard for a while and eventually ended up back at No. 3 Rede Avenue.

Around this time, Dr. Anne Ross, a distinguished scholar and archeologist and an expert on ancient Celtic culture, gave a lecture in the Hexham area. Peter Moth, news reporter for Tyne Tees Television, decided that a piece on the locally famous Heads—with Dr. Ross present to give her thoughts—would make an interesting news segment on "Today at Six." Moth obtained the Heads from the Robsons and asked if Dr. Ross could keep them temporarily for examination. Reputedly, the Robsons agreed, even saying, "We really don't want these back." Thus, after the program, Moth gave the artifacts to Ross. "And the last I saw of them was Dr. Ross putting them in her bag.' [Screeton 2012, p.65]

Ross took the Heads to her house at 6 Rose Road, Bevis Mount, Southampton, where she lived with her husband, Richard Feachem, an archeologist in his own right, and their children, Richard Charles Feachem (5) and daughter Berenice (15).

One night, Dr. Ross woke almost panic-stricken and "very, very cold." Something was at the bedroom door. As she told BBC reporter Luke Casey:

> It was about six feet high, slightly stooping, and it was black against the white door. It was half-animal and half-man. The upper part I would have said was wolf and the lower part was human. It was covered with a kind of black, very dark fur. It went out and I just saw it clearly, and then it disappeared, and something made me run after it, a thing I wouldn't normally have done, but I felt compelled to run after it. I got out of bed and I ran, and I could hear it going down the stairs, then it disappeared toward the back of the house. [Rickard 1976, pp. 4–5]

Husband Richard searched the house but found no sign of an intruder. Anne insisted it was not a dream.

A few days later, Anne and the elder Richard traveled to London on business. Berenice arrived home from school about 4:00 P.M. Her parents returned at 6:00 to find her in a distraught state.

> She had opened the front door and a black thing, which she described as near a were-wolf as anything, jumped over the banister and landed with a kind of plop. It padded with heavy animal feet, and it rushed toward the

The Hexham Heads

back of the house and she felt compelled to follow it. It disappeared in the music room. [Rickard 1976, pp. 5]

Richard Jr. also saw the creature, which was also at his bedroom door, as he wrote to Paul Screeton in April 2011:

> It was stooped, a humanoid shape, pointed ears and glowing, narrow red eyes, I screamed and it turned and jumped over the landing banisters [a drop of 25–30 feet] and that is all the memory I have. [Screeton 2012, p. 246]

The werewolf apparition was seen several more times, but never by Richard Sr. All family members, however, heard the sound of its paws echoing through the halls. Doors burst open without any apparent cause, and there was an occasional "cold presence."

Dr. Ross removed the Heads from No. 6 Rose Road, but the phenomena persisted until she removed her entire collection of Celtic carved heads from the premises. She also, by some accounts, had the house exorcised.

HEAD GAMES

Anne Ross concluded that the Hexham Heads were authentic Celtic relics carved about 200 CE from local sandstone. She along with many others were taken aback in March 1972 when a truck driver named Desmond Craigie announced to the newspapers that he had molded the Heads himself in 1956.

Craigie, a former resident of No. 3 Rede Avenue, told the regional *Evening Chronicle* that 16 years earlier he worked for Alco, a firm that made artificial stone for building sites (which can include materials other than cement). His daughter Nancy asked what he did for a living, and, supposedly during a single half-hour lunch break, he took three handfuls of rock bits and mortar and molded them into three bizarre little heads.

Strange as they looked, Nancy took to the heads and played with them like dolls. One eventually shattered and moved to the waste bin. Eventually, the girl lost interest in the remaining two heads, and they were left in the garden, apparently sinking into the soil after several years.

Unlike many an expert, Dr. Ross admitted she could have been mistaken. However, she asked Mr. Craigie to "show his work" (*i.e.*, create a new head). The truck driver did so, but his new creation seemed hurried and lackluster, having only a line of mouth and two pits of eyes. It was also made of ordinary concrete because he no longer had access to Alco's "artificial stone." There was no real way of comparing it to the Hexham Heads.

So, the Heads were sent to geology professor Frank Hodson, the dean of the Faculty of Science at Southampton University. He reported: "Both heads are made from the same material which is a very coarse sandstone with rounded quartz grains up to 2mm. diameter in a calcite cement." In a nutshell, Hodson believed the Heads to be actual ancient artifacts.

However, the Heads were also sent to Dr. Douglas Robson (no relation to the Robsons of 3 Rede Avenue). Dr. Robson, senior lecturer in geology at Newcastle University, actually cut off fragments of the Heads (apparently without permission) to analyze chemically. A single line from his report will suffice: "The material from which the heads have been formed is an artificial cement." The controversy continued.

The Heads next went to Dr. Don Robins, an associate of Dr. Ross who would eventually collaborate with her on a book (*The Life and Death of a Druid Prince*, 1989). I begin to wonder at the amazing number of Robsons, Robins, and Rosses (who lived on Rose Road) in this saga, but synchronicities and coincidences abound in fortean tales.

Anyway, Dr. Robins held a Ph.D., and he was trained in organic chemistry, solid state chemistry, and archeology. In the 1970s, he grew more and more interested in the paranormal, particularly in the "stone tape" theory—the possibility that scenes of the past can somehow be "impressed" into objects as if onto videotape and "played back" later. This is a favorite theory of parapsychologists, as many ghosts do not exhibit any sign of consciousness but merely repeat events that occurred during their lives as if they were film segments on a loop.

Dr. Robins retained custody of the Heads for two years, during which time he became increasingly "creeped out" by them. He saw no man-animals, but his cats and German shepherd always acted strange around them (the shepherd even seized one and tried to shake it as if it were a rat). The scientist himself felt "electric" and "cold" and "oppressive" presences about the house. When one Frank W. Hyde expressed an interest in the Heads, Robins was happy to be rid of them.

For what it's worth, Robins found no trace of cement in the Heads, bouncing them back into the possibly ancient court.

The Hexham Heads

WINNER OF THE HYDE AND SEEK CONTEST FOR THE FIFTH CONSECUTIVE DECADE

If Dr. Robins seems a little "off" for a scientist, Frank W. Hyde flies well into left field. He was originally "a consultant in technology with special attention to space exploration and space medicine." [Screeton 2012, p. 87] He slowly gravitated to mysticism and the occult, and he gained a measure of fame as an astrologer.

Hyde wanted a dowser of his acquaintance to examine the Hexham Heads, and in February 1978, Don Robins drove the artifacts to the diviner's house in northwest London. Robins was so frightened of the Heads by now that he simply dropped them off and left.

And here our train of thought engages its emergency brakes. Dr. Robins may have wanted to forget the Hexham Heads, but Anne Ross and other scholars did not; Ross especially requested an update, as it was getting on toward two and a half years since Robins had borrowed them from Southampton University.

Robins tried to call and write Hyde throughout the spring of 1978 but to no avail. Finally, a mutual acquaintance reported that Hyde had been seriously injured in a car crash. But even he did not know the scientist-astrologer's current whereabouts.

Over the next five years, friends and acquaintances of Hyde joined in the search—fruitlessly. No one has been able to locate or contact the man since the spring of 1978. And with Hyde went the Hexham Heads. It is admittedly a most unsatisfying end to this saga of artifacts and apparitions.

ANCIENT OR RECENT? DOES IT MATTER?

Some who are mainly interested in the paranormal aspects of the Hexham Heads might snort in disgust and leave were they ever proven to be of recent manufacture; ancient artifacts might be cursed but not globs of concrete some guy molded during his lunch break. Actually, age may not have much bearing on whether or not the Heads caused or allowed anomalous phenomena to happen. Everyone agreed that quartz crystals made up much of their mass, and parapsychologists claim that quartz is a prime substance for absorbing and holding psychic or paraphysical energies—if such powers exist. The Heads may have become "haunted" or "cursed" whether they were new or ancient.

It does feel as if something, some force in Rede Avenue, Hexham, wanted Heads to exist. Remember, Colin Robson created a head out of clay for an art contest six weeks before digging that hole in the back garden. If Desmond Craigie spoke truthfully, a man who dwelt in the same house created a trio of eerily similar heads 16 years before.

There certainly was a "head cult" in ancient Britain that created stone effigies of heads when those of enemy warriors were scarce; Anne Ross's book *Pagan Celtic Britain* contains dozens of line drawings of the baleful stone noggins. Perhaps some spiritual remnant of that ancient religion lingers to this present day, influencing ordinary people to create odd little reminders of a once great civilization.

ON THE TRACK OF THE SHEEP-SQUATCH

As mentioned earlier, everyone knows werewolves, but nobody—in 1971 United Kingdom, at least—understood weresheep. Even people deeply involved in the saga of the Hexham Heads laughed at the Dodds' woolly intruder, downplayed it, or tried to force it into the more familiar lycanthropic mold. The ovine manimal, however, refused to go away.

The slaughterhouse that stood across from the Dodds and the Robsons played an important role in "explaining" the weresheep of No. 1 Rede Avenue. It came into play once more after the Hexham Heads vanished into limbo.

The "weresheep" apparently took up residence in the slaughterhouse, maybe trying to avenge its four-footed cousins. A man named Michael Newton reported to Paul Screeton: "It was said to be haunted by a half-man, half-sheep. The haunting was the talk of the slaughterhouse then [c. 1982]." The manager of the abattoir, Hilton Stonehouse, ran into it one night when he should have been the only one on the grounds: "He saw a dark shape in the slaughterhouse where the carcasses were hanging . . . It was half-man, half-sheep. It scared the hell out of him, and he's a big man. After that he wouldn't go back without someone else." [Screeton 2012, p. 182]

If a haunting "weresheep" isn't enough for you, I suppose I'll have to mention that a "new" cryptid on the fortean scene has been dubbed "Sheep-squatch." One of the earliest reports of this new woolly booger came from—of all places—a wooded area just outside Point Pleasant, West Virginia, home to another infamous cryptid, Mothman.

A woman who signed herself "Tess" was driving from Huntington to Charleston with two friends. The going was slow because snow and ice covered the land.

> "I looked to my left, and about a foot from my window I saw what appeared to be a strange creature, half man, half animal. It had a face very similar to a sheep, horns like a ram, and it was standing upright like a human. I was so stunned, and immediately thought I had lost my mind! My friends started screaming 'What in the hell was that?'"

Tess backed up. The creature was still there, only inches from the driver's side window. "I got a pretty good look at it, it basically had its nose right in my face!" continued Tess. "It was white, furry, and had paws, no hooves, paws like a dog, a sheep-like face, and stood upright like a human, it ran away on human legs."

Despite the wintry conditions, the trio dared to travel a bit faster to Charleston. They discussed what they saw endlessly but could come to no conclusion other than that Point Pleasant really is a weird place.

A fellow named Ed Rollins, who grew up in Gallipolis, Ohio, also saw Sheep-squatch near Point Pleasant. As a boy, he discovered his mom's old scrapbook full of articles about the 1966 appearances of Mothman and UFOs. After a stint in the Navy, Rollins took to hiking through the TNT Area outside Point Pleasant. One day as he was walking along a stream, he heard something crashing through the underbrush. As he reported to the West Virginia Ghosts website:

> "What I saw emerge from the brush was a large brownish-white creature. Its fur looked dirty and matted as if the animal did very little in the line of self-grooming . . . The creature moved on all fours as it breached the brush line and knelt to drink from the creek. Its front limbs, the only limbs I saw clearly, ended in what was markedly paw-like 'hands.' Its head was long and pointed, like a canine, and it had largish horns; not antlers but single point horns.
>
> "I shrunk back into the brush and watched, afraid to stay and afraid to run. It drank for a few minutes, then

crossed the creek and continued on across toward Sandhill Road."

I suppose Sheep-squatch feels quite at home in Point Pleasant, having neighbors like Mothman, Men-in-Black, the Grinning Man, and all manner of UFOs.

SOURCES:

Davison, Wendy ["wendyD"] "Hexham Heads" reply, Sept. 15, 2011. Accessed 1/19/2023. https://forums.forteana.org/index.php?threads/the-hexham-heads.3750/page-3

Ferrol, Stuart, "In Search of the Hexham Heads Part One," *Fortean Times* No. 294 (December 2012), pp. 42–47.

———, "In Search of the Hexham Heads Part Two," *Fortean Times* No. 295 (January 2013), pp. 44–49.

———, "Head Case: A Chat with Paul Screeton," *Fortean Times* No. 295 (January 2103), pp. 50–51.

McCoy, Kurt. *White Things: West Virginia's Weird White Monsters* (Morgantown, WV: OGUA Books, 2008).

McEwan, Graham J. *Mystery Animals of Britain and Ireland* (London: Robert Hale, 1986).

O'Donnell, Elliott. *Werwolves* (New York: Wholesale Book Corp., 1972 [1912]).

Rickard, Bob, "A Celtic Werewolf," *Fortean Times* No. 15 (1976), pp. 4–5.

Rollins, Ed, "Sheepsquatch," West Virginia Ghosts website, accessed 1/18/2023. https://www.wvghosts.com/true-stories/cryptozoology/sheep-squatch/

Ross, Anne. *Pagan Celtic Britain* (Chicago: Academy Chicago Publishers, 2005).

Screeton, Paul, "Curse of the Hexham Heads," *The Unexplained* Vol. 4 (1992), pp. 460–464.

———, *Quest for the Hexham Heads* (Bideford, North Devon: Fortean Words, 2012).

"Tess," "Strange Creature in Point Pleasant," West Virginia Ghosts website, accessed 1/18/2023. https://www.wvghosts.com/true-stories/cryptozoology/strange-creature-in-pt-pleasant/

HOLLYWOOD DOGMEN

"Can your heart stand the shocking facts about Hollywood Dogmen?" as famed psychic The Amazing Criswell might say.

It was not until her fourth book on unidentified bipedal canines that artist/reporter/author Linda S. Godfrey uncovered any reports of "dogmen" or "manwolves" from southern California, and three of those were actually of a creature that "looked like a lynx but was the size of a Doberman." [Godfrey, p. 95] There seem to be few sightings in general of such cryptids in the western United States. Perhaps we have overlooked an early witness to the dogman phenomenon.

Born and raised in the Hollywood area, Paul Marco (1927–2006; birth name, Angelo Inzalaco), went into show business "because I liked acting and being funny, and, well, I didn't know what I was doing," as he said in a 2005 interview. [Sloan, pp. 88–89] Eventually, he became friends with the infamous filmmaker Ed Wood, Jr., who employed Marco in several movies, which may or may not be a success story, depending on your point of view.

Marco appeared in Wood's 1955 film, *Bride of the Monster*, alongside horror stars Bela Lugosi and Tor Johnson. Marco portrayed a timid police officer named Paul Kelton, which eventually became his signature role.

Filmed in 1956 (but not released until 1959), Wood's *Plan 9 from Outer Space*, often dubbed "the worst movie ever made," brought back Marco as Officer Kelton, who bemoans the fact that he gets all the weird assignments. The patrolman knew of which he spoke because he appeared again in Wood's *Night of the Ghouls*, a sequel to *Bride of the Monster*.

Unfortunately, after a few more movie and TV credits, Marco faded from the scene for nearly a quarter century. Then, in the cinema magazine *Cult Movies* (#16, 1995), publisher Buddy Barnett reported: "Ed Wood actor Paul Marco (Kelton the cop) has been admitted to the county psychiatric hospital for evaluation. Allegedly, Marco was seeing men with dog heads invading his property."

Marco summoned the police, and the responding officers, predictably, found nothing. "Marco was taken into custody after a brief altercation with the officers." [Barnett, p.20]

I'm surprised more witnesses of dog- or wolf-headed humanoids don't get taken in for evaluation—or get into "brief altercations" if they don't wish to go. Perhaps after so long out of the spotlight, Marco's life was taking a final sad turn.

Or was it a sad turn? Sometime in 1995, Marco (as Kelton) cut a record with Dionysus Records, *Home on the Strange*. In 2005 he played Kelton in a movie called *The Naked Monster*, a spoof that starred several actors from 1950s sci-fi films. ["Marco, Paul"] In 2006, "Kelton's Dark Corner" was slated to be an independent TV series, directed by Russian rock-and-roll star Vasily Shumov and starring Marco as the bumbling cop who encounters strange beings and situations *à la* the '70 TV show *Kolchak: The Night Stalker*. Unfortunately, Marco died during production, and the existing footage was edited and padded to make one feature-length film, *Kelton's Dark Corner, Trilogy One*. ["Kelton's Dark Corner"] (Marco shared the cinematic fate of his former co-star Bela Lugosi, who died during the production of *Plan 9*, and whose existing scenes had to be padded out by a body double, Ed Wood's chiropractor.)

Perhaps seeing dog-headed men was a prophecy of better times to come. Or perhaps it was just the sort of thing that happened to Officer Kelton.

UPDATE (And let me just say I'm sure few people would expect an update on a fictional character from *Plan 9 from Outer Space*):

In 2017 in a twist Ed Wood himself would have appreciated, Kelton the cop returned. Director Shumov filmed a fourth episode of *Kelton's Dark Corner*. It seems the officer had absorbed so much ectoplasm and mystic energy during a lifetime of running into supernatural creatures that he became one himself: He is reincarnated as "police woman Keltonova," played by Shelley Michelle.

And there is more to come. As *Filmfax* writer Al Doshna tells us: "Utilizing the many shots he took of Paul and using an animated stills technique as in other episodes, Paul Marco has, in a sense, become the first virtual movie star almost ten years after his death." [Doshna, p. 67-68] One is reminded of Bela Lugosi "starring" in *Plan 9* well after he shuffled off this mortal coil.

So beware, dogmen of Hollywood: Kelton the Cop is back from the Great Beyond to put you in the pound!

SOURCES:

Barnett, Buddy. "Cult Movie Stuff," *Cult Movies* No. 16 (1995), p.20.

Doshna, Al, "Kelton's Dark Corner," *FilmfaxPlus* no. 148 (May-July) 2017, pp. 67-68.

Godfrey, Linda S., *Real Wolfmen: True Encounters in Modern America* (NY, NY: Tarcher/Penguin, 2012).

"Kelton's Dark Corner." http://www.keltonsdarkcorner.com/ [link broken].

"Marco, Paul" Wikipedia entry, accessed 1/22/2023. http://en.wikipedia.org/wiki/Paul_Marco

Sloan, Will. "Can Your Heart Stand the Shocking Facts About Kelton the Cop, aka Paul Marco?" *Filmfax* No. 106 (April-June 2005), pp. 88-89.

IMITATE THE ACTION OF THE TIGER

By the 1960s, the abuse of psychedelic drugs had become a prominent social problem in the United States. Professionals in the field of psychotherapy felt that more study of such drugs and their effects on the mind was necessary, because psychedelic substances *do* have therapeutic uses, and demonizing them in the public eye was counterproductive.

Researchers like husband-and-wife team R. E. L. Masters and Jean Houston realized that most records of actual visions and perceptions experienced during drug-induced "trips" came from addicts or hospital patients who were "severely disturbed" to begin with. Masters and Houston, therefore, solicited accounts of psychedelic experiences from relatively normal, healthy, mentally steady volunteers, each (ideally) working with a psychiatrically trained guide.

A volunteer described as a "thirty-seven-year-old anthropologist and author," referred to only as "S-6," took 500 micrograms of LSD "in the privacy of his apartment, with no one else present." [Masters and Houston, p. 76] S-6's trip was surprisingly low-key. Other volunteers described landscapes of alien worlds, awareness of super-slowed time or individual subatomic particles, and all manner of supersensory and extrasensory perceptions.

S-6 seems to have merely puttered around his apartment for a few hours.

Well, he *did* turn into a tiger.

Ten to twenty minutes after dropping the LSD, the anthropologist recalled, "I became conscious of myself moving across the floor of the apartment, moving as best I can recall by propelling myself along on my knees with my flattened palms also pressed against the floor. At about this same instant I found myself before a full-length mirror and, looking into it, was confronted by a huge, magnificent specimen of a tiger!"

The test-subject grew aware of strange emotions. He felt his new body possessed extraordinary power the likes of which he had never felt or experienced in his human form.

S-6's mind and personality apparently became a mixture of human and tiger. He felt immersed in "tigerness," but retained a modicum of human awareness, as well as a "pull" back toward humanness that he—for the moment—fought with all his might. He knew the image in the mirror was his own ("it seemed to me later that there was, in the face of this tiger, something of my face"), yet his body tensed its muscles, and he snarled. "I recall my bafflement when I ran my claws across the glass and touched the hard, flat surface."

Eventually, he forgot the mirror and padded around the apartment. "I looked at the room with incomprehension and a sense that this environment was alien and not at all where I belonged." He had a kind of "flattened vision" that made objects look like paper cutouts. His consciousness he also described as narrow, focused only on immediate perceptions, emotions, and physical sensations.

S-6's human sensibilities returned in stages. The tiger, he felt, had been unhappy, but the anthropologist now considered the animal an essential aspect of his being. He stood erect as the experience ended; then he stepped over to his desk and wrote a rambling missive that read in part: "I am a tiger who has learned to turn himself into a man . . . The tiger will have to become more of a man and less of a tiger if he wants to fulfill his human destiny and realize happiness."

S-6 wondered if there could have been an actual transformation. "Would I have appeared to an observer to resemble in any way a tiger? Somehow, I think the answer to that is 'Yes.'" He was scientist enough to concede, however, that he might just have been crawling around on the floor. [p. 78]

At the end of his account, S-6 expressed his desire, as an anthropologist, to seek out and participate in animal metamorphosis ceremonies as practiced in areas of Africa and Haiti. (Some of these rituals are harrowing indeed, as we will see in "Out of Africa"). One can only wonder how successful he was.

SOURCES:

Masters, R. E. L., and Jean Houston. *Varieties of Psychedelic Experience* (New York: Dell Publishing, 1966).

INVASION OF THE DOGGY SNATCHERS

When she was a child, Ardy Sixkiller Clarke's grandmother told her of the Star People, who came down from the sky and became the ancestors of the Lakota and other Native Americans. After she grew up, Clarke joined Montana State University as an assistant professor. She found herself in a prime position to obtain anthropological data from the Lakota people "from the inside," as it were, being Lakota herself.

She devoted her time to collecting narratives about the Sky People and their aerial vehicles, which in modern times were called aliens, spacemen, UFOs, and flying saucers.

One old man, "Chauncey," told Clarke of a "space man" who seemed extremely interested in his dog. (Clarke changed the names of her sources and obscured their locations to protect their privacy, but we are told the old fellow lived in northern Montana only a few miles from the Canadian border.) Chauncey dwelled in a two-room cabin, alone except for his big black dog, Blue Son. He had lived off the land most of his life, and he still hunted game and raised chickens at the age of 88.

One night during a full moon, Blue Son started whining. The aging Lakota opened the back door, and the dog ran off into the night, barking. Chauncey grabbed his shotgun and followed.

"I caught a glimpse of the space man just as I came round the corner of the house," Chauncey told Clarke. "That's when I seen him. He was bent over Blue Son, and at first I thought Blue was dead." [Clarke, p. 27] The old man fired at the humanoid but was unsure whether he hit him or not.

The "space man" did not seem to take offense. He rose and stepped into the full moon's glow. He wore a jumpsuit of some sort, dark in color but glistening in the lunar light. The suit had a patch on the right shoulder and a belt around the waist. "Instead of a buckle there was a circular contraption of some sort," said Chauncey. The old man and the alien studied each other for a moment.

"He was the slightest man I ever saw in my life," Chauncey continued. "He looked like a ghost, but somehow he explained to me that he was from the stars."

The visitor had not harmed Blue Son, but he was very interested in the canine because he had never seen a dog before.

The alien escorted Chauncey to his ship, which had landed about 50 yards from the cabin. The dog followed his master. As Chauncey was amazed by the UFO, so was the ship's pilot amazed when Blue Son obeyed the old man's order to heel. Chauncey had Blue sit, fetch a stick, and roll over, all of which seemed to astonish the alien. "When we reached his small craft he pointed at Blue Son and his craft. That's when I realized he wanted my dog." The old Lakota fellow refused, and the spaceman left.

After that meeting, however, UFOs continually flew by or hovered over the cabin. The dog would hide under the bed. Chauncey was sure they were after Blue Son. "Maybe they do not have dogs on their planet and if they do, maybe no animal can be taught simple commands like dogs," he concluded.

Two years after Dr. Clarke's interview and just two days short of his ninetieth birthday, Chauncey died. Clarke attended his funeral. Afterwards, Blue Son spent the day lying on the old man's grave. Chauncey's granddaughter Susan allowed the faithful canine time to mourn but promised Clarke she would pick him up in the morning.

"When she went to her grandfather's cabin the next morning, he was gone. Despite hours of searching they never found him." [Clarke, p. 29]

Chauncey's skinny spaceman was not the first alien visitor with an unhealthy interest in our four-footed friends. Early on the morning of November 6, 1957, Everett Clark, a 12-year-old living in Dante, Tennessee,

Invasion of the Doggy Snatchers

let his dog, Frisky, outside to do his business. A strange oblong object sat in an empty field across the road about 100 yards away. The boy thought he was still half asleep and seeing things, so he simply went back in.

Twenty minutes later, Everett went out to find Frisky. The dog—and several other neighborhood canines—were out in the field near the unknown object. There were also two men and two women present. The strangers spoke loudly to one another; the boy said they sounded like "German soldiers" he'd heard on TV shows. One man tried to grab Frisky, but Everett's dog growled and fled. The man tried for another dog but backed off when it snapped at him.

The strange quartet finally had enough. According to the young witness, when the aliens returned to their vessel, they "walked right through the side, as if it were glass." (The ship was, one journalist finally determined after much questioning, "translucent.") The UFO shot straight up noiselessly.

Reporters entering the field found an impression in the grass 24 feet long by 5 feet wide. Everett's father commented, "I don't think he made it up, but I still don't believe it."

The very next day, truck driver Malvin Stevens was traveling from Memphis, Tennessee, to Meridian, Mississippi. While driving his rig along Mississippi State Highway 19, he spotted a strange object ahead. It was round, with a propeller at each end and one on top. Malvin stopped his truck and stepped out; at the same time, three men who stood only four and a half feet tall climbed from the improbable vessel. The trucker said they wore gray uniforms, had "pasty white skin," and seemed to want to talk with him. Malvin, however, could not understand their language. Perhaps disappointed, the little men returned to their ship after only two minutes, and it rose straight up into the sky. [Bowen, pp. 154–156]

There were no dogs in the Mississippi case, but I mention it because around sunset of that same day in 1957, in Everittstown, New Jersey, one John Trasco stepped outside to feed his dog King. To his shock, he found a glowing, egg-shaped object floating in front of his barn. A strange humanoid approached him.

The trend in aliens must have been toward compactness. We go from average height in Tennessee to four-and-a-half feet in Mississippi to a being only three feet tall in New Jersey. He had a "putty colored" complexion and bulging eyes. He wore a green suit with a matching green cap, and "gloves with a shiny object at the tip of each glove."

The invader said, "We are peaceful people. We don't want no trouble. We just want your dog." Mr. Trasco immediately replied, "Get the hell out of here." He yelled this, apparently, because he was frightened and confused, but one can only wonder what a calm, well-thought-out response to this request would be. The creature trotted back to its ship, perhaps startled in turn by Trasco's vehemence, and the vessel rose up out of sight.

Mrs. Trasco saw the UFO from a window but not the tiny humanoid. She did hear its voice and her husband's shout. She later told reporters, "I told John we should have let them take King. He's half-blind and so cross I don't know who else would want him." [Bord, pp. 31–32]

Once in a while news stories report dogs disappearing in groups. Starting around December 10, 1973, for instance, there were numerous reports of "dognappings" in Wisconsin. All the victims were collies. Near the Christmas holidays of that year, two dozen collies disappeared in and around Voluntown, Connecticut, while seven or eight went missing in Rhode Island. The usual explanation given for such incidents is that unscrupulous people catch dogs and sell them to experimental labs for profit. Who knows? Maybe UFO occupants have improved their dog-chasing abilities and now abduct specimens of man's best friend without witnesses. Let us hope they want canines for companionship and not for nasty experiments or tasty alien dishes.

SOURCES:

Bord, Janet, "I Spy Little Green Men," *Fortean Times* no. 91 (Nov. 1996), pp. 30–33.

Bowen, Charles, ed. *Humanoids* (Chicago: Henry Regnery Co., 1969).

Clarke, Ardy Sixkiller. *Encounters with Star People* (San Antonio, TX: Anomalist Books, 2012).

Lorenzen, Coral, "UFO Occupants in the United States," in Bowen, op cit.

THE LAND BETWEEN NIGHT AND DAY

Like most children, I was never enamored with bedtime, but I had reasons beyond merely wanting to stay up late and watch TV or play. Sleep was something I had to prepare for, or else *it* might come again.

I learned early that *it* nearly always came if I slept on my back; the most important part of preparing was to arrange myself on my side or stomach. Overexcitement or too much physical exertion before retiring also seemed to allow *it* in; it was this possibility, not concern for any parental desires for peace, that made me slow down at night. Worry and anxiousness also weakened my defenses; I'd lie in bed some nights, contemplating some upcoming holiday or vacation, and then calm myself by deliberately thinking of nothing—a difficult task for anyone not a student of Zen Buddhism.

Some nights, however, all my precautions came to naught, and *it* would come as it had so many times before.

Some people describe the stages of darkness, from full consciousness through the REM period to deep sleep, as a descent. I think of it more like a train ride—a trip that carries one through a switchyard on the way to peaceful slumber and sometimes gets diverted onto a parallel branch, a track that is neither wakefulness nor sleep as we know it, a frightening and malevolent land between night and day.

Sometimes one wakes up to this uncanny state of affairs; sometimes it occurs as one is waiting for the Sandman, but often I noticed that, though my muscles relaxed and my hearing grew weak (as if I listened to everything from underwater), my mind would be as sharp and focused as ever. I would try to lurch up, twist, and kick, but I rarely fought off the spell. It felt like all my strength, my willpower, my very life essence drained out of a hole in my back. I'd rant and rave inside my skull, but my body remained inert.

I lie in bed staring at the ceiling. The room is dark, but a vague, purple light outlines the furniture. In the corner by the closet, I notice a coat and hat stand. I do not recall ever seeing it before.

I should get up, but I'm very tired. Moving a single muscle is a task so difficult, I don't even wish to contemplate it. Still, I'm sure I must rise.

I roll my eyes and glance around the room. The shades are drawn. A long, slick mackintosh hangs from the coat stand. A broad, black hat sits on top. The stand now suggests an evil, shadowy figure.

I try to lift my arm. I groan. It is not painful, but attempting to move it is an incredible, terrible effort. I can't do it.

I hear whispers. I look at the coat stand. It is a stand no more but a moving form, a black spectre drifting across the room. It mutters about the evil things it is going to do to me.

There is a lamp by the bed. I have to turn it on before the spectre reaches me. It can't take the light. I lift my left arm, gritting my teeth. It weighs a thousand pounds. I hit the lamp clumsily and then fumble with the switch.

Click-click-click. *There is no light.*

The shadow creature squats momentarily like a toad in the middle of the floor. It whispers about how it is going to strangle me slowly, crush me beneath its weight, grope me with a cold rapist's touch before it murders me. I gather all my strength and sit up.

There is a window on the right; I seize the curtains and fall back, dragging them open. The morning light is pale and gray, but it is enough. The spectre is gone.

I wrote the above passage for a short story, and once upon a time I read the story to a writer's group. The listeners did not comment on how accurate or inaccurate my description was, mainly because none of them knew what I was talking about.

Beasts Beyond Belief

This came as one of the most stunning revelations of my existence: A roomful of adults had never heard of a phenomenon that was, to me, as common as dirt. Growing up, I had heard people speak of having nightmares, or a "hag-ridden" night, or just a bad night's sleep in general, and I assumed they were speaking about the paralysis and evil presence I knew so well.[1]

In college I came across a book called *The Terror That Comes in the Night* by David J. Hufford. In the early Seventies, Hufford worked in the Folklore Department of the Memorial University of Newfoundland. He was delighted at the number of beliefs and folktales still extant in the province, and among the accounts of will-o'-the-wisps, ghost ships, and fairies he found reports of a phenomenon that seemed more psychological than supernatural. One university student described it this way: "You feel as if someone is holding you down. You can do nothing, only cry out. People believe that you will die if you are not awakened." [Hufford, p. 2] A 62-year-old woman said, "Yes, the people of ____ did speak of having nightmares. Usually they said 'I was hagged last night.'" [p. 3] Still others referred to "it" as the Nightmare, the Old Hag, or just the Hag, and the rather humorous "having the diddies."

Hufford realized that even the existence of this phenomenon had been muddled by nomenclature, definition, and the inability to properly describe it. It was not a nightmare by the common usage of the term (*i.e.*, a bad dream). It was not an incubus, the medieval demon that came in the night and had sexual encounters with mortals, because there was rarely a sexual component to a "hagging," certainly not an enjoyable one. Nor was it *pavor nocturus*, or "night terrors," typified by the victim literally lurching up out of sleep screaming and struggling. It was not quite either hypnagogia nor hypnopompia, those twilight zones that one passes through just before falling asleep and just before waking up, accompanied often by dreamlike or hallucinatory images.

The term nearest to describing Hufford's "Old Hag" was "sleep paralysis," and in modern times the "Hag" has entered urban legend and the media as a "sleep paralysis demon."

Why is this psychological misfire called a demon (or a hag, for that matter)? The clinical explanation for sleep paralysis is that consciousness has returned during a REM sleep cycle. During REM sleep, most voluntary motor functions are curtailed. This is the body's way of preventing

---

[1] According to the American Sleep Disorders Association, "Isolated sleep paralysis occurs at least once in a lifetime in 40–50% of normal subjects." [p. 166] That means that 50 to 60% of "normal subjects" never suffer from it at all.

The 1781 painting *The Nightmare* by Henry Fuseli portrays many of the mythical concepts of nightmares, including the nightmare horse and a demon sitting on the sleeper's chest.

the sleeper from physically acting out dreams and possibly injuring itself. Victims of sleep paralysis cannot move their bodies, and breathing feels labored as if something fairly hefty is lying or sitting on their chests. This is a disconcerting state to find oneself in, but that is not the worst of it. Inherent in this mental state is a feeling of danger, a certainty that someone or something, a distinct, separate entity, lurks nearby, placing the sleeper in a position of mortal harm.

How could a sleep disorder make one specifically believe that some evil entity is approaching? Is this an exaggeration? Hufford points out that in hundreds of interviews no one ever believed that the danger sensed was the roof about to collapse or the house burning down. The fear was always that a palpable "something" was near.

As the name "Old Hag" suggests, most cultures have historically believed that sleep paralysis was the work of witches, demons, vampires, or other supernatural beings. Earlier societies shaped the phenomenon into some form familiar to local religions and folklore. During the Salem Witch Trials, for instance, witnesses described experiences that were certainly sleep paralysis, and the night attacker would resemble a neighbor

The Land Between Night and Day

with whom they had recently quarreled. "Obviously" the neighbor was a witch, coming in spirit form to vex and smother innocent Salemites.

In 1725, Peter Plogojowitz of the village of Kisilova, Serbia, died. Within a week, nine other villagers died mysteriously, and the rumor sprang up that Plogojowitz had returned as a vampire. Some villagers claimed "that the above-mentioned Plogojowitz, who had died ten weeks earlier, had come to them in their sleep, laid himself on them, and throttled them." [Barber, p. 6] In the infamous case of the Shoemaker of Breslau (1591), the unnamed shoemaker committed suicide by slashing his own throat for undisclosed reasons. Soon afterwards, inhabitants of Breslau reported him back from the grave, an animated corpse attacking people in the night: "[O]ften it came to their bed, often it actually lay down in it and was like to smother the people." [Barber, p. 12]

In David Hufford's microcosm of Newfoundland folklore, his informants spoke of people "hagging" other people (i.e., sending an evil spirit to oppress them during the night). In other tales, the supposed offender appeared personally as the attacking force, presumably via astral projection. Either version of hagging, of course, was enabled by the practice of witchcraft.

THE BEAST IN THE NIGHT

Marra resembles a beautiful girl, but is the worst kind of troll. During the night-time, when folks lie asleep, she comes in and lays herself above them, pressing so hard on the breast that they can neither draw breath nor move limb.

—William Craigie, "The Night-mare"

A magical animal that occasionally pops up in fantasy literature is the "Nightmare," which is usually depicted as a black horse that inhabits or controls or emerges from your dreams. The word *nightmare*, however, has nothing to do with "mare," a female horse, which comes from the Old High German *mariha*, according to the *Random House Webster's College Dictionary*. *Mara, marra,* or *mare*, "a fanciful being thought to induce nightmares," comes from Old Norse. Nevertheless, nighttime attackers often take a zoomorphic guise, as the following anecdotes demonstrate.

NIGHT MONKEY

Jerry Glover emailed *Fortean Times* magazine in 2005 to tell of a strange experience we now recognize as a classic case of being hag-ridden. Age 16 at the time, Glover was scheduled for an interview the next day, which might have provided the stress that triggered the event. At about 1:00 AM, the young man woke to find that he could not move his arms or legs. He lay on his back and felt a tightness in his chest. No wonder, because a monkey sat there.

The "monkey" had red eyes and brown fur, yet it was also slightly transparent. It absolutely exuded evil, "growling and making a mouth-clearing sound."

The creature resembled the dwarfish Incubus in Henry Fuseli's famous painting *The Nightmare*, but even that squat demon looked more human than Glover's night visitor.

The monkey drew closer to the boy's face and spoke: "It wanted me to know how pathetic it held me to be. It knew I was powerless at that time and relished my helplessness." [Sievekin, p. 136] Glover fought to move or speak, but he could barely even breathe. Fearing it would bite his face or throat, he focused on moving above all else. The manifestation slowly melted away as he concentrated, and finally the paralysis passed.

"I am positive it was not a dream," Glover concluded, but what was it? Whatever its nature, he was sure it had been "nourished" into existence by his worry over the upcoming interview, among other troubles.

CURSE OF THE FLY

Esma Percey contacted the venerable *Fortean Times* in 2008 with an account of an even more hideous apparition. In June 1997, Pearcey was a fashion student at a London university. She lived in a residence hall on campus. One afternoon, she returned to her room and flopped onto her bed, napping for about two hours. When she woke, she opened her eyes, her mind feeling sharp and clear, but she could not move.

It was broad daylight. Paralyzed though she was, much of the room remained in her field of vision. In moments, however, she probably wished it wasn't.

"I then saw an enormous fly, about six inches (15 cm) long, buzzing around the room. It was a black, lumpy mass, with stiff bristles sprouting from its body, and small clear wings on its back." [Sieveking, p. 138]

After a few seconds of panic, Pearcey reasoned that the event was just a lucid dream. Once she convinced herself that the fly was part of a fantasy, it did indeed vanish, and the college student could move again. She chalked up the event to "the strange powers the mind can exert over us."

AFRO ANTEATER

After these grotesque visitations, perhaps we need one that is more amusing.

Brenda Ray of Mickleover, Derbyshire, recounted the particulars of an incident that occurred in 2004.

Late one night, she woke up as something small but heavy tried to climb into bed with her. She decided one of her cats had escaped from the kitchen, where they were kept at night. The bedroom invader managed to get atop the mattress. Brenda, half asleep and not even looking, just muttered "Get off!" and shoved it back to the floor. It was far more massive than a housecat, though, whatever it was.

The thing did not give up so easily. Its claws raked the wooden frame audibly as it clambered up again. This time, Brenda watched:

"I saw something resembling a small bear with a long nose and very thick curly hair. It also had long claws, which it dug into my hand quite painfully." [Sieveking, p. 140] When she described it later, her daughter called it "an anteater with an afro."

Ms. Ray claimed to have been paralyzed at some point, but she shoved the creature off a second time, and when it ascended yet again, she was able to turn on a lamp. The entity vanished.

Gail-Nina Anderson of Newcastle-upon-Tyne reported an even more solid bed climber. One night when she was a teenager, she was sleeping in a bedroom in her parents' house when something dropped onto the foot of her mattress. Like Brenda Ray, Gail sensed "it" was much larger than the typical housecat. The intruder ambled up the bed and nearly reached her face.

Like Brenda, Gail was not paralyzed. She explained, "I reached out and closed my hand round its front leg, which felt perfectly palpable and real."

She reached out with her other hand and clicked on a bedside lamp. "Instantly all sensation of its paw in my hand or its pressure on the bed vanished, and, needless to say, there was nothing there." [Anderson, p. 75]

I sympathize with Ms. Ray and even more so with Ms. Anderson, because this "Bed Climber" is a phenomenon I've experienced vividly. In the early Nineties, I lived in the Foxfire Apartments in Tulsa, Oklahoma. A bedraggled white Persian cat roamed the area, perhaps abandoned when its owners moved out. I wasn't the only resident to feed it once in a while. It was notorious for trying to slip past people into their rooms whenever a door conveniently opened.

One night as I lay in bed, I heard the "plip plip" of claws poking into cloth. Our family had once owned a mother cat (then its litter of kittens), so the sound of felines climbing furniture was familiar to me. Also, as the "plipping" continued, I felt tugs on my blanket from somewhere below.

In seconds, something scrambled onto the mattress, pressing down on it enough that I could feel the change in the surface. I reached over blindly and felt a solid body with long matted fur.

"Kitten, how did you get in?" I asked of the darkness. I supposed it had slipped in with me the last time I'd come in.

I sat up and petted the cat. It leaned heavily against my thigh, and its body was warm to the touch. I clicked on a bedside lamp—

And there was nothing on the bed with me. The cat could not even have jumped away at the last second: I was petting it even as I turned on the light, and its solidity vanished beneath my hand.

Ray's "anteater" and my Persian cat do not quite fit the "hagging" archetype. Both of us could move to intercept our visitors. We felt them and heard their claws raking physical objects. I, at least, could have taken an oath that I had touched and petted a genuine animal; I felt its tangled fur, its bony hips, and its bodily heat as much as I've felt any solid object before or since.

We may be edging into the field of "false awakenings" here, wherein the percipient is convinced they awaken and even rise and walk around, starting the day's activities before truly regaining consciousness.

There are many levels between everyday reality and the land of dreams.

The Land Between Night and Day

As intense, immediate, and frightening as "Hag attacks" are, I never believed them to be actual supernormal manifestations. This is partly because the Hag experience, like more mundane dreams, sometimes incorporate stimuli from the surrounding environment. The earliest assault I can remember consisted of three clown-like beings standing beside my bed as I lay paralyzed. They mocked me and laughed at me (silently), capered and stuck out their tongues, and took turns leaning over and blowing at me, as if blowing out birthday candles. Their breaths were icy blasts that would have made me shudder could I have moved.

When the episode passed, however, I realized the window next to my bed was open, and a cold, rain-sodden breeze had sprung up during the night. The clowns were simply the night winds, personified by my subconscious mind.

Another clue that night terrors were a psychological rather than a parapsychological phenomenon was the array of characters that came in the night. Medieval peasants saw vampires; Mormon missionaries saw the Devil; New Englanders saw witches.

I remember vividly—during the short period I rented a house trailer in Stillwater, Oklahoma—entering into a Hag attack and hearing heavy footfalls clump down the hall. Within moments, Michael Myers of *Halloween* fame stepped into my bedroom and sat beside me on the bed. "The Shape" did not assault me in any fashion, but even in my paralyzed state I grew skeptical of this visitation.

Not long after this I was hired by the Cities Service Company, and my nighttime attacker became my boss, who, though sometimes a little overbearing, I would not call a Hag. Later, my visitor became a strange tentacled being that came straight out of a *Weird Tales* illustration drawn by the great fantasy artist Virgil Finlay.

I decided that none of these characters were actually invading my bedroom at night and trying to crush the life out of me. I concluded that night terrors, Old Hag assaults, or whatever one called them were some complicated physiological and psychological phenomena.

This looks like a good point at which to end the discussion, but . . .

The thing is, I've always been a loner, while other percipients are not. Some Old Hag accounts involve witnesses outside the paralyzed victim.

In David Hufford's "Case Twenty" from *Terror that Comes in the Night*, three female college students (called Carol, Ruth and Joan, but not their real names) rented a house near Western Kentucky University in Bowling Green, Kentucky. They soon came to believe the house was haunted. Their story came to the attention of Lynwood Montell, chair of

WKU's folklore department, who contacted Hufford because a lot of the "haunting" phenomena sounded like "Old Hag" assaults.

The three students moved into the house on July 15, 1974. They immediately suffered bouts of nausea and diarrhea, but there was nothing "ghostly" about that.

Two weeks after the move, Ruth lay down on a sofa between 3:30 and 4:00 PM and fell asleep. (Remembering the theme of this book, she suffered through multiple nightmares about being surrounded by "wolfish looking foes.") She woke with the typical paralysis and paranoid feelings of "hagging." In her own words: "I was lying on the couch. And I could see the door. And I was looking at the door trying to get out! Trying to get to the door! . . . But *something* wouldn't let me! I couldn't get out! I couldn't move at *all*." [Hufford, p. 177]

Finally, Joan, Carol, and a young man named Jerry returned, and Ruth broke free of the spell.

As time passed, the inhabitants of the house experienced typical ghostly phenomena (excepting Carol, strangely enough). Carol reported of her roommates, "They would hear, like, voices, and footsteps on the stairs going up into my room. And noises in my room." [Hufford, p. 180] Eventually, Carol also encountered spooky things, such as hearing her name being called when no one else was around.

David Hufford commented on a factor I myself noticed after reading large numbers of ghost stories: Many accounts of hauntings include at least one "hagging," delivered as simply another of the ghostly events. Do hauntings cause haggings? Hufford suggests that, since night terrors are rare for most people, a lone, random hagging would be kept close to the vest, since people would not know how to define or explain it. During a haunting, however, one can simply drop this frightening event into a series of paranormal happenings and blame them all on discarnate entities. Haggings occur; they could occur during a stay in a haunted house as easily as any other time; therefore, a case of night terrors during a haunting *could* be ascribed to coincidence.

WKU student Carol, however, was to suffer a hag visitation with an interesting epilogue.

"I was awakened by this laughter," she told Hufford in an interview. "Like A-ha-ha-ha-ha (high-pitched). This real hysterical, cackling laughter." [Hufford, p. 188]

Sleepy, Carol could only wonder what her roommates found so funny. Seconds later, a noise approached her room from the stairs. It was not footsteps, but a rustling, as from the hem of a long, trailing dress. This was followed by "a really foul odor." Still dazed, the student told herself one of the pet dogs had come in and made a mess on the floor.

Beasts Beyond Belief

Even more disconcerting, the bed started rocking and making an "insane racket." Determined to keep to the mundane, Carol decided the hypothetical dog had jumped on the mattress and was now vigorously scratching fleas.

Finally, something undoglike touched her neck and shoulder. Carol tried to react and realized she could neither move nor scream. She struggled fruitlessly until she shouted "NO!" loudly in her mind. At that point the paralysis lifted. Carol clicked on the light and checked the room. No dog and no dog poop. The floors were hardwood; no canine or human could have entered the room without making more noise than a "rustling." The young woman now screamed for real and ran downstairs to Joan's room. Joan had been asleep, but reported: "I was awakened by this noise in your room. It sounded like someone was throwing your bed around." The three students spent the rest of the night in one room.

Joan was not present for Carol's interview, but when Hufford met with her five months later, she agreed that she had heard "thumping" upstairs minutes before Carol descended screaming.

This account makes one raise one's eyebrows. As noted, a major component of Old Hag assaults is the paralysis of the victims, which is quite all encompassing, except for the eyes. Spouses and other bedmates have witnessed this frequently; at best, victims can only moan and breathe erratically. Victims perceive malignant entities, hear voices and noises, smell odors, and feel movement of mattresses. These phenomena are basically subjective, however.

So, what do we make of Joan hearing the bed being "thrown around" well before Carol broke free of the paralysis? Could there be a malignant entity involved in night terrors after all, or at least something that affects the physical world? The eminent Dr. Franz Hartmann would say, "Yes!"

In February 1896, Dr. Hartmann, a German physician and theosophist, wrote to *Borderland*, a magazine devoted to psychical research, regarding a horribly tangible night terror. In that careful nineteenth-century manner of not exposing anyone's identity, Dr. Hartmann tells us: "A miller at D____ had a healthy servant boy, who, soon after entering service, began to fail." The boy ate well yet grew weak and emaciated. He finally admitted that something invisible yet material crawled onto him every night, "drawing all the life out of him." When the entity settled on him, he could neither move nor yell.

The miller shared the young man's bed, and one night thereafter the thing returned. "The miller grasped an invisible but very tangible substance that rested upon the boy's stomach, and, although it struggled to escape, he grasped it firmly and threw it into the fire." [Hartmann, p. 355] The nightmarish entity was apparently physical enough to burn and mortal enough to die because after this the boy recovered and was assaulted no more by the invisible nemesis.

Dr. Hartmann called this night attacker an "astral tumor" and claimed that it was a curable as a physical tumor. He added that the tale of the miller's apprentice, along with many other similar cases, were no old folktales but events that involved "people still living in this country."

A tumor, of course, is a mass of cells that have deviated from normal patterns of bodily growth, whether due to toxins, radiation, genetic predisposition, or other factors. Tumors can be benign or malignant (cancerous). They do not serve their intended biological functions, and once they become malignant they can spread cancer throughout the body.

I find the concept of an "astral tumor" fascinating yet terrifying. Imagine part of your psyche, astral form, spirit, or life-force splitting away from the totality that is "you," yet continuing its existence. Not being a proper "entity," it may have to draw power from you or others to continue "living." Perhaps the European vampire identification of sleep paralysis isn't so far from the mark after all. If the "tumor" retains some psychic remnant of the original sufferer, that residue might appear as a ghostly image of the person. Victims of the wandering tumor might indeed see specific persons attacking them and accuse the originals of being "Hags"—yet the originator would be innocent of evil-doing.

Calling the creators of "astral tumors" innocent of wrongdoing inevitably brings to mind the opposite question: What about people who *do* want to control immaterial beings? The trances of spirit mediums, shamans, and wizards world-wide are designed to allow intelligences from beyond the physical realm to enter our own. Such studied and practiced states of consciousness are meant to allow contact with specific beings, whether those are genii, demons, the Great Raven Spirit or your late Aunt Mabel. There are many levels of consciousness, however, about which we know little, let alone control.

I am put in mind of the usual random contents of my own dreams, like how I will be in high school again, naked and unable to recall my locker combination. I think of the typical antics performed by stage hypnotists, or rather, their hapless volunteers. I think of Victorian era séances and of the spirits who had nothing better to do than blow trumpets and bang tambourines. I think of all the altered states of consciousness brought on by hallucinogens, brain damage, dementia or simply struggling out of a deep sleep and answering the TV remote rather than the phone. Perhaps there are beings that can piggyback on uncommon but powerful altered states and enter our reality through them. The Hag experience is certainly powerful and impressive, at least as intense for the victim as a shaman's channeling is to him or her. If immaterial beings draw power from humans in the form of strong emotions, well, the Hag experience certainly generates those.

Another possibility: There exists a level of mind on the edge of sleep that seems to possess no function but to generate fear, inspire in one the certainty that something horrible lurks nearby, something inimical that is closing in on one with the intention of hurting and killing one. A weird mechanism of the human subconscious that generates monsters.

Back in the story of "The Aura of an Ape," I mentioned the idea of the thought-form, or *tulpa*—a being created when enough mental power devoted to the image of a person or creature could actually create a facsimile of it—one that could eventually take on a life of its own. To quote Janet and Colin Bord again: "So are they solely hallucinatory, taking shape from the archetypal monster image? They might sometimes originate in this way, but then take on an independent existence, feeding by vampirism on whatever energy source is available." [Bord p. 192]

Perhaps future cryptozoologists will not have to finance expeditions to the African jungles, the high Himalayas, or the primeval forests of British Columbia to hunt for monsters. They won't even have to get out of bed.

And they will not need to set out traps or food. The monsters will come to them.

SOURCES:

American Sleep Disorders Association. *International Classification of Sleep Disorders* (Rochester, MN: ASDA, 1990).

Anderson, Gail-Nina, "Invisible Cats," *Fortean Times* no. 323 (February 2015), p. 75.

Barber, Paul. *Vampires, Burial, and Death* (New Haven, CT: Yale University Press, 1988).

Bord, Janet and Colin. *Alien Animals* (Harrisburg, PA: Stackpole Books, 1981).

Craigie, William A. *Scandinavian Folk-Lore* (Alexander Gardner, 1896).

Glover, Jerry, "Gothic Night Terror," in Sieveking, Paul. *It Happened to Me!* Vol. 3 (London: Dennis Publishing, 2010), pp. 135–136.

Hartmann, Franz, "Vampires," *Borderland* Vol. III, no. 3 (July 1896), p. 355.

Hufford, David J. *Terror That Comes in the Night* (Philadelphia: University of Pennsylvania Press, 1982).

Pearcey, Esma, "The Fly," in Sieveking, *op cit.*, pp. 138–139.

Ray, Brenda, "They Came by Night," in Sieveking, *op cit*, pp 139–140.

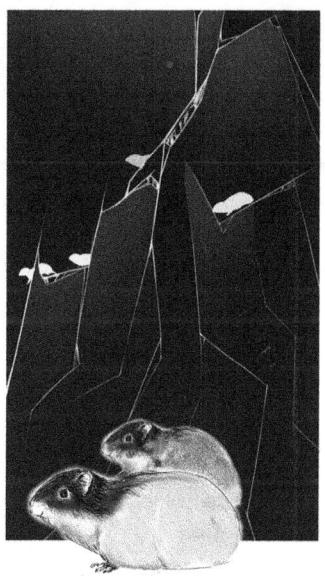

LEMMINGS FROM HEAVEN

In 1949 and 1950, nature writer Sally Carrighar lived in Alaska, where she gathered material for a book on Arctic animals. She focused her attention on the small, plump rodents known as lemmings. Lemming populations grow explosively every few years, after which their numbers then dwindle to the point of near extinction. During their population spurts, local predators live almost exclusively on them. Despite their ecological importance, little was known about these bob-tailed rodents.

"In every far Northern country, on every continent," writes Ms. Carrighar, "the primitive people call lemmings 'mice from the sky.'" As she mingled with the Inuit (Eskimo) inhabitants of the village of Unalakleet (on the shore of the Norton Sound in western Alaska, near the 64th parallel), she soon learned why they were called this: Several witnesses claimed to have seen lemmings drifting down from on high, "falling in bigger and bigger circles that turned same way as sun" (that is, clockwise when looking at the ground). Even those who did not witness actual falls were familiar with lemming footprints that started from nowhere and led away to the nearest grass or hiding place. Reggie Joule, a native bush pilot Carrighar held in high esteem, claimed to have seen such tracks on the roofs of cabins at Point Hope, where he grew up. "I think lemmings fly," was his final word on the subject.

One day in April 1950, Frank Ryan, the native postmaster of Unalakleet, told Carrighar that lemmings had just landed at (appropriately enough) the local airstrip. The nature writer hurried out and found fifteen spots where the rodents had apparently coasted in. "The blacktop was covered with less than an inch of new, light, soft snow—too shallow for any lemming to tunnel under it without thrusting up a ridge on the surface." The tracks continued "more deeply" on from the landing points, as if the animals had been nearly weightless in transit. They were definitely lemming tracks because mice left tail marks between their footprints and there were none here. The tracks were so new and sharp that even the imprints of long, dragging hairs on the animals' paws were visible.

"In each case the tracks led off the blacktop to a clump of grass, where the lemming evidently had burrowed down among the roots." [Carrighar, p. 27]

The naturalist tried and failed to think of an explanation for her flying lemmings. They possess nothing like a flying squirrel's membranous "wings." A powerful wind might scoop them up by their long, fluffy fur, but "the snow was as light as eiderdown and it lay as level as it had fallen." An owl might have dropped one struggling lemming, "but hardly fifteen in a space about twenty yards square."

While certainly an odd story to the man on the street, reports of small living things falling from no visible source are numerous. The books of Charles Fort are full of them. Even the apparent lack of weight (until touching the earth) is not unusual. It is rare for mammals to be the subject of sky falls, however. Fish, frogs, snails, and other so-called lower life-forms are much more common.

Ms. Carrighar had the misfortune of spending her first year in Alaska during a population crash of lemmings. Despite the sky fall, not even the native children could find any. Carrighar even convinced the Coast Guard to ferry her out to St. Lawrence Island to seek them, but no one could locate any at all. She left Alaska for the winter and returned the next spring.

Do lemmings sometimes vanish as strangely as they appear? During her 1950 hunt for lemmings, Sally Carrighar visited the small village of Shishmaref, located on a mere sandbar a few acres in size. She and her Inuit assistant found lemming burrows easily and dug into a dozen or more. Even as she admired the intricate construction of the tunnels, Carrighar wondered where the animals were. It was summer, food was plentiful, trails in the grass had been used quite recently, but not a lemming was to be found. "Since this was a small, narrow island, the only direction the lemmings could have taken was toward the sea. They could only have crossed the wide, smooth beach." [Carrighar, p. 33]

When she finally did obtain five lemmings (one of which eventually produced two litters), Carrighar had two habitats built in a large house

Lemmings from Heaven

she occupied in Nome, one on the first floor and one on the second. She studied the animals for several months before they, too, began to disappear. One, kept upstairs, ended up in a drip pan beneath an oil heater on the first floor (it died from its oily bath). The writer slowly transferred the lemmings downstairs, and finally there were four left topside. "What became of the final four never was known. I had heard them regularly, running about, spinning their wheel, chirring—and then from a certain day on there was silence." [pp. 164-165] An Eskimo youth helped her take apart the whole room and sift through the soil, grass, and sticks of the animals' environment, to no avail. "They were just gone—a fact to be added to the rest of the lemming mysteries." Perhaps Ms. Carrighar underestimated the abilities of small animals to escape captivity, but the consensus still seems to be that lemmings are strange little critters.

There is one legend associated with these rodents that almost everyone has heard: their "suicidal" tendency to march to the sea and drown. This myth was helped along by the 1958 Walt Disney film *White Wilderness*. (When the lemmings being filmed refused to march over a cliff into the sea, off-screen grips with push brooms shoved them over the edge!)

A more scientific view is that when the lemming population explodes, the animals are forced to migrate to find food. Sometimes they wander over cliffs or into rivers in their marches. Even this idea is not accepted by many modern biologists, who believe the whole legend to be greatly exaggerated.

Naturalist Dennis Chitty, who studied the animals for nearly 50 years, seemed to think there is something odd about lemmings. The notes that he and his fellow naturalists took between 1935 and 1949, such as the following, make interesting reading:

> "Bake Lake. Lemming were abundant in the summer of 1943. In November they migrated, presumably toward Eskimo point. In May 1944 they were practically non-existent. Numerous carcasses were seen lying in the glare ice on the lakes as if they had frozen to death. [Chitty, p. 8]

Chitty admits that lemmings that move out onto sea ice will die from starvation and exposure, thus they "in a sense are committing suicide."

SOURCES:

Carrighar, Sally. *Wild Voice of the North* (New York: Doubleday, 1953).

Chitty, Dennis. *Do Lemmings Commit Suicide?: Beautiful Hypotheses and Ugly Facts* (New York: Oxford University Press, 1996).

MAMMAL 411

*It was told in the **New York World**, July 29, 1908—many petty robberies, in the neighborhood of Lincoln Avenue, Pittsburgh— detectives detailed to catch the thief. Early in the morning of July 26th, a big, black dog sauntered past them. "Good morning!" said the dog. He disappeared in a thin, greenish vapor.*

—Charles Fort, *Wild Talents*

Over the past two decades, former law enforcement officer David Paulides has documented hundreds of missing person cases in wild areas and national parks in a series of books called *Missing 411*. Critics argue that it is only natural for the occasional hiker, hunter, or camper to get lost or die in the wilderness, but Paulides outlines specific criteria that place these missing person accounts beyond the norm. One sign of an extraordinary disappearance has to do with animals.

I don't know whether to think of this aspect of disappearances as amusing in a Disney-ish way or as exceptionally creepy. I refer to the subset of missing people (mostly children) who, when located, describe seeing—or who were seen by witnesses in the vicinity of—animals that do not act like normal animals. As a matter of fact, witnesses often have trouble identifying the species of the creature in question, though they are usually described as dog-, wolf-, or bear-*LIKE*. The poster girl for this phenomenon was Katie Flynn of Wallaha, Michigan.

Henry Flynn ran a lumber mill near Wallaha, and a large part of the operation consisted of hauling logs up to the sawmill at the top of a hill, depositing the load, and going back down for more logs. Three-year-old Katie would ride one of the horses on the way up, and as the men unloaded the lumber, she would trot down a separate trail through the trees and pop out at the base of the hill, ready to ride up again.

One day in June 1868, Katie ran down the trail but didn't appear at the other end. Henry Flynn assumed she had gone home, so the alarm did not go out until late evening. Henry, his workmen, and two hunters who happened by searched the woods with torches well into the night.

The next day, the hunt began again. At about 4:00 P.M. the searchers heard faint cries coming from the underbrush near a river. As the men neared the river, a huge black hairy "bear" plunged into the water and swam furiously for the other bank. It disappeared into the woods before anyone could get a better look at it.

In the underbrush, they found Katie standing on a dead tree that had fallen partially across the river.

The Flynns asked their daughter what had happened. According to the *Ludington Daily News*, the three-year-old replied, "Big dog came up to me, took me in his arms and walked away with me." One of Katie's shoes was missing; "Big dog ate it" was her explanation.

Another *Ludington Daily News* article expanded on the event. The black creature—whatever it was—had come out of the woods and played with Katie. It "held out its paw and she caught hold of it and it had walked away with her." It picked berries, which it brought back to her in its paw, and it lay next to her all night to keep her warm.

As David Paulides pointed out, "Bears are not nurturing warm creatures that cuddle children." Some accounts called the unknown animal a wolf, but "A wolf cannot pick berries, place them in its paw and carry them back in that paw." We can only agree with Paulides, who said that "Katie Flynn had something very unusual happen to her in the summer of 1868." [Paulides *Eastern US*, pp. 55–57]

Here for your perusal are some more very unusual animals.

THE TALKING BEAR

It seems that Greg and Stephanie McKay of Enumclaw, Washington, were camping near Greenwater in July 1985. On the morning of the 6th, their camp was invaded by an eight-foot-tall "bear-like animal."

"'You may think this sounds crazy, but the bear talked to us,' Stephanie, 35, said in a telephone interview. In a very high-pitched voice that didn't sound human it asked them their names and whether they had permission to use the campsite. They said they had permission, but the bear told them to get off the property immediately." ["Talking Bear," p. 34]

The bear started throwing stones at them. Understandably, the couple fled at top speed. Greenwater Fire Department officials visiting the site found only the paw prints "of a large dog," though saying the creature was an eight-foot-tall talking dog isn't much better. "The case was eventually dismissed as a product of over-active imagination."

I remember seeing this story in the *Weekly World News*, which did not help its credibility. However, the story appeared on July 10, 1985, in the *Boston Globe, Houston Chronicle, San Francisco Chronicle, San Diego Union*, and the *Seattle Times*, among other newspapers.

A TED WITH A 'TUDE

Cryptozoologist Scott Corrales described a bizarre ursine creature in "Monster Hunting in Latin America and Spain" (*Fate*, April 2004). In April 1997, two sisters were walking beside the AO-12 highway near Roldan, Argentina. They were near a silo factory when they suddenly noticed "a diminutive creature, entirely covered with hair and with shiny eyes." [p. 38] The younger sister felt a sudden unshakable urge to walk toward the being. The older sister grabbed her arm and yelled at her to keep her from going to it.

For a time, the creature simply stared at the women, but eventually it made an amazing leap entirely across the road (about 40 feet) and disappeared into a soybean field.

A few nights later, Mrs. Coronel, in her house in the country, felt a "strange compulsion" to open the door and step outside. She did so and spotted a small "bear," about 65 feet away, staring intently at her. She described herself as being "mesmerized," only snapping out of the spell when her husband yelled for her from the house. Mrs. Coronel described the creature as having a bear's face, but it stood upright.

Several other people (all women) also saw the creature, which author Corrales called a "Teddy Bear with a bad attitude." One can only wonder what would have happened if either of the first two witnesses had been alone. Maybe they would have simply wandered off with their little ursine friend, like Christopher Robin with Winnie-the-Pooh . . .

SEMEEL THE GUARDIAN

In the February 9, 2008, edition of the *Liverpool Echo*, Dawn Collinson told of uncovering an old story of a mysterious animal that may have actually *prevented* a tragic disappearance. Early in November 1953, two boys—David, age 12, and Alan, age 11 (last names withheld)—were playing cowboys and indians south of Liverpool in a section of forest called Little Woods. At about 4:20 P.M. they built a campfire. As Alan (with questionable wisdom) fired flaming arrows into the trees, David spotted an enormous tabby cat, four feet tall (presumably while on all fours) only 20 feet away. The creature said, "Hello, children," "in a clear, well-spoken voice," according to Collinson. The boys ran in terror and stumbled out onto a nearby street, where they were almost hit by a bus. Predictably, their parents did not believe the story.

The boys girded up their courage and ventured out to the woods the very next day, lighting a fire at about 4:20 again. "The enormous cat came slinking out of the woods, arched its back and sat by the fire opposite the boys." It gave its name as "Semeel" and said it was something called a "Guardian." It warned the boys to stay out of the forest because a local man (whose name they recognized) was lurking there, waiting to kill them. Then it padded off into the trees.

The boys' parents were still unimpressed because the man "Semeel" accused was in Wales at that time. However, several days later, the police discovered that the man had returned secretly from Wales. He had built a rough dwelling in Little Woods and was living there while the boys unknowingly played nearby. He confessed that he had been planning to abduct David and Alan.

The boys encountered the guardian Semeel three more times, but the giant feline apparently did not like the way the forest was being cleared for a housing project because after its fifth manifestation it never appeared again.

THE VULPINE VISITOR

Adventure/travel writer Richard Curle was living in Scotland "on the Borders" when he was a boy. One winter night in the 1890s, "over forty years" before the publication of his autobiography, *Caravansary and Conversation* (1937), at about 2:00 A.M. young Richard Curle woke and watched the swirling snow and waving tree branches outside his window. "I was wide awake, as wide awake as I am now." He became aware of "steady, unhurried" footsteps approaching the house. They appeared to pass through the back yard gate and cross the courtyard to the kitchen door. They then entered the house and climbed the stairs. Familiar with the layout of the house, Curle mentally marked their passage as they reached the top of the stairs, turned left, left again, took a few steps down, passed through the room next to Curle's, and finally stopped before the boy's door. The boy watched in horror as the handle turned and the door opened, revealing "a creature with the face of a fox, which walked on its hind legs. It was dressed in some sort of way and, would you credit it, wore a top hat, which added to its appearance an indescribably macabre touch."

The creature was larger than a normal fox. It possessed a bushy vulpine tail, but Curle detected no foxlike odor. It stared at him silently for several moments. Curle yelled, "Go away!," and the entity obediently turned and marched off. Its footsteps followed the same path they had in approach, leisurely but steadily, "until at last they died out on the road leading to the woods."

The episode bears some resemblance to "hag assaults" and "night terrors" as described in "The Land Between Night and Day." Some night terror cases do include loud, approaching footsteps as well as the appearance of a bizarre, usually evil creature. People being "hagged" suffer from temporary paralysis, however, and Curle maintained that he sat up in his bed and shouted at the fox-thing. A similar phenomenon called "false awakening" can lead one to believe one is awake, when in fact one is still dreaming. Curle wrote that "if one does not know when one is wide awake, what does one know?" He dismisses the idea of a hoax because the creature's legs were too small in proportion to be a human's. He conceded that he might have had a once-in-a-lifetime hallucination.

A new class of humanoids with animal heads, usually those of dogs, has been the subject of much discussion on fortean message boards and podcasts in recent years. Jonathan Downes, the director of Great Britain's Centre for Fortean Zoology, dubbed these animal-like entities "zooforms." A fox with a top hat, though, is like something out of a cartoon. It is tempting to dismiss Curle's childhood memory as a hypnogogic dream, but perhaps it bears some relationship to the modern "dogmen" and other creatures. Poor thing made a long trip for nothing, though.

THE FOOTBALL BEAST

On January 12, 2002, two boys just into their teens, "Jean F" and "Nelson C," both of Calama, Chile, were on a sleepover. Just before midnight, Jean discovered that his pet snake had escaped from its cage. The boys searched for the reptile, eventually remembering that dogs had been howling on some nearby waste ground about 30 minutes before. The youngsters got it into their heads that the escaped snake had made it all the way out there and that the dogs were announcing its presence.

Jean and Nelson ventured out into the night As they explored the empty lot, they noticed what appeared to be a dog watching them from about 100 feet away. Rather unsportingly, they threw rocks at it to make it leave.

The "dog" did not flee but hopped toward them like a rabbit. The animal finally stopped and rose on two legs, and the boys felt an unpleasant sensation, "a kind of electric shock in the stomach."

The animal continued approaching, dragging one leg as if injured (perhaps a rock had struck home). It glowed slightly in the dark, so the young men were able to describe it thoroughly. Its body was rather wide at the waist and narrow at the neck and tail, "like a rugby football with legs." ["Hopping Horror," p. 16] It had a head, canine but broad like a bulldog's, and big round Mickey Mouse-like ears. Its eyes were red and slanted, only visible when it turned its head, as they were placed on the sides like a herbivore's. Its arms and legs ended in three digits, webbed like a duck's feet. It was covered with coarse gray hair like a wild pig's, with bristly clumps jutting out along its spine like a boar's crest. Its stubby, white-tipped tail was about two inches thick.

Jean ran away, but Nelson felt a weird desire to approach the creature just like in the stories of the Argentine "teddy bear." This did not last long, for Nelson heard a voice in his head say, "Don't stare, just run away." He did so, feeling a burst of extreme cold as he fled the waste ground. Again, we can only speculate as to what might have happened if the beast *wanted* Nelson to approach.

The boys were interviewed separately by members of the Calama [Chile] UFO Center, and their accounts agreed completely. The South American UFO center sent the report on to the Miami [FL] UFO Center.

A SHAGGY DOG STORY

A man who identified himself only as "John" sent an email to the *Fortean Times* in 2013 concerning what he called a "dog mechanic."

"It was a Saturday night in February 2010 at around 11:45 P.M." John and his girlfriend opened the front door of their house in Pendle, Lincolnshire. John had stopped smoking three years previously, and his girlfriend accommodatingly only smoked outside. They stood on the threshold, looking into the cold, dark, quiet night (what some researchers would call a "liminal spot," halfway between one place and another, which seems to attract odd events).

Suddenly, a large shaggy "Digby"-type dog ran across the street. It kept tripping over its own legs. John's girlfriend said, "Poor thing, it looked terrified... what's it doing out at this time of night?"

The dog had no collar (at least, none that was visible in its thick fur), but it looked well groomed. It disappeared into the darkness.

Moments later, another figure sauntered along the opposite side of the street. "It was the same dog we had seen running across the top of the street, but this time it was wearing baggy work-style jeans, a long grey T-shirt and a dark red baseball cap. It looked like an American mechanic."

The creature walked upright, but very badly. Rather than being shocked or horrified, the witnesses found it "hilarious that it was trying to pass as human."

The canine "mechanic" glanced at the couple as it walked off down the street, and the weirdness of the sight finally hit them. The woman tossed her cigarette away, and then she and John shut and locked the door, "both stunned and shaking at what we had seen."

A THROBBING GIANT AND A FRIENDLY TREE

One of the most frustrating details of 411 accounts is the lack of information as to what happened during the missing period. Most victims never return or are found dead, and of those who are recovered alive, most are too young to explain or have medical conditions that prevent lucid communication.

A two-year-old boy named Jackie Copeland, however, gave an account of his vanishing in 1950—and what an account it was!

The Copeland family, parents, four daughters, and son, Jackie, attended an oil company picnic on the company grounds outside Pleasantville, Pennsylvania. The date was May 14, 1950. Around 1:00 P.M., the family noticed that Jackie was not in evidence. Everyone at the picnic looked for the toddler.

State police, bloodhounds, and hundreds of volunteers joined the search but could not find the boy. The next morning, two miles away from the picnic grounds, a Mr. Bevier led a group of searchers through what were described as "impassable" swamps. As the volunteers called for Jackie, someone peeked out from behind a tree. It was the missing two-year-old, scratched and tired but otherwise in good health.

After being reunited with his parents, reporters interviewed the Copelands, and Jackie proved to be quite talkative.

According to the *Logansport Press*, "He saw something peering at him from behind a big tree. When he approached, the creature scampered into the brush." Jackie did not say why he followed it. Eventually, he "recounted in child talk his adventure in an awful blackness, peopled by a great throbbing giant and a tall friendly tree and wild animals howling in the distance and the unfamiliar shouts of strangers prowling nearby." [Paulides *Eastern US*, p. 201]

Most people dismissed Jackie's tale as a dream or fantasy, but researcher Paulides wrote that it "could be a very sobering narrative of what might possibly be occurring with the plethora of missing children outlined in this book from the Pennsylvania area."

THE THREE-LEGGED RACE

In recent interviews, Paulides backpedals a little from tales of helpful animals. As he said to host George Noory on *Coast to Coast AM* (Sept. 28, 2022, at approximately 45:55 onward), "I try to tell people, don't put a lot of credence into what kids say . . . you don't know if they're making it up, or if it's truthful." Yet what are we to make of stories like that of another two-year-old, Ida May Curtis?

The redundantly named Curtis Curtis and his son, Mortimer, worked for the Leigh Creek Camp as loggers. The camp was located in Kootenai National Forest, Montana. On holidays, families of the loggers were allowed to visit the camp and set up tents, so the loggers could remain nearby.

On July 4, 1955, Mortimer's family erected tents with other families in the designated camping area. Around 1:30 in the afternoon, little Ida May said she saw something moving through the trees at the edge of the campgrounds. Her brother Cecil, aged nine, accompanied her a short distance into the woods without finding anything. Cecil escorted her back to a tent where other children were playing.

Suddenly, a bear poked its snout into the tent. It scooped up the two-year-old Curtis girl in one foreleg and fled, loping awkwardly on its other three limbs.

Meanwhile, the girl's grandfather Curtis Curtis, happened to be walking near the tree line. He saw what he thought was a bear, and yes, it was hobbling along on three legs, apparently clutching something close with one foreleg. It crossed a stream, and the older Curtis chased after it, though he did not yet know Ida May was missing. Despite its clumsy mode of locomotion, the bear outran Curtis and vanished into the forest.

Search parties quickly formed, eventually growing to a total of 250 men. Strong rain followed by snow rolled in at an amazing speed (sudden bad weather is a common factor in Missing 411 stories). The search had to be postponed.

The next day, at about 4:30 P.M., Ida May was found about 300 yards from the camp. She showed her rescuers a crude shelter made of cedar limbs, and she told them a "mama bear" kept her warm during the night.

She suffered from neither scratches nor bites, and she was not wet from the creek, the rain, or the snow. Need we say it? A bear carrying any item any distance would certainly hold it in its teeth; bears don't build lean-tos, and they don't cuddle children overnight then release them unharmed. At least, no normal bear does.

Bears snatching children—and doing very unbearlike things—is not a recent phenomenon. Loren Coleman wrote on his *Cryptomundo* website about a "bear" that kidnapped a young shepherdess in seventeenth century France ("Abduction by Modern Neandertals").

"France, Savoie, the village of Naves. 1602 Female abduction, cited in writing already in 1605. Seventeen-year-old Anthoinette Culet was herding animals when she disappeared." Months later three lumberjacks working on a nearby mountain heard a voice echoing from a cave, the entrance of which was blocked by a boulder. The person calling out proved to be the abducted Anthoinette Culet. According to her testimony an "ugly but amorous monster with enormous strength" carried her off and occasionally brought her "baskets of bread, fruit, cheese, linen and thread."

The girl was escorted home, but that night the beast, whatever it was, tracked her down and attacked the village. It was shot to death. It was described as a bear, but it "had a navel like humans and almost looked like a human."

What are we to make of these helpful, if mischievous, 411 animals? One theory is that the beasts are Bigfeet or Dogmen, mistaken for bears and wolves by small children and adults who glimpse them from a distance. Both of these cryptids show a disturbing amount of interest in human children. Some children they keep, perhaps even adopt for all we know; others are released as the kidnapping creatures lose interest.

A second theory is that the animal forms are screen memories created by UFO aliens, an aspect of many abduction accounts. The most common culprits in this scenario are the "Grays," and their disguise of choice seems to be oversized owls.

And yet . . .

I've read accounts where searchers become worried because they *do* find prints of bears. Ida May Curtis spent over 24 hours with her abductor and said it was a bear. The other children she was playing with insisted it was a bear. Grandfather Curtis, before he even knew Ida May was missing, saw a bear acting just like the creature at the camp, hobbling along with something hugged to its chest, which in turn was a very strange thing for a bruin to do and which attracted attention.

Can those nasty old Grays control that many minds at once? If they can, why not just knock everybody unconscious and grab who they want?

For all I know, there are intelligent, anthropomorphic animals in the woods that snatch children, whether on their own or under the direction of other entities. I might add my own theory that regular animals are sometimes possessed by an outside intelligence and used to abduct children in ways that are very un-animal-like.

CRIKEY!

I begin to think the key to comedy is to add a kangaroo because this last tale sounds like a joke. Girraween National Park straddles Queensland and New South Wales in Australia. On June 15, 1975, a neighborhood group from a town called Lota visited the park to have a picnic. The group consisted of the O'Malley family, including three-year-old Justin O'Malley, plus four of their neighbors. Sometime that afternoon young Justin wandered away from the group and could not be found.

By sundown, nearly 200 people were searching for the boy. Dogs sought his trail, boats plied the surrounding ponds, but Justin was nowhere in evidence. After a subfreezing night, searchers found the boy atop a high rock outcropping. According to the Sydney *Morning Herald* of June 16, "His mother said he was dressed in a red jumper and long pants but he had lost his shoes and socks. 'He told me he met a big kangaroo and the kangaroo took them.'" [Paulides *Off the Grid*, p. 268] Was *this* a misidentified Dogman or Bigfoot (or Yowie, to use the correct vernacular)? Or are Grays strapping on marsupial pouches Down Under?

SOURCES:

Coleman, Loren, "Abduction by Modern Neandertals," *Cryptomundo*, November 5, 2006. https://cryptomundo.com/cryptozoo-news/abductions-neandertals/

Corrales, Scott, "Monster Hunting in Latin America and Spain," *Fate Magazine*, Vol. 57 no. 4 (Apr. 2004), pp. 32–39.

Curle, Richard. *Caravansary and Conversation* (New York: Frederick A. Stokes Co., 1937), pp. 271–274.

"David Paulides Missing 411: Some Come Back." *Coast to Coast AM*, September 28, 2022 (accessed 1/22/2023). https://www.youtube.com/watch?v=PdHH3rN29Ns&t=5758s

"Hopping Horror," *Fortean Times* no. 158 (June 2002), p. 16.

"John—," "Dog Mechanic?," in Sutton, David, editor, *It Happened to Me!* Vol. 6 (London: Dennis Publishing, 2014).

Paulides, David. *Missing 411: Eastern United States* (North Charleston, SC: CreateSpace, 2011).

———, *Missing 411: Western United States* (North Charleston, SC: CreateSpace, 2011).

———, *Missing 411: Off the Grid* (North Charleston, SC: CreateSpace, 2017).

"Talking Bear," *Fortean Times* no. 45 (Winter 1985), p. 34.

"Uncanny Encounters," *Fortean Times* no. 237 (special issue 2008), p. 23.

MY NAME IS SU

Alexander, I thought, might have been encountered while crossing the Granicus, and elephants might be driven into the sea; but how could anyone face a beast with a man's head?

—Leigh Hunt, *The Life of Leigh Hunt*, Vol. 1 (1878)

The Mantichore, a tigerlike creature with a human head, is one of the less convincing mythical animals. After all, could the following be real? According to the ancient Greek writer Ctesias, the Mantichore was said to have "the face of a man and the bulk of a lion; to be of red-colour, having three rows of teeth in each jaw, with human ears but larger, and grey eyes; equipped with a tail above a cubit long, pointed with a sting like that of a scorpion." [Costello, p. 104]

This must be a monster of pure imagination. However, Ctesias claimed to have seen the beast himself in Persepolis, after its capture in India.

Modern researchers suggest Ctesias merely saw a tiger. T. H. White, author of *The Sword in the Stone* and translator of *The Bestiary*, suggests that the Mantichore may only be a were-tiger. *An American Werewolf in London* comes to mind, wherein David Naughton's character changes into a four-footed beast, but his face remains relatively human until the very end of the transformation. Perhaps the Mantichore is a were-tiger who never quite made it. White added, "In Haiti at the present day there is a voodoo animal called the *cigouave*, which resembles the Manticora." [White, p. 52]

LEAPIN' LEMURS!

Andre Thevet was a French clergyman and explorer of the sixteenth century. He was almoner (one who distributes alms to the poor) for Catherine de Medici and historian to Charles IX. He introduced tobacco to France after a sojourn in Brazil. In 1571, he penned the *Cosmographie Universelle* in which he had this to say:

> At the time when I was on the Red Sea, certain Indians came from land, from the banks of the River Vachain ... They brought a monster the size and shape of a tiger, with no tail, but a face just like a well-proportioned man's except the nose was a snub: the hands in front like a man's and the feet behind like a tiger's, all covered with tawny fur. [Heuvelmans, p. 507]

In his classic text *On the Track of Unknown Animals*, Bernard Heuvelmans theorizes that Thevet's monster was a lemur. ("A monster the size and shape of a tiger"? That's some lemur!) Some species of lemurs, the earliest of the primates (prosimians, technically), resemble monkeys with pointed, foxlike snouts. Other writers, oddly enough, suggest that the fabulous *Cynocephali* (dog-headed people) were based on lemurs. Could the same animals inspire legends of humanoids with *animal* heads and of quadrupeds with *human* heads?

Perhaps these are merely travelers' tales from centuries ago. However, human-headed beasts were reported in the nineteenth and twentieth centuries—in North America, yet.

THE MISSOURI "GHOST"

One evening in 1864, Judson K. Mason spent some time at a neighbor's house across the street. As he headed home, he met something untoward right in the middle of the avenue, according to the St. Louis [MO] *Post-Dispatch* of June 2, 1889: "He says it had the body of a dog with a human head and face attached." Mason kicked at it and ran back to his neighbor's house. The two ventured out but found no trace of the human-animal. Mason told no one of the encounter for decades.

STUMPY

W. W. Wilson provided this story to the Ohio Valley Folk Research Project in the early 1960s. It seems a bizarre creature haunted the Norwich, Ohio, area in the nineteenth century.

"Coming home from church one Sunday evening with her brothers and the neighbor's children, my grandmother felt something tugging at her dress." The woman was used to her brother John teasing her, so she called out, "John, let me be." To her surprise, John popped up from the crowd ahead. He was several yards away, so he certainly had not grabbed any part of her apparel.

Suddenly an animal of some sort shot out from behind her, dashed past the people ahead, and vanished in the fading light. "Comparing notes they agreed it looked like a dog except it had a man's head." [Woodyard, p. 101]

Somehow the creature received the name "Stumpy."

The strange being next showed up at a local farm. At the time, only a hired girl was at home. She glanced out a window while attending her chores and noticed cows trotting in from the pasture and heading for the barn. It was a strange thing to see when no one else was supposed to be there, so the girl stepped outside. Wilson continues:

> Driving the cows was a large dog, a dog with a man's head! Naturally one presumes the girl did not linger long to make observations, but she got a good look at it and she recalled that it looked at her with [a] fixed gaze.

One night, a local doctor, riding his horse-drawn buggy home after a house call, dozed off at the reins. Suddenly he woke—possibly from the jolt of something climbing aboard. Whatever the reason, he realized the human headed dog was sitting right beside him, staring hard at him. After a long, uncomfortable moment, the canine chimera jumped out, hitting the ground with an audible "thump." It then dashed into a field and disappeared into the night.

That was the last known sighting of "Stumpy."

EVERY SEMBLANCE TO A MAN

In July 1901, according to Jerome Clark and Loren Coleman, three men—Milton Brint, Taylor Brint, and Tom Lukens—were raccoon hunting in Stewart's Woods, Pensbury township, Pennsylvania. Their hunting dogs ran ahead, barking wildly at first then growing silent. After a long moment, the animals turned tail and fled.

The puzzled hunters shone their lantern up into a cedar tree. "A low dismal sound" came from high in the tree, which now shook as something descended. According to Milton Brint:

> "[I]t was impossible to tell precisely just what it was.... I got a faint glimpse of the thing before it struck the ground, however, and while its head and neck bore every semblance to a man, it had the body and legs of a wild beast. [Clark and Coleman, pp. 63–64]

The hunters ran for home. The dogs did not show up for nearly a week, and they refused to enter Stewart's Woods thereafter.

Later, two other men, Lewis Brooks and Jack Murphy, riding through the area on a wagon, saw "something with a manlike head and an animal-like body" cross the road in front of them. "Brooks emptied a revolver into the thing but with no apparent effect."

THE VIRGINIA "GHOST"

A man named Charlie Cooke packed up and left after a frightful entity wreaked havoc on his property in Henrico County, Virginia, in April 1903. The creature appeared for several nights in succession, showing up around 10:00 P.M. It was a "ghost, which takes the shape of a dog with a woman's head," according to the Richmond *Times Dispatch*. "It gets into the yard and scatters the milk pans and the woodpile, uttering the while the most horrible noises." [Paijmans, p. 31] It even came up to the house and rattled the doorknob.

THE PALO ALTO "WEREWOLF"

"Something big, black and hairy" terrified people in the Palo Alto, California, area in May 1943. Deputy Sheriff Nicholas Rose described the beast as "a hairy thing with a man's head and a wolf's body." It wandered lonely back roads and jumped out at passing cars. Professor Ira Wiggins of the Stanford Museum of Natural History tried to stem the hysteria by saying that "there just isn't such an animal." [Paijmans, p. 31]

WEREWOLF/OGRE

In May 1961, a bizarre "ogre" supposedly stalked the streets of Compton, California. It had the body of a dog and the face of a woman. ["Rumors"] A local journalist pointed out that a "werewolf" had been reported lurking around nearby Palo Verde since 1957.

THE MOBILE WOLF-WOMAN

In Mobile, Alabama, April 1971, a "wolf-woman" was supposedly on the loose. The *Mobile Register* claimed to have received 50 calls in one week concerning a bizarre creature haunting the area around Davis Avenue and the Plateau neighborhood. One witness said that "the top was a woman and the bottom was a wolf. It didn't seem natural." [Paijmans, p. 30]

A FAMILY OF MONSTERS

A trio of creatures, reputedly a male, female, and cub, haunted the area around Albany, Kentucky, in 1973:

> Its tail, which it carried like a cat's, was long, bushy, and black. According to one witness, its head was shaped "like an ape/human with a flat face and nose with large nostrils. Its ears are like mule ears and will perk up." [Clark and Coleman, pp. 115–116]

Compare this description with that of the legendary South American creature, the Su, or Succarath, described by early European explorers as "a very emaciated sort of lion with a plume of a tail like an anteater's and a grotesque head somewhat reminiscent of a bearded man." [Heuvelmans, p. 279] Particularly intriguing is Father Andre Thevet's drawing (*ca.* 1558) of the Su, with its bushy tail and long pointed ears.

The Kentucky creatures reportedly killed many pigs, calves, and dogs. Livestock ran around their pens in panic when they approached, and wildlife disappeared from the local forests. One witness, Rick Hall, reported: "My girl's aunt went home one evening and found it just outside their back door eating old table scraps. She shot at it six times with a pistol and 17 times with a .22 rifle and she says she missed it." [!]

The thing ran but paused at the edge of the woods, one hundred yards away, to watch the woman. It fled when her husband started after it. This woman was either the world's worst shot, or the Su-beast possesses some werewolf-ish resistance to ordinary bullets.

Most anthropomorphic animals and were-beasts are depicted with animal heads on humanlike bodies. They seem almost natural. In fact, in a psychological study of preschoolers, who were shown pictures of the Minotaur, Anubis, mermaids, and other animal-human characters, it was noted that most children found nothing unusual in bipedal, anthropomorphic animals, rarely referring to them as "monsters," "half-human," or the like. They were, to the toddlers, just animals. [Nash, *passim*.]

The opposite idea, however—a human head with an animal body—has always struck the present writer as less aesthetically pleasing. If I should ever meet a Su or Mantichore, I may take a tip from H. P. Lovecraft:

"I glimpsed—and ran in frenzy from the place, / And from a four-pawed thing with human face." [Lovecraft, p. 121]

SOURCES:

Clark, Jerome, and Loren Coleman. *Creatures of the Outer Edge* (New York: Warner Books, 1978).

Costello, Peter. *Magic Zoo* (New York: St. Martin's Press, 1979).

Heuvelmans, Bernard. *On the Track of Unknown Animals* (New York: Hill and Wang, 1959), p. 507.

Lovecraft, Howard Philips. *Fungi from Yuggoth and Other Poems* (New York: Ballantine Books, 1971).

Nash, Harvey. *How Preschool Children View Mythological Hybrid Figures* (Dominguez Hills, CA: California State University, 1982).

Paijmans, Theo, "Wolf-Woman of Mobile and Other Human-Headed Hounds," *Fortean Times* No. 369 (August 2018), pp. 31–32.

"Rumors of Ogre Pour into Police," Long Beach [CA] *Press-Telegram*, May 4, 1961.

White, Terence H. *Bestiary: A Book of Beasts* (New York: Capricorn Books, 1960 [1954]).

Woodyard, Chris. *Haunted Ohio II* (Beavercreek, OH: Kestrel Publications, 1992), quoting *Ohio Folk Publications*, New Series, no. 94 (1962).

OUT OF AFRICA

THE LEOPARD SOCIETY

As far back as the seventeenth century, rumors of cannibalism emerged from the Sierra Leone area of Africa. Explorer William Finch wrote in 1607: "To the South of the Bay, some fortie or fiftie leagues distant within the Countrey, inhabiteth a very fierce people which are man-eaters." Rumors of a slightly different nature emerged two centuries later. Bishop Ingram wrote in 1894: "The Temnes believe that by witchcraft a man may turn himself into an animal, and, in that form, may injure an enemy. A man was burnt at Port Lokkoh in 1854 for having turned himself into a leopard." [Beatty, p. 14]

One of the most enduring and frightening legends of Africa is that of the Leopard Society, an organization involved with witchcraft, crime, murder, and cannibalism, yet curiously it may be of relatively recent vintage. In 1901, T. J. Alldridge, an expert on the Mende tribes, expressed his belief that the Leopard Men as a group formed only half a century earlier. The British colonial government was stunned in 1891 when reports came from Mende country that as many as 80 people had been burned alive in the Imperri chiefdom (without consulting said colonial government). The Mende had been suffering murderous predations for so long that they had summoned in "Tongo players" to uncover the perpetrators.

The Tongo players were themselves a secret society of medicine men—reminiscent of the clichéd witch doctors of old Tarzan movies—and they were employed by African villages as witch finders. When called upon (and paid), they sent spies ahead to find out information about the most suspicious individuals. Afterwards, the medicine men themselves arrived in force, and they ordered all the men, women, and children to meet at a cleared area of the settlement on an appointed day. The names of those most likely to be guilty were given to the witch doctors, who, disappearing into the bush, "professed to go through the ordeal by which the guilt or innocence of these suspected persons might be determined." [Beatty, p. 14]

When the Tongo men "discovered" a guilty party, the accused had as little hope for escape as a medieval European peasant grabbed by the Inquisition. At best they would be allowed to greet their family members one last time (if they paid for the privilege), but all the "guilty" parties were eventually thrown into a huge fire.

Occasionally, the Tongo performed a much more elaborate ritual, perhaps to impress outsiders. They dressed, ironically, in leopard skins with bells hanging from the tails. Their headman and his assistant each carried a club with jutting spikes called *Tongora*. The Tongo danced, and during this dance the men with the Tongoras would run up to the ones accused and strike them powerfully on the head. It didn't matter if the accused survived or not because they were thereafter thrown into the fire.

It was the 1891 incident that brought both the Leopard Society and the Tongo players to the notice of the colonial government. The Leopard Men were secretive in all their dealings, however, while the Tongo were quite open (to the local natives they were the "good guys.") The British did not agree, so on May 5, 1892, they issued a statement which read in part:

> His Excellency the Administrator of the Government of the Colony aforesaid doth hereby publish, proclaim, and make known—That from and after this date the play or dance of the Tongo People commonly called and known as "Tongo play," being contrary to law, must at once cease throughout the Colony. [Beatty, p. 17]

Unfortunately, with the Tongo removed, the Leopard Society carried on unchecked. During 1894, the number of murders skyrocketed, and virtually everyone—white or black, farmer or chief—agreed that the crimes were the work of the Leopard Men.

The Leopard Men were infamous for taking victims while dressed in leopard-skin suits and wearing mummified paws on their feet to leave catlike prints. They proved to be as elusive as their feline namesakes. Most of the time, they were ordinary-looking members of the community, numbering respected citizens and even chiefs among them. Such important men were able to bribe witnesses, destroy evidence, and convince the populace that most of the killings were the work of actual leopards, which abounded in Sierra Leone.

If all this was not bad enough, authorities discovered that there existed a splinter organization, the Human Alligator Society, that met near rivers infested with crocodilians.[1] Finally, after the murder of a young girl in May 1913, informers reported that a small but deadly Baboon Society rose spontaneously after normal citizens argued with a local chief. These "commoners" decided that the only way to strike back at a powerful ruler was through witchcraft.[2]

In July 1912, at the village of Imperri, a group of Leopard Men were interrupted in the commission of a murder, and one of their number was captured. He admitted to being of the Society, but he was no killer. It seemed the Leopard Men inducted some people merely to be servants, menial workers, and kidnappers.

This lowly leopard fellow proved to be a fountain of knowledge, and most of the information he provided, when it was possible to vet it, proved accurate. He knew details of some 30 Leopard Society murders committed since 1907, which resulted in the arrests of almost 400 people, some of whom were tribal chiefs or sub-chiefs. Of these, 108 stood trial.

The British authorities in Sierra Leone soon learned more than they ever wanted about the premiere terror organization of West Africa, a group they did not know existed just 20 years earlier.

---

[1] The new Society might have been more properly called the Human Crocodile Society, as alligators are not native to Africa, but "alligator" and "crocodile" meant pretty much the same in the local dialects.

[2] Fursuiters from the furry fandom would have had problems in this era. In 1895, the British Colonial government passed a number of laws meant to cripple the Leopard Organization, one of which stated it was against the law to have in one's possession "a leopard skin shaped so as to make a man wearing it resemble a leopard." After learning about the Human Alligator Society, new laws were passed in 1901 making it "a felony for any person without lawful authority or excuse to have in his possession, custody, or under his control an alligator skin shaped or made so as to make a man wearing the same resemble an alligator." In 1912, after the Human Baboons surfaced, you guessed it, it became illegal to own "a dress made of baboon skins." Likely anyone dressed as any animal would have been met with suspicion or outright hostility.

The Leopard Men knew one another by, as corny as it sounds, a secret handshake that involved one member raking the middle finger in a special way over the palm of another; this signal was hidden from outsiders by the participants' hands. Members also bore a scar that was made by "piercing the flesh with an iron needle, raising it, and shaving off a thin slice of flesh." [Beatty, p. 49] This mark was usually made on a buttock, which would be hidden by a loincloth, the one item of clothing nearly everyone wore.

Both the Leopard Men and the general population believed in the magic of an artifact called the *Borfima*, a "medicine bag" that contained the most powerful sorcery of the Society.

The word actually is a contraction of *Boreh fima*, which means "medicine bag" in the local language. It consisted of a leather bag containing "amongst other things, the white of an egg, the blood, fat, and other parts of a human being, the blood of a cock, and a few grains of rice; but to make it efficacious it must occasionally be anointed with human fat and smeared with human blood." [p. 39] Individual Leopard Men possessed their own Borfimas, but local leopard "chapters" revered a communal object called the Mother Borfima that ruled over all the others. These medicine bags brought their owners wealth, power, good luck, the love of the people, and victory in the white men's courts. They also withered the hearts, livers, and kidneys of those who opposed them.

I write Leopard Men "possessed" Borfimas, but effectively the opposite was true. The Borfimas, according to Leopard cultists, were living beings with minds and desires of their own. If they were not "fed" with human blood and fat on occasion, the artifacts would withdraw their magic boons.

The Leopard Men's victims were rarely picked at random. Each member of the Leopard Society was expected to produce a sacrifice, which was usually a close relative. Once chosen, the victim was either lured to a lonely area by some ruse or simply set upon by a group of Leopard Men and slain. After "feeding" the Borfima, according to Captain Beatty, "the body is divided up among the members, and, according to the evidence of the ex-members of the Society, the flesh is either eaten raw on the spot or taken away and cooked." [p. 50]

So great was the fear of the Leopard Men, the families of victims did not strongly pursue their loved ones' killers. Some even explained away the perpetrators' guilt: "They look upon the 'medicine' as being responsible, and hold the view that the members of the Society are forced into killing a victim in order to 'feed' the Borfima."

Once captured, the typical human leopard was quick to accuse others, often claiming to be innocent of actual murder. In a series of trials stretching from December 1912 through May 1913, 108 accused Leopard Men stood trial at Gbangbama in the Imperri chiefdom. E. M. Merriweather, the colonial governor of Sierra Leone, summed up the trials in a statement released in July 1913: "Of the persons brought to trial, nine were convicted of murder and 10 others of lesser offenses, the remaining 15 being acquitted." He ended his report with a warning about the Leopard Society, however: "It has held sway for many years—possibly for centuries—and the task of stamping it out will undoubtedly be one of great difficulty."

Yet worse than Leopard Men was to come.

WATUSIMBA: THE LION-PEOPLE

In 1920, Officer Hitchens of the East African Game Department learned that "rampaging lions" were killing hundreds of local villagers each year. This seemed like an incredible number, but there *were* lions in the district, and some did become man-eaters on occasion, so he accepted the reports, however appalling.

Rumors reached Hitchens, however, that witch doctors in the area were willing to "eliminate" people for a fee. They did this, it was said, by directing lions to their chosen targets. Hitchens soon noticed that the bodies of the victims of the so-called man-eaters were not, in fact, being eaten. Those killed had only been clawed or bitten, and some mutilations looked more like knife wounds. The maulings were so savage, however, that even the medical examiners could not be certain.

The inhabitants of one village finally had enough. The moment news came of a new killing, they took to beating the bush and succeeded in driving the marauder into the open.

To their amazement, the "lion" "turned out to be a youth dressed in a lion skin with paws tied on to his hands and feet." [Cowie, p. 72] The witch doctors had been sending out human assassins after all.

In the mid-1930s reports of man-eating lions were on the rise again, but these seemed to be actual big cats. With the coming of World War II, the predations became epidemic, resulting in nearly 200 human deaths in a single year. An officer named Rushby, a ranking official of the Game Department, was sent to oversee the hunting down of the man-eaters.

Rushby's war against the lions seemed doomed to failure. Wherever he placed himself and his men, the animals struck elsewhere, as if they read his mind. Entire villages were abandoned due to the carnivores' depredations, yet the native inhabitants would give Rushby no aid or information—once again, the people feared the power of the witch doctors.

When Officer Rushby finally shot down a few lions, they proved to be in perfect health. It was commonly accepted that only old, sick, or injured lions turned to hunting humans, so this made no sense.

The predations amped up even more in 1946. That year, 36 people were killed, virtually torn to pieces, in the village of Dodoma, Tanzania. Perhaps there really was something supernatural about the perpetrators. The people turned to the witch doctors for protection, paying well for "anti-lion amulets."

The first clue to the unbelievable truth came in 1947, when a man turned himself in to the authorities and admitted that he had once been a "lion-man." At the age of 12, while watching over his family's cattle, the boy had been kidnapped by persons unknown and dragged off to an undetermined location. There he was dressed in lion skins and fitted with claws. He was then given a long course on the fine art of killing people in a fashion that made it look like the work of lions.

He lived with four other abductees, all women, who were already full-fledged "lions." Eventually, a teacher/keeper led the boy out to perform his first leonine murder. The would-be victim, however, clubbed the youth on the head and also injured his leg. The pseudo-lion's injuries proved to be so severe he was no longer useful as an assassin, and he was basically dumped in the jungle.

The story gave the Game Department a better understanding of the situation, and Officer Rushby and his companions actually captured a few of the pseudo-lions. Just as importantly, the local villagers cooperated with the European officers because the witch doctors now looked more like ordinary gang leaders than omnipotent sorcerers.

A new officer assigned to the Game Department, Tulloch by name, ferreted out more details about the lion-man cult, and what he learned proved to be more horrible and grotesque than any tale of witch doctors' magic. The lion-cultists preferred young female recruits over males. When a suitable girl was found, she . . .

> . . . would then be imprisoned in a cave, too low for her to stand upright. She would be plied with drugs, mostly hashish, to render her insensible. Her hands and feet were then mutilated so as to be more suitable for fitting a lion's feet and claws, and at a suitable stage she would have a fresh lion skin put upon her and stitched so that it could not be removed. She would be fed only on raw meat and water and after some months would be so demented that she believed she was a lion.[Cowie, p. 75]

These miserable creatures lost the ability to speak, but they understood and obeyed their masters, who sometimes led them on leashes like hunting hounds. The lion-people were allowed to run loose two or three times a week, sometimes to target specific individuals but mostly just to raise havoc and engender superstitious terror.

By June, 1947, the number of victims around Dodoma totaled 103, all of whom were mutilated and sometimes partially eaten. Fortunately, by the end of that same month, police tracked down a cell of the cult, and no less than eight witch doctors and 45 lion-people were captured. The Tanzanian government held a mass trial, and the law made no distinction between the cult leaders and the pathetic, barely human lion-people who were as much victims as the murdered villagers. Twenty-nine of the pseudo-felines were hanged, many others imprisoned, and one is said to have bitten his own tongue off and bled to death.

WERE-HYENAS

The myths and legends of Africa are full of stories of proper therianthropy (i.e., of people who actually transform into animals). "Well, of course," says the Thoroughly Modern and Civilized Individual. "Every primitive culture believed in such things. Nowadays we know that these superstitions were perpetuated and exploited by so-called witch doctors and wizards as in the story of the Leopard Society."

I might agree, if only members of "primitive" societies ever reported such creatures, but that is not the case.

Richard Bagot was an English writer and a member of the Society for Psychical Research. In 1899, he published a novel entitled *A Roman Mystery*, which predominantly featured lycanthropy (the psychological disorder). Bagot had researched werewolfery thoroughly, and because of this a friend of his who held a high position in the West African government sent him the report of a Lieutenant F____, the commander of a detachment of troops in Northern Nigeria. (Bagot withheld the officer's name as a courtesy to his friend.)

"To understand the situation clearly, you must know that in this particular part of the Empire one lives in grass and mud houses," writes Lieutenant F____. "Doors did not exist."

Among other animals, Lt. F____'s compound housed two goats and two sheep. In mid-July 1915, a hyena carried off one of the goats. By a bizarre coincidence (if coincidence it was), the next day the second goat died of an apparent snake bite. F____ and his soldiers hauled the second goat out into the bush, built a wall of thorns around it, leaving only one opening, and set a steel trap in this entrance. That night, the trap was sprung without catching anything, and to add insult to injury one of the *sheep* went missing. Hyena prints were everywhere.

F____ put the second sheep in a mud hut and secured the doorway as best he could with grass mats. Awakened that night by a "rustling," he stepped out with his rifle but saw nothing. Before falling asleep again, however, a servant boy ran in to tell him the last sheep was dead.

Hyena tracks indicated the culprit, but the dead sheep presented a bizarre spectacle: "The poor sheep was standing up, but the whole of its head was gone. The lower jaw only was whole, and stuck out in a horrible manner. The wound was so clearly cut it looked as if it had been done with a knife." [Bagot, p. 355][3]

The next day Lt. F____ bought a new goat, which he staked out as bait. That night he concealed himself nearby, and at about 1:00 A.M. a hyena dashed out of the bush at the goat. The officer fired twice from only yards away, but the predator escaped.

About 25 minutes later the beating of drums started at the nearest native settlement, a village of the Yungeru people, indicating that someone had died.

In the morning, F____ and an orderly followed a trail of blood and pawprints to a river. The beast had apparently drunk there, then it trav-

---

[3] A bit off topic, but the headless sheep still standing may not be some omen of the supernatural. William R. Corliss, a physicist and collector of scientific anomalies, gathered together several accounts of "attitudes after death" for his books *Strange Life* and *Incredible Life*. Basically, sudden, violent death—particularly any causing fatal trauma to the chest cavity or the head—can cause a body to freeze in position, as if it has entered rigor mortis in a split second. Dr. Rossbach of Wurzburg came upon a striking example of such a frozen corpse after the Battle of Beaumont in 1870: "He found the corpse of a soldier half-sitting, half reclining, upon the ground, and delicately holding a tin cup between his thumb and forefinger, and directing it toward a mouth that was wanting. The poor man had, while in this position, been killed by a cannonball that took off his head." [Brown-Sequard, p. 115]

Though not unheard of, it is curious that such an odd phenomenon would pop up among all the other, stranger events listed by Lt. F____.

Beasts Beyond Belief

eled upstream and lay on a white sandy patch marked by numerous ant-hills.[4] Blood stained the patch.

From there, all signs of the hyena vanished. However, bare human footprints led back to the Yungeru village.

The next day, news came from the settlement that an important villager had died, but the Yungeru would not let anyone examine the body.

The following October, a donkey died in a town inhabited by the Hausa tribe. F____ had the carcass dragged out into the wilderness and sat up in a nearby tree for two nights. Nothing happened. On the third night, he set up a gun trap with a .308 carbine and left. At midnight, the carbine went off. Minutes later, the death drums pounded again in the Yungeru village.

In the morning, F____ followed a trail of blood and hyena tracks toward the village. About 300 yards out, the trail stopped. It looked like people with brooms and rakes had swept the dirt clean all the way back to the settlement. Later, Lieutenant F____ was informed that the Yungeru chief's mother had died mysteriously during the night.

In November of the eventful year of 1915, a horse died in the Hausa village. Again, Lt. F____ had the carcass dragged into the wilderness, had a wall of thorn bushes built around it, and set up a gun trap in the entrance. After about 36 hours, the carbine went off. F____ once more followed copious amounts of blood to the ant-infested sand patch, and again the hyena prints ceased, replaced by human prints that led off into the bush.

In the Yungeru village the death drums boomed.

Lt. F____ had further stories to tell, but the incidents outlined above should give one the flavor of his strange adventure in Africa. He commented, "Of course to the educated mind these things appear at first to be absolutely impossible, but there is evidence, and good evidence too, that there may be something in this unusual power."

---

[4] Ordinary black ants have something to do with were-hyena transformation. How? I can do little but repeat Richard Bagot's own note: "In Somali-land, and in other parts of East Africa, a wide-spread belief exists that it is perilous to sleep on ground thrown up by ants. The sleeper runs the risk of being 'possessed' by evil spirits which may change him into some wild animal. When once this metamorphosis has taken place, it infallibly recurs, and the victim is never freed from the evil obsession."

THE JACKAL DANCE

Everyone has heard of the dread "Society of the Leopard"... They put on their bodies the skins of leopards, and they laid upon their perverted souls the nature and habits of leopards—but they did not BECOME leopards.

—Frederick Kaigh, *Witchcraft and Magic of Africa*

The rationalist would argue that Lt. F____ never actually saw anyone change into anything or vice versa. Some sort of trickery must have been involved, as in the case of the Leopard Men creating prints with mummified paws strapped to their feet.

What do you do, though, when a witness, a European who does not—or at least once *did* not—share native beliefs, reports seeing something even more spectacular than hyena tracks apparently becoming human tracks?

Frederick Kaigh was a medical doctor and author based in London, England. For seven years, he held the position of government medical officer and deputy sheriff in the African Service. This position allowed him to see much of the African continent firsthand and become familiar with its people. He was very vocal in his desire to end colonialism and let Africa become the master of its own fate. "At present the native can only be gainfully employed by working for the white, and this is a wrong principle. He must be encouraged towards a social and economic independence," he wrote in his 1947 memoirs.

Native education, technical training and a legal system that took into account the traditions of the African peoples themselves were necessary, but there was another factor Kaigh considered more important even than social reforms. "Witchcraft must be attacked first. Every government official knows this," he wrote [Kaigh, p. xxiv]. To Africans south of the Sahara, magic, divinations, hauntings, curses, and strange events of every stripe were as common as births, deaths, weddings or dances. They were as "unnoteworthy as our early morning cup of tea."

"Of course!" exclaims the rationalist. "Primitive superstitions hold sway over less civilized people the world over! Belief in such nonsense must be squelched, or people will always fear so-called witch doctors and other charlatans!"

This was not what Frederick Kaigh meant, however. "The things we shall see are actualities." Perhaps the most spectacular of these actualities was a rite called the Jackal Dance.

Beasts Beyond Belief

Dr. Kaigh's personal assistant was a young native sergeant in the British South African Police (a branch of law enforcement in Rhodesia [now Zimbabwe]). The sergeant warned that there might be trouble in the area during an upcoming night because a Jackal Dance was to be held in the jungle. Kaigh was determined to observe this normally secret ritual, and after much "cajolery, bribery and corruption" the sergeant agreed to smuggle him unseen to the site of the ceremony.

After letting it be known that Kaigh was extremely ill with malaria, the doctor and the sergeant waited until nightfall and crept into the brush.

"The spot was on the Rhodesian-Congo border near the north-eastern border of the Jiundu Swamp." [Kaigh, p. 31] A natural clearing, an almost parklike expanse, had formed in the otherwise thick and tangled jungle foliage. The sergeant pointed out a tree that would provide concealment, and the stealthy pair climbed high into it.

After an agonizingly long time, natives started arriving by one and twos. Eventually, a *nyanga* (witch doctor) arrived, attired in jackal skins and with stripes painted on his face and body in a crude outline of a skeleton. He began a long incantation. Now men pounded drums: "A rhythm which beat inside one and tingled down the spine: a rhythm which seemed gradually to take on itself a bestial quality." [Kaigh, p. 31]

Suddenly, the drums and chanting ceased. The witch doctor started a fire and tossed various concoctions into it. He also drank some potion from a wooden bowl.

A jackal howled in the brush. The *nyanga* jumped up and padded about like a dog sniffing. Eventually, he kicked out the fire and howled. Jackal calls answered him out of the night.

The witch doctor danced a wild, frantic dance. "It was the cleverest imitation of a crazy jackal I have ever thought to see." At the height of this dance he dropped to the ground like a log. Jackals howled everywhere.

Now a young man and woman sprang completely over the circle of watchers and landed in the clearing. Kaigh described the shocking climax:

> They danced the dance of the rutting jackals. As the dance progressed, their imitations became more and more animal. . . . Then, in a twinkling, with loathing unbounded, and incredulous amazement, I saw these two turn into jackals before my eyes. [p. 32]

The were-jackals mated multiple times in the clearing. Finally, they finished their display and crept off into the jungle. The watching people paired off and began their own frenzied mating. The orgy lasted amazingly long, but eventually even the most virile participants dropped in exhaustion. "That is what I saw with the same disillusioned eyes now glued to my very ordinary Oliver typewriter in a very ordinary study in Essex."

"Every magistrate and native commissioner" knew rituals like the Jackal Dance were held once in a while, but Frederick Kaigh's close-up view was unique in the Colonial annals. The doctor considered that the whole affair might have been mass hypnosis brought on by the *nyanga's* chanting and dancing, but, as Kaigh concluded, "All my experience rebels against so convenient and specious an 'explanation.'"

What does that leave, though? Did actual shapeshifting occur amid the horrible outbreaks of Leopard (and other society) atrocities? For now, we can only observe, as Pliny the Elder did 2,000 years ago, *"Ex Africa semper aliquid novi."* There is always something new out of Africa.

SOURCES:

Bagot, Richard, "The [?] Hyenas of Pirra," *Cornhill Magazine* Vol. 45 no. 268 (full Vol. 118), (October 1918), pp. 353–361.

Beatty, K. J. *Human Leopard Society: Ritual Murder and Cannibalism in Colonial Africa* (London: Notoir Books, 2020 [1915]).

Brown-Sequard, C. E., "Attitudes After Death," *Knowledge* Vol. 6 (1884), pp. 115–117.

Corliss, William R. *Strange Life* (Glen Arm, MD: The Sourcebook Project, 1976).

Cowie, Mervyn. *World of Animals: The African Lion* (London: Arthur Barker Ltd., 1966).

Godwin, John. *Unsolved: The World of the Unknown* (Garden City, NY: Doubleday & Co., 1976).

Kaigh, Frederick. *Witchcraft and Magic of Africa* (London: Richard Lesley & Co., 1947).

Seabrook, William. *Witchcraft: Its Power in the World Today* (New York: Harcourt, Brace and Co., 1940).

THE PACING WHITE MUSTANG

The first recorded account of the legendary animal known variously as the White Steed of the Prairies, the Pacing White Stallion, the White Mustang, the Ghost Horse, and Shunka-tonka-Wakan comes from Washington Irving's *A Tour on the Prairies*. In his diary for October 21, 1832, Irving wrote:

> There were several anecdotes told of a famous gray horse which has ranged the prairies of this neighborhood for six or seven years, setting at naught every attempt of the hunters to capture him. They say he can pace and rack (or amble) faster than the fleetest horses can run. [Irving, p. 116]

Note it is a gray, not a white stallion. Perhaps the animal turned white with advancing years, or the white steed was the offspring of the gray. Or both "white" and "gray" were attempts to describe a shimmering, shifting silver, like the Lone Ranger's famous steed.

In 1841, the Santa Fe Expedition set out from Texas to annex New Mexico. This enterprise did not fare too well—the men became lost in the wide open spaces and were marched into Santa Fe at last as prisoners of the Mexicans—but journalist George W. Kendall recorded the activities of the expedition in his 1844 book, *A Narrative of the Texan-Santa Fe Expedition*. He wrote:

Many were the stories told by some of the old hunters of a large, white horse that had often been seen in the vicinity of the Cross Timbers, and near Red River . . . so game and untiring is the White Steed of the Prairies, for he is well known to trappers and hunters by that name, that he has tired down no less than three race nags sent expressly to catch him, with a Mexican rider well trained in the business of taking wild horses.

The most famous White Mustang tale is certainly "Gretchen and the White Mustang," told to Western writer and folklorist J. Frank Dobie by Dr. J. O. Dyer of Galveston, who got it from a woman named Gretchen. As an eight- or nine-year-old, Gretchen was part of a group of Germans who crossed the Texas plains around 1848 looking for a place to settle. The wagon train followed the Guadalupe River upstream. Gretchen asked to ride an old gray mare that bore sacks of corn meal. Her father tied her loosely amid the sacks, but in the mid-afternoon a wheel broke on the family wagon, so the train had to halt. Gretchen fell asleep, the family was busy with the repairs, and the mare wandered away.

Gretchen awoke to find herself in the middle of nowhere. The mare was following "a neighing, pacing white horse with cream-colored mane and tail." The mare would not stop, nor could Gretchen reach the knots of the rope holding her on.

Eventually, they ran into a herd of mares. The wild mares nibbled at the meal sacks and bit the girl. She screeched. "But at her cry the Pacing White Stallion was with one bound beside her. He was as considerate as he was intelligent. He drove the wild mares off. Then he chewed in two the ropes that bound Gretchen. Next he took her gently by the collar of her dress, very much as a cat takes one of her kittens, and set her down upon the ground."

The girl spent the night on the plains, sleeping in a nest of grass and drinking water from a spring. Morning came, and all the horses had vanished. By noon, Gretchen found only a few wild currants to eat. She cried a lot. Another night came, and on the second morning she awoke to find the gray mare back. Unfortunately, the girl was too short to climb aboard the animal herself. "She was leaning against the shoulder of the old mare sobbing, when she heard swift hoofbeats, rhythmic and racking. She looked up and saw the beautiful White Steed . . . He paced right up to where she stood, gently grasped the collar of her dress and the scruff of her neck in his teeth and lifted her upon the mare." The mare carried her back to the wagon train, which had remained at the same place as the colonists searched for the girl.

The Pacing White Mustang

A Irishman named Mayne Reid was 20 years old when he emigrated to New Orleans in 1838. He worked with traders on the plains and served in the American army during the Mexican War. In his book *War-Trail; or, The Hunt of the Wild Horse* (1861), Reid mentioned that:

> I had heard of the white horse of the prairies . . . For nearly a century has he figured in the legends of the prairie "mariner," a counterpart of the Flying Dutchman . . . Some say he cannot be taken, that he is so fleet as to . . . glide out of sight in a glance . . . on the open prairie. There are those who assert that he is a phantom. [Reid, p. 92]

Folklorist David Wilson collected a number of narratives on tape (as folklorists are wont to do). Jack Thompson had an interesting tale about his great-grandfather, Jock. It seems old Jock and his family lived in Paradise Valley (Montana) in the 1870s. When wild mustangs wandered into the valley, Jock and his son Archie would catch them, break them, and sell them to the army. Jack told Wilson: "Archie said that one night he woke up and heard a lot of noise out around the pens. He got up and went outside to see what the hell was going on. He said he saw a big white horse running back and forth close to the pen." The great beast would run up, whinny, and run away, as if trying to get the mares to follow him. "Archie ran out to try to scare him off, but the damn thing just stood there, lookin' at him, shakin' his head, and pawin' the ground." [Wilson, p. 159]

Archie went for help, but by the time he returned, the horse was gone, and the mares had knocked down the fence to follow him. This happened three or four more times that summer (sometime in the early 1870s). Jock and Archie finally went looking for the stallion. They found him by a river after a few days' search.

> Well, he stood in one place long enough for Jock to get a rope over him. He set his horse and threw another rope, and Archie tied that one to a tree. But before Archie could move away from the tree and let the horse wear himself out or choke himself to death, he took off running around the tree and wrapped Archie up in the rope. Archie said he thought he was about to get squeezed to death, but one hand was free, and he remembered he had a knife; so he grabbed the knife and cut the ropes. The horse took off like a bat out of hell, and that's the last they saw of him.

SOURCES:

Dobie, J. Frank. *Mustangs* (NY: Curtis Publshing Co., 1934).

Irving, Washington. *Tour of the Prairies* (Norman, OK: University of Oklahoma Press, 1956 [1835]).

Wilson, David L., "The Legend of the Pacing White Mustang," *Folk-Lore* (Volume 90, Part II. 1979), pp. 153-166.

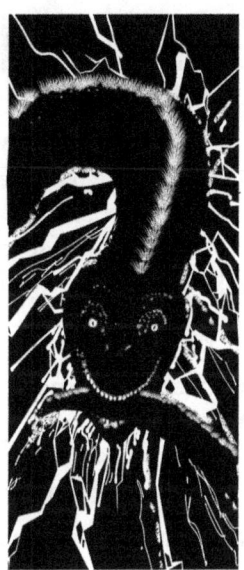

THE PENNSYLVANIA OUROBOROS

While Annie Whitney and Caroline Bullock collected folklore from Maryland and Pennsylvania in the 1920s, along with the usual witch and haunted house stories they received this truly eerie report from a local named William Johnson.

When William Johnson was a boy in Somerset County, Pennsylvania, the schoolhouse stood in the middle of a field in such an out-of-the-way location (even for a country school) that students lost much of each morning merely walking there. When Johnson was about 16 (c. 1886), a new building was erected at Jenner ("16 miles west of Johnstown, in Somerset Co., Jenner township, at the Cross roads"). One gray-haired old man warned that the crossroads were haunted; apparently, he was right. No sooner was the building completed than a terrifying entity manifested itself:

> Every month in the dark of the moon, an immense snake would appear. While its head and tail seemed to be hidden under the school-house, its long scaly body, over a foot in diameter, was laid across all public highways leading to the place. He [Johnson] said they often had evenings at the school-house, and spelling schools and the like, and had to get over the serpent before entering the house. [Whitney and Bullock, p. 193]

Johnson said the scales on the creature were "sharp" rather than slick, and that if anyone touched it in stepping over, he or she would "stick" to it and get thrown to the ground.

Not everybody could see the thing, but everyone could feel it, and even those blind to it were thrown down if they stepped on it. The creature was so long its body ran across several people's properties. One such landowner, a man named Frame, became so frightened that he sold his holdings and moved away. The purchaser, Joe Leverson, raised a large family on the "snake" property with no problems. The local children lost their fear of it as well. Occasionally, men who had bolstered their courage with drink would attack the serpent with fence stakes or other weapons, to no avail. Along with Leverson, Johnson provided other witnesses' names, such as Joe Boyer and Jeremiah Mowery, a preacher, lifting his tale out of the "friend of a friend" category.

No one ever saw this bizarre apparition's head or tail tip. It seemed to be a single, endless loop of serpentine body. Its immense size—the implication is that it must have been miles long—calls to mind the colossal serpent Jormungandr from Norse mythology, which encircled the world.

William Johnson moved away from the area at the age of 30. The "snake" still appeared at that time around the turn of the twentieth century. No one he knew had any explanation for the entity. (I tried hard not to write, "They could make neither head nor tail of it.")

An old drawing of a dragon-like creature with a long neck and tail can be found in T. H. White's translation of *The Bestiary*. Both neck and tail terminate in small, doglike heads, and the front head holds the tail head in its jaws. The text explains, "This is called an AMPHIVENA (Amphisbena) because it has two heads. . . . With one head holding the other, it can bowl along in either direction like a hoop."

This medieval monster sounds like the ancestor of the good old American Hoop Snake, a fabulous reptile that bites the end of its tail and rolls after its prey like a loose bicycle tire. *The Bestiary* in turn lifted its information from older sources like Physiologus and Pliny. (In an odd echo of the trouble people had in crossing the Pennsylvania entity, Pliny reported of the Amphisbena that "a pregnant woman will miscarry if she steps over it." [White, 177]

These legendary creatures, along with the aforementioned Jormungandr, are all permutations of the Worm Ouroboros, the serpent with its tail in its mouth, a universal symbol of wholeness, totality, and the cycles of nature. Yet it seems such things can be more than symbols.

We might take a science-fictional view and suggest that the Pennsylvania Ouroboros was a multi-dimensional being. Such a creature could project part of its body into our universe while the rest of it remained in a higher spatial dimension. Or we could draw upon occult lore. The trouble people had in merely stepping over the Ouroboros, along with its circular outline, reminds one of the "magic circle" used for protecting oneself from or caging a spirit. Also, the spirit power of serpents in general is an ancient and universal belief. Perhaps in some primordial time the two were one: the Magic Circle personified as a huge, curled snake, protecting or imprisoning what lay within its coils.

A sign like that would warn *me* away, certainly.

SOURCES:

White, Terence H. *Bestiary: A Book of Beasts* (New York: Capricorn Books, 1960 [1954]).

Whitney, Annie Weston, and Caroline Canfield Bullock, "Folk-Lore from Maryland," in *Memoirs of the American Folk-Lore Society*, Volume 18, 1925, pp. 192–193.

THE RAT-KING

There have been some strange court cases involving animals over the centuries—birds and cats accused of being witches in disguise, for instance, and pigs and donkeys tried for murdering their human owners. A case involving a "creature" known as a Rat-King was convened in Leipzig, Germany, in 1774.

On January 12 of that year, a young man named Christian Kaiser, who was employed at the windmill at Lindenau a few miles from Leipzig, was working as usual when he heard squealing noises from the staircase. He spotted several rats on and around the risers and clubbed them to death with a chunk of firewood. He still heard squealing, so he climbed a ladder to reach a high ledge, this time armed with an ax. He found a hairy gathering of rats only inches from his face and raked at it with the implement.

To his surprise, the rodents slid out as a single mass and fell to the floor. There were 16 rats altogether, and most survived the fall. They did not flee, however. Their tails were "plaited together" in a dirty, scabby knot.

Kaiser showed the remarkable tangle of rodents to his employer, Tobias Jaeger. Jaeger kept the bizarre "Rat-King," and some of the animals forming it survived for a short time (we do not know if the miller and his assistant tried to keep them alive).

News of the freakish entity swept through Lindenau, and eventually Johann Adam Fasshauer, a neighbor, visited Jaeger's windmill. Fasshauer asked to borrow the Rat-King so he could paint its portrait. Jaeger agreed. Fasshauer left with the 16 tiny corpses, and no one saw or heard from him for a week.

Finally, the good miller discovered that Herr Fasshauer was publicly exhibiting the Rat-King and charging admission. Herr Jaeger thus petitioned local officials to have Fesshauer return the Rat-King to the miller and turn over any money collected from its exhibition.

The results of the proceedings have been lost to history, but during the legalities a court-appointed doctor examined the Rat-King to determine if it was a real anomaly or a fake. The physician concluded that the "said sixteen rats were not one organism which is called a Rat King but sixteen individual rats of different size and coloration and (in my opinion) different age and sex." The unfortunate rodents "had their tails knotted together in a large knot in such a manner that most tails were completely in the knot except for a piece one or two inches in length near their bodies," [Ley, p. 30]

This entanglement, wrote the doctor, had somehow occurred without the intervention of humans. He theorized that the rats had huddled together that winter for warmth, facing outward to guard against predators. Urine and feces from rats higher up had spilled onto the overlapping tails and frozen, and as the rats struggled to get loose, they somehow entwined their tails in an ever-tighter knot. The scenario seems unlikely, but biologists and zoologists have not come up with a better explanation for Rat-King formation in the centuries since. "Rat Kings fabricated by tying the tails of live rats together look nothing like real kings," as Robert Hendrickson observed in his *More Cunning Than Man.* [p. 92]

About 60 Rat-Kings have been reported in Europe since the mid-1500s, the largest being composed of 32 rats. The usual number of rodents entrapped varies between five and ten. The phenomenon has become increasingly uncommon over the years, and for once we do know the reason: Rat-Kings only form among members of the species *Rattus rattus*, the black rat or roof rat, an animal best known for spreading bubonic plague across all of Europe in the fourteenth century. In the early eighteenth century, however, a new species, the brown rat or Norwegian rat (*Rattus norvegicus*) appeared in great numbers from Central Asia. Brown rats attacked and killed black rats whenever the two strains met, and the larger newcomers usually triumphed over *Rattus rattus*. The number of black rats dwindled, and with that the number of Rat-Kings.

Science writer Willy Ley admitted in an essay for *Galaxy* magazine (October 1963) that he could find no example of a Rat-King more recent than one found in the village of Capella, Westphalia, in January 1907. Hendrickson wrote of one found in, curiously, 1963. Ley published just a tad too soon. In the modern era, Wikipedia reported a Rat-King being found as recently as October 2021 in Polvanaa, Estonia.

> Dr. Ray S. Youmans, a veterinarian from Brunswick, Maine, was called in recently to untangle a half-dozen young squirrels with their tails in a knot. Youmans thinks the squirrels got pine pitch on their tails and became tangled as they grew more active in their nest.
>
> —Pittsburgh *Post-Gazette*, June 4, 1985.

Nature, they say, abhors a vacuum. It looks like the Rat-King shortage may be offset by a new zoological spectacle: Squirrel-Kings. The largest Squirrel-King found so far has consisted of a mere seven squirrels. Unlike Rat-Kings, which can include rats of any age or sex, Squirrel-Kings are nearly always composed of young squirrels, not yet weaned, and their tails always seem to be stuck together with tree sap.

These minor differences aside, it feels almost like some higher power, some godlike being somewhere, wants tail-fused creatures to exist. Perhaps *Homo sapiens* should consider itself lucky it (normally) possesses no caudal appendage. The world is ass-backward enough as it is.

Legend speaks of another kind of Rat-King:

> The name was known to Conrad Gesner, the great Swiss zoologist of the sixteenth century. In his book on the four-footed animals, which was printed for the first time in 1551, he said in his chapter on the rat . . . that "some say that the rat, in its old age, grows enormously large [so that it can no longer move around] and is fed by the younger rats; it is called a Rat King by our people." [Ley, p. 28]

Ley goes on to write that, while tail-tangled Rat-Kings are certainly real, nothing like a single giant King Rat has ever been captured. Yet stories of super-rodents persist. According to *More Cunning Than Man*, published two decades after Ley's article, "sewer workers in London and other large cities have told of sighting the fabulous beast, who is usually attended by a bodyguard of huge white rats and causes his subject rats to grow silent and motionless when he appears in their midst." [Hendrickson, p. 15]

An article in—of all things—*The Wall Street Journal* for August 25, 1969, combines the mysterious super-rodent with another favorite anomalous phenomenon—animal falls (see "Lemmings from Heaven," or, even better, the *Complete Books of Charles Fort*).

For several months, the already poor Island of Lombok, just east of Bali in Indonesia, had been suffering from drought. Then a plague of rats descended upon the rice fields—literally. "'They came six months ago, before the rains stopped,' says [a] farmer. How did they come? 'They fell from the sky.' From the sky? 'Yes, in bunches of seven and then they spread out across the land,' the farmer adds matter-of-factly. 'They are led by a great white rat as large as a cat.'"

This albino King Rat seemed to be supernaturally intelligent—even psychic. "'If we plan to harvest a field the day after tomorrow the rats will eat the field tomorrow night. If we plan, in secret, to harvest the field tomorrow then the rats will eat it tonight.'" ["Life in Lombok," p. 1]

SOURCES:

Hendrickson, Robert. *More Cunning Than Man* (New York: Dorset Press, 1983).

Ley, Willy. *On Earth and in the Sky* (New York: Ace Books, 1967).

"Life in Lombok—Hunger, Starvation Are Day to Day Worries on Plague-ridden Isle," *Wall Street Journal* (August 25, 1969), p. 1.

Michell, John, and Robert J. M. Rickard. *Living Wonders* (London: Thames & Hudson, Ltd., 1982).

"Rat King." Wikipedia entry accessed August 3, 2023. https://en.wikipedia.org/wiki/Rat_king

Sanderson, Ivan T., "Rats Again," *Pursuit* Vol. 2 no.4 (October 1969), pp. 65-66.

"Squirrel King." Wikipedia entry accessed August 3, 2023. https://en.wikipedia.org/wiki/Squirrel_king

THE RED DRAGON STAMPS

On April 4, 1928, Rhys Evans, 71, an expert on old books, left his home in Swansea, Wales, to visit a colleague, Professor Jenkins, at University College. He carried with him an ancient Welsh book of stories and legends that contained strange drawings or maps he hoped Jenkins could help him decipher. He never made it to the college.

On April 6, his wife received a letter from Cardiff. On the front were two penny-ha'penny stamps, which at that time was twice the necessary postage. One stamp had a further stamp of its own—a picture of a dragon in red ink. (It was just as well there were two stamps, as the postal service wouldn't accept the inked-over one.) The letter, written in Welsh, stated that Evans was well and not to worry. Evans himself had signed the letter as proof. Below that was another signature of sorts: "*Trigolion y ddraig Goch*," which means "Natives of the Red Dragon."

On April 11, 1928, Evans was found by the picturesque lake in Brynmill Park, Swansea. He no longer had the old book of legends. He would not or could not explain what happened to him. He *did* say something to this effect: "There are dragons in Wales today," but he would not explain that, either.

Over the next few months, many other people received postcards and letters with one normal stamp and one "dragon" stamp. They had been posted from different communities, including Cardiff, Cardigan, and Wrexham. About 20 such pieces of correspondence showed up altogether, according to an article in the philatelist magazine *The Stamp Lover*.

Meanwhile, at Llandegley, Wales, near Radnor Forest, three children reported seeing "a huge beast in the forest." One tried to follow it. "His way was blocked by two men who escorted him part of the way home. They were dressed in white with red dragons emblazoned on their chests." [Sieveking, p. 32]

One of the stories in the missing book of legends, by the way, was "an account of a secret sect or clan responsible for the guardianship of five sacred dragons." Yes, it's important to keep those kids away from the dragons.

SOURCES:

Andrews, C. H. R., "The Red Dragon Stamps," *Stamp Lover* (1928), cited in: Sieveking, Paul, "Natives of the Red Dragon," *Fortean Time* no. 48 (Spring 1987), p 32.

RETURN OF THE MEGAFAUNA

PLEISTOCENE PARK

Pleistocene Park is the brainchild of Sergey Zimov, a Russian geophysicist (born 1955) who specializes in arctic-subarctic ecology. Although Zimov's experiments in animal reintroduction in Siberia began in 1988, it was not until 1996 that the Russian government devoted 144 square kilometers of land near the mouth of the Kolyma River in the Sakha Republic to the project. The idea was to re-create the "mammoth steppe ecosystem" that arose during the Pleistocene ice ages. First, numbers of yakutian horses, moose, and reindeer—animals already native to northern Siberia—were introduced. The animals dwelled in a 50-hectare fenced-in area. By 2006, a 2,000-hectare area was fenced, and by 2010, in the words of the Pleistocene Park website, "North-East Science Station grew big enough to be able to fund transportation of animals from other regions. Since then, we have introduced musk ox from Wrangel Island; European bison from the nature reserve near Moscow; yaks, Kalmykain cows, and sheep from the Lake Baikal region to the park." [https://pleistocenepark.ru/territory/]

What is this "mammoth steppe ecosystem" Zimov and his compatriots are trying to create? In a nutshell, at the end of the Würm glaciation, the last major ice age, around 10,000 to 12,000 years ago, the "megafauna extinction" occurred, during which mammoths, mastodons, giant ground sloths, and many other sizable mammals disappeared from Earth for reasons that are still not completely understood. Up to that point, millions of square miles of the Arctic landscape were open grassland, supporting a vast population of herbivores. After the extinction event, however, pine forests spread across Eurasia.

Few animals can feed on pine needles, so pine forests are relatively empty compared to grasslands. Trees in general absorb heat more than grasses; the heat transfers to the permafrost, which melts and allows carbon dioxide, methane, and other greenhouse gases into the atmosphere. When trees die, their wooden corpses pile on the surface of the ground and rot, releasing more greenhouse gases. Grasses do not heat up the climate as much, and new grass simply grows over and covers up dead grass, keeping the ground cold and carbon trapped beneath the surface.

Many other details factor in—millions of hooved animals crush down snow and plants, allowing the Arctic cold to penetrate deep into the soil; the mere existence of snow fields instead of forests reflects sunlight back into space; grasses dry out soil quickly and slow the creation of methane, etc. All in all, the Pleistocene Park experiment seems to be destined for success.

There is one important factor missing, however. The personnel at the park use a modified tank to knock down trees to open up new land for grasses (and the animals that feed off them). This is because no modern Arctic animals have the strength or inclination to topple trees. The one animal that did is not available—that being, of course, *Mammuthus primigenius*, the wooly mammoth.

This is where Colossal Laboratories and Biosciences comes in. Founded in 2021 by geneticist George Church and entrepreneur Ben Lamm, Colossal's goal is to "de-extinct" certain vanished species by manipulating CRISPR ("clustered regularly interspaced short palindromic repeats," a class of repeating DNA sequences) and the enzyme Cas9 ("CRISPR-associated protein 9"). They intend to start with everyone's favorite prehistoric pachyderm, the mammoth.

Understanding the science and technology behind the cloning project is daunting, but basically it goes like this: fragments of mammoth DNA have been discovered in frozen bodies; missing sequences can be replaced by genetic material from the Asian (aka Indian) elephant, the mammoth's nearest living relative. Colossal's list of reasons for reviving woolly mammoths is even longer than Pleistocene Park's, and I wish them success, but . . . well, we've all seen movies.

EMPERORS OF THE NORTH

Yet perhaps woolly mammoths need not be cloned. There have been hints during the past 250 years that these mighty rulers of the ancient North are not quite extinct. In 1889, the journal *American Antiquarian* passed on an odd tale from Alaska. Specifically, the story came from H. von Beyer, an engineer from Washington, D.C., who was staying in Port Townsend in December 1887. It seems that a group of Indians followed the Yukon River upstream well into the interior of Alaska. They came upon a series of strange footprints. "They followed these tracks for miles and miles, and finally they came in sight of *hairy* animals, which they supposed to be mammoths. They were frightened at the enormous size of these creatures, whose tracks always described *circles*." ["Mastodon or Bufflo?," p. 65]

Von Beyer concluded that that last detail meant the trail of prints wandered around in a big circle, but if the native explorers believed they had encountered mammoths, they were probably describing the prints themselves as circular, which one would expect from elephant tracks.

Across the Bering Sea, in March 1920, a Monsieur Gallon worked for the French Consulate in Vladivostok. An employee of the Russian Asiatic Bank called upon Gallon and introduced his brother, a hunter who had just returned from four years in the expanse of stunted forest called the *taiga*. The French diplomat was interested in natural history and wanted to hear of this all-but-unexplored region, which covers several million square miles of northern Russia. He invited the brother, a tanned, scarred old fellow with white hair and beard, out to lunch.

The elderly hunter told Gallon about a strange encounter he'd had in the autumn of 1918 at some point south of the Gulf of Ob. The temperature still rose above freezing during the day, so the snowfall had melted, leaving open land with plenty of mud. In a small valley, near the shores of a lake, he came across some shockingly huge footprints. Each track "must have been about 2 feet across the widest part and about 18 inches the other way." [Gallon, quoted in Heuvelmans, p. 350]

The hunter followed the incredible spoor. The tracks led east from the lake into a forest of elms. Branches ten feet above the ground were broken by the unknown beast's passage.

"I followed the track for days and days," the old man recalled. They headed eastward. Finally, one day the hunter found a second set of prints that led down from the north and intersected the first. "It looked to me from the way they had trampled about all over the place for several hundred yards, as if they had been excited or upset at their meeting."

Whatever their differences, the two behemoths finally continued eastward together. The nights were growing bitterly cold, and the hunter possessed only five more shells for his rifle, but he trudged on. Finally, one afternoon he spotted something in the distance among a stand of young saplings:

> It was a huge elephant with big white tusks, very curved; it was a dark chestnut colour as far as I could see. It had fairly long hair on the hindquarters, but it seemed shorter on the front. . . . I've only seen elephants in pictures, but I must say that even from this distance (we were some 300 yards apart) I could never have believed any beast could be so big. [Heuvelmans, p. 351]

The second creature, as large as the first, was partially visible in the forest.

The old man spent a cold night on the taiga with rifle and ax close by. The next morning, the monsters were gone, and the hunter slogged back west. Due to the political climate of Russia and France over the following years, Gallon did not get an account of this sighting into print until after the World War II.

TEMPUS MAMMUTHUS

There may be a third way to obtain living specimens of mammoths and other extinct animals, but it carries us further into science fiction territory than even Colossal Labs' cloning project. On September 18, 2008, Jill O'Brien, a bookstore employee and amateur photographer from Oklahoma City, Oklahoma, was visiting Wrangell-St. Elias National Park and Preserve in Alaska, the largest national park in the United States, containing 20,587 square miles of untamed wilderness. Specifically, she found herself at the base of Mount St. Elias near the Yukon border.

She particularly liked photographing mountains, and St. Elias proved irresistible.

She started setting up her equipment for a shot when, as she explained to British monster hunter Nick Redfern, she heard "a funny crunching and thudding on the ground" off to her left. She glanced in the direction of the sound, and a tiny woolly mammoth, perhaps four feet tall at the shoulders, galloped by, glancing at her as it passed. After a few seconds, it jumped into a "small, black cloud of smoke that sucked into itself and was gone." [Redfern, p. 4]

Ms. O'Brien admitted that hers was one of the craziest claims ever made, but she never backed down from her story. "It was a mammoth, it was a baby mammoth. It was there one second, then it looked at me, and it was gone, like it went invisible or just vanished."

Many paranormal stories are rehashed in books and on podcasts due to their frightening or weird content, but Ms. O'Brien's baby mammoth report pops up occasionally due to its cuteness. The story sparks some interesting ideas. Many of our cryptids resemble prehistoric life-forms—Sasquatch might be some particularly robust proto-human, sea-serpents and the Loch Ness Monster certainly bring to mind Plesiosaurs, Thunderbirds resemble the ancient condors called Teratorns, etc. Could these creatures be popping through portals that reach not across space but across time?

The idea is extreme even in the realm of the paranormal. Most researchers opt for a middle ground, *i.e.*, something paraphysical yet not jumping straight into time travel. Retrocognition, for instance, might explain things.

Also called place memory, retrocognition suggests that certain historical events, particularly those involving strong emotions, are somehow impressed on the local environment. These events are occasionally replayed in the present like DVD recordings for reasons unknown. This is why so many hauntings involve tragedies like murder or fatal crashes and why the majority of apparitions mindlessly repeat the actions they performed in life.

In his earlier works, Andrew MacKenzie, a careful and conservative psychic researcher, was perfectly willing to accept retrocognition as the explanation for visions of the past. As such, however, the people and animals observed had to be mere images, so he dismissed the occasional claim that the characters of yesteryear seemed to see modern-day witnesses in turn. The baby mammoth of Mount St. Elias pointedly glanced at Jill O'Brien, for instance.

In his 1997 book, *Adventures in Time*, however, after years of studying similar cases, MacKenzie admits that it does seem that the people of the past are sometimes aware of modern witnesses. "This accords with Stephen Hawking's statement . . . that the laws of science did not distinguish between the forward and backward directions of time." [MacKenzie, p. 67]

Which seems to be a roundabout way of saying that time travel is possible!

SMILE FOR THE SMILODON

By an amazing coincidence, the same month that author Nick Redfern first heard of Jill O'Brien and the baby mammoth (January 2009), another woman, Jenny Burrows, contacted him about a far more terrifying encounter.

Burrows had been walking with her Labrador dog, Bobbie, only days before through a dense woodland area not far from Seattle, Washington. Bobbie suddenly whined, dropped flat to the ground, and shook uncontrollably. The dog's actions were so violent that the woman thought it was having a seizure. She knelt to comfort the Lab and noted that it seemed to be staring off into the trees. Jenny looked, too.

Something crouched in the underbrush only yards away. At first, the witness thought it was a mountain lion ready to pounce, which was bad enough, but as the creature surged out of the bushes she saw that she was wrong. It was larger than a cougar, for one thing. Also, two vast, knifelike fangs framed its mouth. Yes, it was the carnivore of carnivores, the feline of felines, a monstrous smilodon.

Was she mistaken? As Burrows told Nick Redfern, "You don't have to work in a zoo or [be] an archaeologist to know what a saber-tooth looks like; *everybody* knows." [Redfern, p. 6]

As terrified and confused as she was, Jenny noticed that the beast seemed to be somewhat translucent. "The bottom of its front paws were missing or invisible," she said.

Burrows must not have been its original target because the cat seemed surprised to find her on the trail. Things could still have turned nasty, but suddenly the saber-toothed cat disappeared: "it was gone, just like that."

Jenny decided the animal "had to be the ghost of a saber-tooth" still patrolling its hunting grounds thousands or millions of years after death.

Return of the Megafauna

She found the experience frightening, of course, but the monstrous cat was beautiful. She considered it a privilege to have had the encounter.

Bobbie the Labrador's views were not recorded.

WHAT ARE YOU TRYING TO DO, START A PANIC?

If anyone inherited the title of "Dean of Cryptozoology" after the passing of Bernard Heuvelmans in 1996, that person was probably Dr. Karl Shuker of West Midlands, United Kingdom. An alumnus of the University of Leeds and the University of Birmingham, Dr. Shuker has tried to steer the search for hidden animals into serious scientific waters by founding the *Journal of Cryptozoology*, expressing the "hope that cryptozoological researchers will submit papers to the journal that are totally worthy of publication in mainstream zoological journals." [Wikipedia entry]

Shuker has referred to a curious story from South America in several of his volumes, starting with his 1989 effort *Mystery Cats of the World*.

A large feline beast was shot in Paraguay in 1975. The local authorities called it a "mutant jaguar." A zoologist named Juan Acavar examined the body and was shocked to find that it possessed incisors no less than 12 inches long. Dr. Acavar suggested that the animal was a smilodon, somehow alive in modern times. Also, if there was one, then there were probably others.

In the best tradition of monster/science fiction movies, the authorities decided the local townsfolk would panic if they actually announced that saber-toothed tigers roamed the surroundings forests, so the strange beast became officially a "mutant jaguar," now dead. [Shuker 1989, p. 199] Unfortunately, Shuker has never been able to locate Juan Acavar or discover what happened to the remains of the long-fanged carnivore.

SABER-TOOTHS ARE ALL WET

"I hate water! Especially wet water!"

—Meowth, *Pokemon: the Series*

We have more luck finding modern saber-toothed creatures if we turn our eyes to Africa, where such animals, if they exist, seem to have gone against the feline trope of disliking water and have taken up an amphibious lifestyle like oversized otters.

As fearsome as smilodon and its toothy cousins looked, they fared poorly against competitors like lions, leopards, and tigers. They had smaller brains, for one thing. Their iconic dagger-fangs were rather thin, like actual knives, and broke fairly often. Even intact, their huge canines interfered with biting attacks, despite the fact that some species could open their jaws over 110 degrees. They eventually lost out to more modern forms of the genus *Panthera*.

At least they did on the savanna and in the jungle. A semi-aquatic existence in a new ecological niche might have fit the fanged felines quite well. In *Les Derniers Dragons d'Afrique*, Bernard Heuvelmans makes an analogy between an amphibious smilodon and a walrus that is quite convincing:

> Walruses use their huge tusks for anchorage in flowing waters. They use them to help drag themselves ashore [or onto ice floes in the Arctic]. The canines' plowlike cross-sections are good for raking through submerged sediment, thus stirring up small prey animals.

Saber-teeth would be easier to deploy as weapons by an aquatic beast. A neo-smilodon could probably slash even hippos and elephants to the point they would bleed to death. Furthermore, some paleontologists believe the saber-cats drank the blood of their kills, so an amphibious version might feast on such downed animals like an oversized lamprey. A large carcass would decompose faster in the water, and the hypothetical water-feline could tear off chunks of meat more easily. (Walruses opportunistically feed on beached whales for this reason.)

Even if such a beast makes evolutionary sense, the question remains, does any evidence exist for water-dwelling saber-tooths? Well, if one accepts that certain legends, native tales and hunters' reports from Africa refer to saber-tooth cats, most indicate amphibious versions.

Michel Raynal made a particular study of unknown felines of Africa. The Zagaoua people of northern Chad know of a beast called tigre de montagne, larger than a lion but with no tail (close to the bobcat-tail of Smilodon?). It possesses reddish fur with white stripes and "teeth that protrude from its mouth." In the 1960s, a French hunting guide in the Ouanda-Djaibe region heard roars from a large grotto unlike any animal call known to him—and he was a hunter of long experience. His hunting companion identified it as *tigre de montagne*.

Return of the Megafauna

A year later the French game tracker returned with drawings of various animals, both modern and prehistoric. His former companion picked out a picture of Machairodus, a saber-tooth cat of ancient Africa, as *tigre de montagne*. [Shuker 1989, p. 142]

A remarkable number of African peoples have a name for a huge catlike beast that dwells in river and lakes. Rivers in the Central African Republic, for instance, are reputedly home to a strange beast variously referred to as the *nze-ti-gou* ("water panther"), *mourou n'gou* ("water leopard"), *dilali* ("water lion"), and *mamaime* ("water lion"). Zaire is supposedly home to the *simba ya mail* ("water lion"), Angola has the *coje ya menia* ("water lion"), and Kenya has the *dingonek*. [Shuker 1995, p. 150]

Lucien Blancou, who was once chief game inspector in the former French Equatorial Africa (and an expert in African fauna) spent years chasing one beast in particular, the *dilali* of the Ubangi-Shari. His quest began on May 26, 1930.

On that day, Blancou shot a hippopotamus in the River Mbari, which is several days' march from the nearest village. He and his native trackers camped overnight, waiting for the carcass to bloat and rise to the surface. The next morning, his trackers declared they had heard the roar of a "water panther" during the night (Blancau slept through this). When the hippo finally was dragged ashore, its body was covered with bite marks, which Blancau attributed to a crocodile, but which the natives insisted were those of the "water panther."

As the years passed, the chief game inspector made many inquiries about the *dilali*, the "water panther" or "water lion." A native guard informed him that it had tusks like a walrus. An old African chief told of finding the bodies of a hippo and a crocodile killed by a *dilali* and dragged two miles from the river, indicating the monster was as much at home on land as in water.

When Blancou was stationed at Ndele in 1934, the natives told him of a water-lion living near the source of the River Bamingui. It was a beast so mighty that it killed elephants and hauled them off to its cave in the jungle.

One event Blancou confirmed, at least partly, occurred in 1934. A Morouba Banda tribesman of about 60 years of age named Moussa visited Blancou accompanied by an interpreter. It seems that in August 1911 Moussa was a porter with a detachment of soldiers marching from Fort Crampel to Ndele. Near the junction of the Bamingui and Koukourou Rivers, two soldiers tried to cross the latter in a canoe. A monstrous beast rose from the water and seized one of the men. According to Moussa, "The animal was shaped like a panther, a little larger than a lion but with stripes, about 12 feet long." The creature capsized the canoe as it dragged the man under. It breached the surface once with the unfortunate fellow in its mouth, then vanished. The other man swam to shore.

The detachment decided to march onward three more days before trying to cross the river again.

"This story struck me at once," Blancou wrote to Bernard Heuvelmans later, "because I had just been checking the records of the outpost at Ndele and found signs that a rifleman had been lost about this time." [Heuvelmans, p. 465]

Blancou collected information on unknown African creatures well into the 1950s, when he passed his cryptozoological information on to Dr. Heuvelmans.

Returning to South America, we collect legends of aquatic monsters that now sound familiar: "The water-dwelling *yaquaru* or water tiger of Patagonia, for example, with strong tusks, shaggy yellow pelage, and savage disposition." Then there is the *aypa* of Guyana, "a tiger-headed water beast with extremely large teeth," and another creature from the same area, the *maipolina*, a ten-foot long, fawn-colored anomaly "said to inhabit riverbank caves" and to possess "enormous fangs whose appearance as described by one eyewitness apparently compared to those of a walrus." [Shuker 1995, p. 150]

Comics and movies depict the classic "saber-toothed tiger" as the most vicious, unstoppable engine of destruction this side of *T. rex*. As we have seen, the tigers and lions of today could probably out-hunt and out-fight the mighty smilodon.

If the legends of these "water lions" have a basis in fact, however, and some long-fanged felines do dwell in jungle rivers, dragging off hippos and even elephants to their deaths, then Mother Nature may have imitated—perhaps vastly exceeded—art!

GROUND SLOTH

Nothing at all is known of the history of the tree sloths, **Bradypodidae.** *The ground sloths, on the other hand, have an impressive fossil record.*

—Bjorn Kurten

Return of the Megafauna

PART ONE

In 1789, bones of some unknown beast were found in the muddy banks of the Rio Luyan near Buenos Aires, Argentina. The bones were sent across the sea to the Royal Museum of Madrid, where a naturalist named Jose Garriga assembled and mounted the skeleton. Soon, the scientific world would puzzle over the classification of this strange, colossal animal, which in life would have been more massive than an elephant.

A young scientist from France, Georges Cuvier, who would one day be known as the "Father of Paleontology," correctly identified the monster as a huge ground-dwelling sloth equipped with long, sickle-like claws that allowed it to uproot shrubs and even trees.

The influential Cuvier popularized a theory called "Revolutions of the Globe," which provided a compromise of sorts between science and religion. Instead of a single Creation, ran the theory, a series of Creation events passed over the earth, one for each major geologic era. Each new Creation wiped out all inhabitants of the previous world, thus God paved the way for more advanced species to thrive. One of the precepts of Revolutions of the Globe was that Man as a species had never met any fossil animals; they were all destroyed before the present epoch.

New discoveries, however, proved Cuvier wrong. Giant sloth bones were discovered with crude knife marks, indicating the meat had been cut from the bones after the animal was killed. Far more spectacular was a cave discovered in the far south of Argentina near the Straits of Magellan called Cueva Eberhardt. Here, a wall of boulders had been built across the mouth of the cave, with a narrow opening to allow people access. The floor of the grotto was covered with hay, dung, and bones. The bones were those of mylodons, a buffalo-sized ground sloth. The skulls had been crushed by rocks, and the limbs had been cut by stone tools. Not only had ground sloths lived at the same time as human beings but humans had corralled and butchered the beasts like cattle.

The story grew more interesting still: In 1898, Professor Florentino Ameghino of the Buenos Aires Museum received a pile of small, bean-sized bones. The man who brought them asked what kind of animal they could have come from. "They had been extracted from a piece of leather ¾ inch thick and covered with long reddish-grey hairs in which they had been embedded like small cobbles in a road. This skin belonged without the slightest doubt to a large ground sloth." [Heuvelmans, p. 260] Prof. Ameghino identified them as coming from the skin of a Mylodon. Unlike the tremendous Megatherium, the Mylodon and its close relatives grew these bone nodules in their skins as a sort of armor—eventually, the bones might have evolved into solid plates like those of their distant kin the armadillos.

The shocking part was that the skin and the bone nodules were not fossils. They seemed relatively fresh, the epidermis pliable, with remains of muscles and ligaments visible.

Ameghino remembered a story told to him by Ramon Lista, an adventurer and explorer who also happened to be Argentina's secretary of state. On an expedition into Santa Cruz in southern Patagonia, Lista's party had crossed paths with a strange beast shaped like a pangolin, only it was covered with reddish hair instead of the bony scales of that ant-eating monotreme. The explorers shot at it several times, but it simply shambled off into the bush apparently uninjured.

Ameghino realized that an Asian pangolin covered with red hair would closely resemble a Mylodon, and its bone-nodule armor might indeed repel gunshots. At the time, however: "In spite of the authority of Lista, who, besides being a learned traveller [sic] was also a skilled observer, I have always considered that he was mistaken, the victim of an illusion." [p. 263]. Perhaps Lista had encountered a ground sloth after all!

Where had the bone-studded hide come from? Several scientists who had also been given pieces of the skin converged on the area and found that the samples had all come from a single hide hung from a tree on the holdings of a German sea captain near the Straits of Magellan. His name was Eberhardt, and the hide had come from the same Cueva Eberhardt that proved that man had semi-domesticated ground sloths.

Dr. Francisco Moreno of the La Plata Museum took a chunk of Mylodon skin with him to England in 1899 and displayed it for the Zoological Society of London. The find was certainly amazing, but controversy broke out immediately. Some scientists accepted that the Mylodon might still exist, while others believed that the conditions in the Cueva Eberhardt, where the skin had been buried under hay, dung, and dirt, might have preserved it for millennia.

Ameghino and other authorities pointed out that the Tehuelche Indians of Patagonia speak of the *iemisch*, a fearsome beast with curved claws like an anteater, which arrows and bullets will not kill—a good description of a Mylodon. However, subsequent expeditions brought back no specimens of living ground sloths. There the matter rested for nearly a century.

PART TWO

Decades later, several expeditions ventured into the Amazon rainforest seeking a monster known as the *mapinguary*. The mapinguary is described as hairy, standing over seven feet tall, with a second "mouth" in its abdomen that emits a noxious gas and with which it eats people who cross its path. This seems to have little to do with ground sloths, but David C. Oren, former director of research at the Goeldi Institute in Belém, Brazil, believed the monster to be a Mylodon, the second "mouth" being a large scent gland with which it marks its territory. Oren led an expedition after the mapinguary in 1994 and interviewed "a couple of hundred people" who claimed to have encountered the creature in remote areas of the Amazon basin.

The jungle beast seems to share the amazing bone-armored hide of the Mylodon, because it is reportedly all but bullet-proof. "The only way you can kill a mapinguary is by shooting at its head," says an Amazonian tribal leader named Domingos Parintintin. "But that is hard to do because it has the power to make you dizzy and turn day into night." ["Manimal Watch," p. 16]

A young man of the Karitiana tribe, Geovaldo Karitiana, encountered a mapingaury in 2004. There is an area near his village actually known as "the cave of the mapinguary," and the 27-year-old was hunting the region. A "big noise" indicated the monster was wandering nearby, then the creature's horrible stench made him faint. The mapinguary must not have been hungry because Geovaldo eventually came to and wobbled home. His father, Lucas, visited the site of the encounter and said that it was "as if a boulder had rolled through and knocked down all the trees and vines."

Dr. George Shepard, Jr., an American anthropologist, did not believe in the mapinguary until he worked with the Machiguenga people of Peru. They claimed that the mapinguary inhabited the forested hills nearby, and one tribesman said he had seen one displayed in the natural history museum in Peru. Shepard investigated; the diorama the tribesman referred to featured a model of a giant ground sloth.

If no one can catch a ground sloth in Patagonia, then maybe one can be found in the Amazon jungle. At the rate the rainforest is disappearing, however, there may be no need to mount an expedition. Cryptozoologists can just stand around until the last of the jungle is burnt or bulldozed.

PART THREE

Finally (again), there is the possibility that the Megatherium and its relatives might return along more esoteric routes, passing through portals or windows from some other time or place.

John Keel's *Strange Creatures from Time and Space* is one of my favorite books, and the chapter "Creatures from the Black Lagoon" is one of the most fascinating sections. In this chapter, Keel lists dozens of tales of Sasquatch-like humanoids that lumber through the forests and swamps of North America. At least, most of them are Sasquatches or reasonable facsimiles. A 15-year-old boy from Sherman, New York, wrote Keel in 1969 about a huge white monster that lived in the swamp near his house. He first saw it three or four years earlier [1965-66]. "One night it came down in our yard. It stands between twelve and eighteen feet high, it has a long tail between six and eight feet long. It is covered with hair."

Soon, two or three of these gargantuan beasts would appear at the same time. They were all white-furred, and they could walk upright or on all fours. Eventually, everyone in the family as well as two other local men saw the monsters. "It is almost a double for a Prehistoric Sloth." [Keel, p. 113]

Most scientists doubt a breeding population of ground sloths could hide in the Amazon jungle or the plains of Patagonia. It's even harder to believe one exists in the wilds near Sherman, a town of fewer than 2,000 people near the western tip of New York state.

Perhaps they and their megafauna pals are being imported from—somewhere else.

SOURCES:

"Colossal Biosciences" Wikipedia entry accessed 3/4/2023: https://en.wikipedia.org/wiki/Colossal_Biosciences

"CRISPR" Wikipedia entry accessed 3/4/2023: https://en.wikipedia.org/wiki/CRISPR#Notes

Gallon, M., "Mammouths," *Saint-Hubert* (Paris) October 1946, quoted in Heuvelmans.

Heuvelmans, Bernard. *On the Track of Unknown Animals* (New York: Hill and Wang, 1959).

Keel, John A. *Strange Creatures from Time and Space* (Greenwich, CT: Fawcett Publications, 1970).

Kurten, Bjorn. *Age of Mammals* (New York: Columbia University Press, 1971).

MacKenzie, Andrew. *Adventures in Time: Encounters with the Past* (London: The Athlone Press, 1997).

"Mastodon or Buffalo?" *American Antiquarian* Vol. 11 (1889), p. 65.

"Manimal Watch," *Fortean Times* no. 232 (March 2008), pp. 16-17.

"Pleistocene Park" website: https://pleistocenepark.ru/

"Shuker, Karl," Wikipedia entry accessed 3/15/2023: https://en.wikipedia.org/wiki/Karl_Shuker

Shuker, Karl P. N. *Mystery Cats of the World* (London: Robert Hale Ltd., 1989).

Ibid. In Search of Prehistoric Survivors (London: Blandford Books, 1995).

"Zimov, Sergey," Wikipedia entry accessed 3/4/2023: https://en.wikipedia.org/wiki/Sergey_Zimov

REX OF SUNNYBANK

Albert Payson Terhune was famous for his books about dogs. The Terhunes and their many canine companions lived at Sunnybank, an estate near Pompton Lakes in northern New Jersey. Most of his animals, like Lad, Lady, Wolf, and Bruce, were thoroughbred collies, but in 1916 there lived at Sunnybank a dog named Rex. Rex was an unlikely cross between a collie and a bull terrier, "a giant, a freak, a dog oddly out of place among a group of thoroughbreds," as Terhune wrote in *Lad: A Dog*. The two breeds did not mix well; although slavishly devoted to Terhune, Rex was unpredictable in many ways. He was larger and more muscular than even the big collies, with short, fawn-yellow hair and powerful, "killer" jaws.

Although *Lad: A Dog* was a fictionalized account of life at Sunnybank, Terhune's autobiographical *Sunnybank: Home of Lad* states that the story of Rex in *Lad* was essentially accurate. During a late blizzard in March 1916, Rex and Wolf (a young collie) slipped out the kitchen door and made their way into the nearby forest. Later, the collie Lad slipped out as well and followed their trail. Apparently, Rex injured (and angered) himself in the woods because upon his return he attacked Lad for no apparent reason. The dogs fought at the edge of the estate, and Lad, being 13 years old at this point, lost. Terhune and his wife rushed out into the snow to help him only to have Rex turn savagely on them. The writer was forced to kill Rex with a hunting knife.

In the fall of 1917, a no-nonsense businessman, Henry A. Healey, "a high official of the so-called Leather Trust," visited Sunnybank. He had seen Rex numerous times over the years. On this evening, Healey and Terhune spent hours before the living room fire, sitting in easy chairs and talking. Late in the night, as Healey put on his coat to leave, he remarked, "I wish some animal cared for me as much as Rex cares for you," and described how the dog lay beside Terhune's chair, looking up at the writer. Terhune burst out:

"Good Lord, man! Rex has been dead for more than a year. You know that."

The businessman seemed dazed. He *did* know that, yet somehow he had forgotten. "Just the same," he finished, "*I saw him lying on the floor beside you all evening!*"

During the summer of 1918, the Reverend Appleton Grannis, an old college chum of Terhune's, spent a week at the estate. He had not visited for many years and had never seen or heard of Rex. Neither did he know Healey. One blazing hot afternoon, the Reverend and Terhune sat in the dining room drinking cold beer. The writer sat with his back to the tall windows opening onto the yard.

Eventually, the men stood up to leave the room. The clergyman asked about the dog that had been "out there on the veranda looking in at you" for nearly an hour. He was certain it wasn't a collie, and he went on to describe Rex perfectly, down to "a crooked scar across his nose." "Which dog is he?"

Terhune could only stutter that he didn't know.

The writer also mentioned a patch of hallway "just to the left of the door of my study," where Rex always slept. Rather than walk straight into the room, both humans and dogs had to make a detour of several feet to avoid the animal. After Rex's death, the collie Bruce, whose "domain" was the study, would carefully step around Rex's "spot" on the way in or out. Terhune often tested this aversion before guests, "Ray Long and Sinclair Lewis and Bob Ritchie, among others." Bruce inevitably circled around the spot in the hall.

Bruce avoided Rex's "spot" for years to come, but no one else reported seeing Rex himself.

Terhune knew of no earlier ghost stories at his estate. He had no previous interest in ghosts and did not know anything about psychic phenomena. The fact that Rex looked markedly different from Terhune's thoroughbreds brings up an interesting point, however: There might have been other ghost dogs at Sunnybank for all we know, but since they would have been collies, visitors would not have given them a second thought!

This is not a spectacular ghost story, but it is interesting due to its association with Terhune's dog tales. Not so famous today, they were a worldwide sensation in the early twentieth century, read and adored even by soldiers in the muddy trenches of World War I. We shouldn't make too much about Healey's "forgetting" Rex was dead, though these curious cases of micro-amnesia seem to allow some phenomena to operate (as in phone calls from then dead, wherein the percipient "forgets" that the caller has recently died).

SOURCES:

Terhune, Albert Payson. *Lad: A Dog* (New York: E. P. Dutton & Co., 1947 [1919]), pp. 263–283.

Ibid. Sunnybank: Home of Lad (New York: Grosset & Dunlap, 1934), pp. 120–130.

SNEAKY WEREWOLVES

Douchan Gersi (1947–2015), an explorer, adventurer, actor and producer/director of the TV series *Explore* (shown on PBS and the Discovery Channel), had quite a bit to say about werewolves in his book *Faces in the Smoke*.

In a small village somewhere in Haiti, Gersi came upon a group of men carrying a coffin with a "werewolf" in it. The coffin contained only a little man in his fifties, wearing pajama bottoms and a shirt. The man had a crucifix driven into his chest, another driven into his forehead, and his hands and feet had been nailed to the coffin. A couple of villagers claimed to have seen the man, named Sophocle, change from werewolf to human, so he was slain in this weird fashion.

A week or so later, in the town of Saint-Marc, Gersi struck up a friendship with the mayor, the chief of police, and the local army commander. The mayor had been educated in Paris and the other two in the USA, so they were not backward villagers. Gersi told them of Sophocle the unfortunate werewolf, "concluding with a remark to the effect that I was amazed at what people living in the back country could believe in. The mayor looked at the men sitting at our table and then at me and said, very seriously, 'You shouldn't laugh about that. Werewolves really do exist!'"

One night, he continued, the three important men of Saint-Marc were driving through the town, the commander at the wheel and the mayor and the police chief with him in the front seat. They were looking for a street vendor, hoping to buy a late dinner. At an intersection they spotted a glow shining several feet above the macadam of a side street. Food peddlers in Haiti carried a pan of burning coals on the tops of their heads, so they assumed that was what they saw.

When they turned down the cross-street, however, the car's headlights lit up something that was not only not a peddler but not even human: "It was completely covered with long, black hair and had a long, hairy tail. Its head was the head of a huge dog, with red, luminescent eyes, and a glow emanating from it." [Gersi p. 192]

The creature ran off on two legs. The commander gave chase, and the police chief pulled out his revolver and shot at the thing. "It stopped, turned to face the car for a few seconds, and then crossed the street, running on all fours, and vanished between two houses. Despite their search, they could not find the beast again."

The officials knew such beast-men existed even before this eyewitness sighting because they had been called out to local villages to examine the mutilated victims. The manner of these violent deaths convinced them that werewolves were not a product of the imagination.

"I began reading the local newspapers more carefully," finishes Gersi, "and found that, indeed, more often than I would have thought, there were many official reports of people who had seen werewolves, as well as reports of murders supposedly committed by werewolves."

Gersi's story is a rare example of modern werewolfery. For some reason, I found myself mulling it over, along with other legends of lycanthropy from medieval and early modern Europe. I had the curious image in my head of old "Sophocle" puttering around innocuously in his cottage when suddenly an angry mob of villagers broke in and killed him.

I had a vague memory of several old werewolf stories in which witnesses chased after a horrible predatory monster, lost it momentarily in the trees or shrubbery, then found some bedraggled fellow who was obviously the bloodthirsty shapeshifter in human form.

YE OLDE WER-WOLFE

> It is said that he was hunted down with mastiffs, and that at the moment they were closing in on him he metamorphosed before their eyes from the shape of a wolf into that of a man. . . . What probably happened was that

the men and the dogs pursued what they thought was a wolf into a woods or thicket. More likely they never saw a wolf at all.

Thus described Bernhardt J. Hurwood the capture of Peter Stubbe (or Stump, Stumpf, Stube, along with other variants), an infamous lycanthrope of sixteenth-century Germany. There is no doubt Stubbe was a serial killer and cannibal, and he was so practiced at necromancy and sorcery that, as described in his trial manuscript (1590):

The Devil gave him a girdle which, being put around him, he was transformed into the likeness of a greedy, devouring wolf, strong and mighty, with eyes great and large, which in the night sparkled like brands of fire, a mouth great and wide, with most sharp and cruel teeth, a huge body and mighty paws. [Otten, p. 69]

It was fortunate for his pursuers that he turned into a mortal man when they caught him but poor timing on Stubbe's part. Did they really see a wolf—or something like one—when searching for the local monster?

Another famous lycanthrope was Gilles Garnier of Dole, France, who was put on trial for murder, sorcery, and werewolfery in 1573. Witnesses claimed to have seen something "in the form of a wolf" attack several young children, and once the beast was "hindered" from eating a girl by three brave locals. They must have been close enough to see whether the monster was human or animal. However, during his last attack upon a boy of the village of Perrouze, "the said Gilles Garnier was then and at that time in the form of a man and not a wolf." [Summers, p. 227]

Again, a lupine beast was seen, but once captured the perpetrator was conveniently in human form.

Then there's the 1584 case of Perrenette Gandillon, a female of the species: "Benoist Bidel of Naizan [France], a lad some sixteen years old, and his younger sister were attacked, whilst plucking wild fruit, by a huge wolf without a tail." Several peasants ran up and fought off the beast; too late for Benoist, who died from his wounds. The shaggy killer, however, was mortally injured as well: "the animal . . . in its last throes crawled behind a thicket, where when it was followed they discovered no wolf but the dead body of Perrenette Gandillon." [Summers, p. 229]

Jacques Roulet, 1598: "[S]ome countrymen came one day upon the corpse of a boy of fifteen, horribly mutilated and bespattered with blood. As the men approached, two wolves, which had been rending the body, bounded away into the thicket. The men gave chase immediately, following their bloody tracks till they lost them; when suddenly crouching among the bushes, his teeth chattering with fear, they found a man half naked, with long hair and beard." [Baring-Gould, p. 81]

I'm starting to see a pattern.

Reports of "dogmen" have been increasing over the past 30 years, too. Researchers use the word dogman instead of werewolf because, although the creatures are bipedal and very wolflike, there is no evidence they are people who transform into lupine monsters. And yet...

Dogmen appear to have no fear of human beings whatsoever. They are often seen lurking around houses and mobile homes, peering into windows. Perhaps they watch us as we watch television. They may know quite a bit about certain individuals.

Let's say a dogman, usually Ninja-like when skulking about human habitations, is less careful one night and gets seen by the locals, who gather quickly to chase the monster. It lopes toward a house or cottage it has watched before, where some poor schmoe lives alone. It trots up to the house and then vanishes into the darkness in whatever fashion dogmen use to elude humans. To the approaching mob, however, the beast has run back home to hide. So they kick in the door and find the owner, who has obviously just changed back into human form. Then the poor guy is dragged out of bed and killed in some painful fashion. *That* would be a dirty trick. Those sneaky werewolves!

Heck, a werewolf or dogman doesn't even have to be involved in a case of mistaken identity. *The Land Beyond the Forest* by Emily Gerard is the book about Transylvania and its folklore that inspired Bram Stoker to write *Dracula*. Gerard reported that the Romanian word for werewolf is *prikolitsch*. Apparently, it didn't take much to get those Transylvanian peasants stirred up:

> This superstition once proved nearly fatal to a harmless botanist, who ... was observed by some peasants, and, in consequence of his crouching attitude, mistaken for a wolf. Before they had time to reach him, however, he had risen to his feet and disclosed himself in the form of a man; but this in the minds of the Roumanians, who now regarded him as an aggravated case of wolf, was but additional motive for attacking him. They were quite sure that he must be a **prikolitsch**, for only such could change his shape in this unaccountable manner, and in another minute they were all in full cry after the wretched victim of science. [Gerard, p. 322]

The botanist, fortunately, gained his carriage and fled before the peasants caught him. One wonders if pitchforks and torches were involved.

SOURCES:

Baring-Gould, Sabine. *Book of Were-Wolves* (London: Smith, Elder & Co., 1865).

Gerard, Emily. *Land Beyond the Forest: Facts, Figures, and Fancies from Transylvania*, Vol. 1 (New York: Cambridge University Press, 2010 [1888]).

Gersi, Douchan. *Faces in the Smoke: An Eyewitness Experience of Voodoo, Shamanism, Psychic Healing, and Other Amazing Human Powers* (Los Angeles, CA: Jeremy P. Tarcher, Inc, 1991).

Hurwood, Bernhardt J. *Vampires, Werewolves, and Ghouls* (New York: Ace Books, 1968).

Otten, Charlotte F. (editor). *Lycanthropy Reader: Werewolves in Western Culture* (New York: Dorset Press, 1986).

Summers, Montague. *Werewolf* (Secaucus, NJ: Citadel Press, 1973 [1933]).

THE STEEDS OF POSEIDON

And then the Minyans witnessed the strangest of portents: out of the sea a monstrous horse sprang landward, gigantic, with golden mane flying high about his neck; and lightly shaking the streams of brine from his quarters set off at a gallop, wind-swift.

—Apollonius of Rhodes, *The Argonautika*
(translated by Peter Green)

Some stories that pop up in the modern era sound like nothing found in previous human experience. For instance, South African newspapers in 1997 were full of stories about the "Mamlambo," a "half-fish, half-horse" that reportedly sucked the brains out of its victims.

This scaly chimera lurked in the Mzintlava (also called the Umzimhlava) River near Mount Ayliff, 110 miles southeast of Durban, South Africa. "It eats their faces off and sucks out the people's brains," according to an elderly gentleman named Mr. Matshunga, of the village of Lubaleko. The inhabitants of this frightened community claimed the creature was 20 meters (67 feet) long.

The river-dwelling horror was even discussed in government meetings: "Agriculture and Land Affairs MEC [Member of the Executive Council] Ezra Sigwela raised the issue for the attention of the house, saying the 'half-fish, half-horse monster' was believed to have killed at least seven people trying to cross the Mzintlava River." [Johannesburg *Star*, April 30, 1997] The Cape Town *Argus* put the body count at nine.

Bizarre, right? Yet the concept of a water-dwelling, horselike creature goes back thousands of years. I'm not referring to that amusing little fish known as the seahorse, nor to the hippopotamus (the name of which means "river horse" in Greek), but to the Hippocampus.

The Hippocampus was known to the ancient Phoenicians, Greeks, and Etruscans. It looks like the front half of a horse attached to the somewhat elongated back half of a fish. Their main function in mythology was to pull the chariot of Poseidon. (I always found it odd that the God of the Sea was also the Patron of Horses, a notoriously land-based animal, but there you go.)

In the Celtic world, Water-Horses or Kelpies were nasty customers that dwelled in rivers and lochs, like prototypes of the modern Nessie-type monster. A favorite trick of theirs was to climb onto land disguised as an ordinary terrestrial horse complete with bridle and saddle. If some wayfarer decided to ride this convenient mode of transportation, they would find themselves stuck to the creature as if by a powerful glue. The Kelpie would then plunge back into the water and devour its victim.

In western Ireland, the aquatic equines take a step closer to the modern concept of lake monsters. When interviewing witnesses for a book on water-dwelling creatures, F. W. Holiday commented, "Some people called it the Peiste or Piast; others spoke of the Horse-eel or Eel-horse. Old books called it the *Payshtha More*." [Holiday, p. 32] As you might guess, the beasties have horselike heads and eel-like tails.

Lady Augusta Gregory, a great friend of W. B. Yeats' and a dedicated collector of Irish lore, received the following information from "A Man on the Height near Dun Conor":

> This boy here saw a horse one time out in the sea, a grey one, swimming about. And there were three men from the north island caught a horse in their nets one night when they were fishing for mackerel, but they let it go . . . One year at Kinvara, the people were missing their oats that was eaten in the fields, and they watched one night and it was five or six of the sea-horses they saw eating the oats, but they could not take them, they made off to the sea. [Gregory, p. 16]

The Steeds of Poseidon

In his cryptozoological classic *In the Wake of the Sea-Serpents*, Bernard Heuvelmans examined 358 sea monster reports from across the world and hypothesized that there were nine basic types or species. One of them he christened the "Merhorse." "The head, somewhat tapering in profile, looks like a horse's or a camel's, but is also very wide," wrote the Father of Cryptozoology. The creature's eyes are very prominent (indicating that it dives to immense depths), and the skin is smooth and shiny, perhaps covered with short fur. The name comes from the "long, floating mane" that grows along its neck. [Heuvelmans, p. 552]

Heuvelmans listed a creature called the San Clemente Monster as a Merhorse—a big one. Maybe the biggest sea monster of them all. Between 1914 and 1919, rumors spread among sports fishermen that "something" was appearing in the sea between San Clemente Island and Santa Catalina, about 50 miles south of Los Angeles. Ralph Bandini, secretary of the Tuna Club, felt it his duty to investigate the story.

He did more than investigate—he saw the creature itself. One day while fishing for tuna he watched something huge bulge up from the surface of the San Clemente Channel. Later, however, in September 1920, Bandini had a very close encounter.

He was fishing for marlin with fellow sportsman Smith Warren about two miles out of Mosquito Harbor when a monstrous head on a thick, slightly tapering neck rose up right in front of him.

"It lifted what must have been a good twenty feet," Bandini wrote. "Widely spaced in the head were two eyes—eyes such as were never conceived of even in the wildest nightmare! Immense, at least a full foot in diameter, round, slightly bulging, and as dead looking as though they had seen all the death the world has suffered since its birth!"

Bandini yelled for Warren, who had stepped into the cabin. He grabbed a pair of binoculars as Warren brought the boat around and headed for the oceanic colossus. The creature's neck was at least six feet thick. Its skin was covered with bristly hair, dark with a slightly reddish tinge.

"The bulk of the Thing simply cannot be told," he continued. "To this day, I don't believe that I saw anything but the head and a section of the neck—if it had a neck. What was below the surface only God knows. But listen to this. You will recollect that I mentioned a little roll coming down the island? The Thing did not rise and fall in that roll as even a whale would. The waves beat against it and broke." [Bandini, p. 92]

The daring fishermen chugged up to within 100 feet of the creature. The San Clemente Monster turned toward them with its soul-freezing eyes and simply sank back into the cold waters without so much as a ripple.

Perhaps, then, it isn't so strange that horses were associated with Poseidon. Second in power only to Zeus, the bringer of earthquakes, storms, and floods, the King of the Sea required an equally mighty steed, and if the ancients ever saw a real-life Hippocampus comparable to the San Clemente beast, well! A seahorse fit for a sea god.

But if the Merhorse shares the Mamlambo's appetite for brains, I'm afraid my gray matter would serve as little more than one "sprinkle" on a donut for it.

SOURCES:

Bandini, Ralph, "I Saw a Sea Monster," *Esquire* (June 1934), pp. 90–92.

"Brainsucker in South Africa," *Fortean Times* no. 100 (July 1997), p. 7.

Gregory, Lady Augusta. *Visions and Beliefs in the West of Ireland* (Gerrards Cross, Bucks: Colin Smythe, 2006 [1920]).

Heuvelmans, Bernard. *In the Wake of the Sea-Serpents* (New York: Hill and Wang, 1968).

Holiday, F. W. *Creatures of the Inner Sphere* (New York: Popular Library, 1973).

"Mamlambo on the Loose," Cape Town *Argus* (May 16, 1997).

"Nature Conservation Called to Hunt East Cape 'Monster'," Johannesburg *Star* (April 30, 1997).

"South Africans Fear 'Half-Fish, Half-Horse' Monster," Johannesburg *Star* (April 29, 1997).

TALES TO MAKE YOUR SKIN CRAWL

In an article called "Central Pennsylvania Legends," folklorist Henry W. Shoemaker passed on a strange story he heard from an old man named Henry Rau from Penn's Creek, Snyder County. It seems that in April 1864 a farmer named Jake Sansom shot a male panther (mountain lion) as it raided his chicken coop. "He took the hide, which was a very fine one and very dark in color, and stuffed it with straw and leaves. We did not know of taxidermists or glass eyes in those days, so the completed job looked rather uncanny with the great empty eye sockets."

Mr. Sansom set the stuffed hide on the ridgepole of his woodshed. The cougar's mate lurked in the area for months thereafter.

That August, there was a revival meeting held near New Berlin. Jake and his sons rode off in their wagon, leaving Mrs. Sansom and the physically handicapped Sansom daughter to mind the house.

As if awaiting this opportunity, the female cougar invaded the farm, killed half a dozen hunting dogs, and hauled the stuffed skin of her mate down from the woodshed. She dragged the hide into the forest as the women watched.

Henry Rau emerged from his house to investigate the commotion. Mrs. Sansom told him what happened, and Rau gathered several men to chase the mountain lion. The Sansom men, encountered as they returned home, joined them. The panther's trail led to a pine forest on the slopes of Jack's Mountains. The hunters reached a spring and found, not one, but two cougars.

> When the larger brute wheeled, we noticed it had very imperfect eyes. We recognized it as the animated form of the stuffed carcass that for six months had been fastened to the ridgepole of old Jake's woodshed. . . . I who had faced death at Malvern Hill and Chancellorsville allowed the two brutes to get away from me, without turning a finger to prevent it.

The men retreated. The whole neighborhood talked about the cougar dragging off its stuffed mate, "but our part of the adventure we kept dark." [Shoemaker 1949, p. 202]

A wise move.

In an article entitled "The Werwolf [*sic*] in Pennsylvania," Mr. Shoemaker briefly noted a similar story he heard in 1927 "of 'spook wolves' (stuffed wolves which went out at night and hunted)." Despite the title of his article, Shoemaker remarked, "These revived wolves could hardly be werwolves." [Shoemaker 1951, p.155] Still, there might be a connection.

Whoever heard of animal furs coming to life? Well, the Inuits of Greenland speak of artificial creatures called *tupilaks*. *Tupilaks* are often simply animal hides into which human and animal bones have been thrown. An *angakok* (shaman) brings the Frankensteinish thing to life with sorcery. A *tupilak* doesn't even have to be made from the hide of a single animal or from skins of a single species. The Smithsonian publication *Greenland Mummies* displays a native drawing of a *tupilak* as a dog with a human head. On the same page is a photo of an Inuit carving; this *tupilak* has the head and upper body of a bear and the lower torso and legs of a man. [Hansen, p. 63]

Lawrence Millman's *A Kayak Full of Ghosts* relates the legend of a woman becoming a *tupilak* for revenge. There were once two hunters, Papik and Ailaq. Ailaq would harvest many seals, while Papik often came home with nothing. Jealous, Papik murdered Ailaq during a hunt. Ailaq's mother swore revenge. "The woman went down to the sea. She took along her bearskin rug and draped it over her entire body and let the incoming tide sweep her away." Later, a group of hunters out on the ice saw "a she-bear twice the size of a house, with burning coals for eyes and sharp knives for claws." The bear invaded Papik's village, mangled the killer in his hut and dragged him away "by his own intestines."

The bear lay down. When the people approached it, they found only a bear skin and human bones. [Millman, pp. 161–162]

Suppose no one thinks to stuff a living animal skin to resemble a cougar, wolf, or bear? What would we have then? An animated fur rug? Strangely enough, there are stories of such things.

Manly Wade Wellman, the American fantasy writer famous for his tales of John the minstrel, created a pantheon of bizarre creatures for his Appalachian story-cycle, including "the Flat": "It lay on the ground like a broad, black, short-furred carpet rug. It humped and then flattened, the way a measuring worm moves." [Wellman 1963, p. 104]

The Wellman book *Worse Things Waiting* contains an account called "Up Under the Roof," which he said "is as close to autobiography as I have ever come." If so, it would appear that Wellman's boyhood was haunted by a creature similar to the Flat.

Wellman was the only child in a large, crowded household, and his relatives seemed to resent his youthfulness. He was forced to sleep in a high, dusty, uncomfortable garret. In the summer of his twelfth year, he started hearing something between the ceiling and the peak of the roof.

> Years afterward, I was to see through a microscope the plodding of an amoeba. The thing up under the roof sounded as an amoeba looks, a mass that stretches out a thin, loose portion of itself, then rolls and flows all of its substance into that portion, and so creeps along.

The humping, flowing noise returned every night: "I was certain that it crouched there, almost within reach of me, that it gloated and hungered, and that it turned over in its dark sub-personal awareness the problem of when and how to come and take hold of me." [Wellman 1973, pp. 4-8] The one time he explored the area under the roof he found nothing, but it appears another young boy had a physical run-in with an entity like the Flat, in Ireland, as described in Diarmuid MacManus' book *Between Two Worlds* (1977).

"Mr. George Hallet, a prominent professional man in the old city of

Limerick, had a very queer experience when he was a youngster," during a summer holiday at Mount Temple House, several miles outside that city. Twelve-year-old Hallet slept in a bedroom on the second floor, next to a room full of old furniture and junk. He had no rug in his room.

Hallet had developed the habit of sleepwalking, but he always woke after taking a few steps, whereupon he would scramble back into bed. One night he found himself at the opposite end of the narrow room. It was so dark he had to feel his way back.

> He had not gone half way when one bare foot, put gingerly down as he felt his way, just touched something that was very soft and furry but by the feel of it flat like a rug. . . . The next moment, in spite of himself, he lost his balance and his bare foot came down solidly on the thing he was so anxious to avoid, whereupon it let out a deafening, reverberating and blood-curdling scream and the fur, though still flat, seemed to come to life under his foot. [McManus, p. 18]

Hallet jumped into bed and pulled his blanket over his head, waiting through long, agonizing hours until the sun rose. Adult members of the household searched the room but found nothing.

(I wonder if it is significant that both accounts of "Flats" concern boys aged 12, and that they take place during the summer in old houses where the layout of the building is important [to show how the boys were isolated near old junk]. The stories are even close chronologically: Wellman would have been 12 in 1915, and MacManus' 1977 book claims that Hallet's encounter occurred "fifty-five to sixty years ago," or between 1917 and 1922.)

In the folklore of North America there is a bizarre critter called the Rumtifusel, an entity that resembles nothing so much as a flat, furry skin with a fine, rich texture like that of a mink coat. Sometimes an unsuspecting person investigates the Rumtifusel: "With a lightning-fast flick of its blanket-like body the Rumtifusel completely envelops its victim." [Tryon, p. 35] Off the coast of Chile, according to Jorge Luis Borges, fishermen must beware of "the Hide." The Hide resembles a stretched-out cow hide. "Its edges are furnished with numberless eyes, and . . . whenever persons or animals enter the water, the Hide rises to the surface and engulfs them with an irresistible force." [Borges, p. 100]

Many legends of shapeshifters mention furry hides or belts used to incite the change. The Norse warriors called "Berserks," for example, were thought to become wolves or bears in battle; the name "Berserk" means "bear shirt," referring to the furred skin believed to become an actual pelt when they transformed.

Some legends are a little blurry as to whether characters actually transform or simply wear quasi-living suits. The Selkies of Ireland are described as people who slip on sealskins to become water-dwellers. Many stories speak of a man hiding the sealskin and taking a Selkie as a wife—until she finds the skin again. The Navajos of the American West speak of "Skinwalkers." William Morgan's famous paper "Human-Wolves among the Navaho" lists many tales of Skinwalkers. A Navajo named Kejoji claimed to have seen one in his hogan one night during his youth. "The witch was after my mother. He was looking at her. He was in a mountain lion skin." [Morgan, p. 29] Another Navajo, Hajogo, told Morgan:

> [S]ome older men put on skins at night, a wolf skin or a lion skin . . . I have always looked for tracks but I haven't ever found a wolf track or a lion track. (What kind of tracks would one of those men make?) They would be big, like a big paw . . . How do you think they work the tail? (I guess they just let it hang down.) No. They stuff clothes in it and then it stands out. [Morgan, pp. 12–13]

These excerpts make it sound like Skinwalkers are merely evil men dressed as animals. Other Navajo stories indicate that they take on wholly animal form.

Perhaps certain costumes made of animal skins are "alive," conferring upon their wearers the senses and powers of the original beasts. Perhaps there is a spectrum of were-ness here: A would-be werewolf might start out with a costume that mimics an animal—eventually, he or she absorbs its power or vice-versa. A new stage might be transforming with the aid of the skin. Finally, a full lycanthrope might appear that is able to change without the pelt.

But what if a living skin is cast aside, or its master is killed? Such an entity might not accept life as a groping rug, humping and sliding like a hairy amoeba. More likely it would seek another human host. Perhaps Messrs. Wellman and Hallet just missed becoming Skinwalkers. Perhaps victims of the Hide and the Rumptifusel are not so much devoured as hijacked.

So, if you ever hike down a forest trail and see an expensive-looking fur coat that is draped over a stump—well, you shouldn't take what isn't yours. It just might take you, instead.

SOURCES:

Borges, Jorge Luis, and Norman Thomas di Giovanni. *Book of Imaginary Beings* (New York: Avon, 1967).

Hansen, Jens Peder, *et al. Greenland Mummies* (Washington, DC: Smithsonian Institution Press, 1991).

MacManus, Diarmuid A. *Between Two Worlds* (Gerrards Cross, Buckinghamshire: Colin Smythe, 1977).

Millman, Lawrence. *Kayak Full of Ghosts* (Santa Barbara, CA: Capra Press, 1987).

Morgan, William. "Human-Wolves among the Navaho," in *Yale University Publications in Anthropology* No. 11 (New Haven, CT: Yale University Press, 1936).

Shoemaker, Henry W. "Central Pennsylvania Legends," in George Korson, ed., *Pennsylvania Songs and Legends* (Philadelphia: University of Pennsylvania Press, 1949), pp. 195–202.

Ibid, "Neighbors: The Werwolf in Pennsylvania," *New York Folklore Quarterly* 7:2 (Summer 1951), p. 155.

Tryon, Henry H. *Fearsome Critters* (Cornwall, NY: Idlewild Press, 1939).

Wellman, Manly Wade. *Who Fears the Devil?* (Sauk City, WI: Arkham House, 1963).

Ibid. Worse Things Waiting (Chapel Hill, NC: Carcosa, 1973).

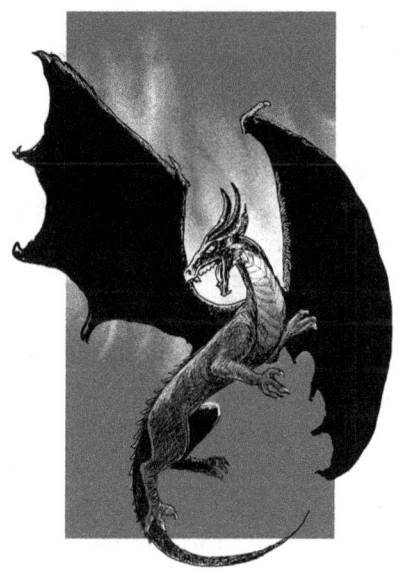

THE TEXAS DRAGON

Susie Mills owned ten acres of land on the eastern edge of Denton, Texas, off Mills Road. She promoted the 14 houses on her land as a "Writers' and Artists' Retreat." She ended up renting to anyone she found amiable, although most of the 47 residents did work in the university town of Denton. The land, once the property of her ex-in-laws, was rumored to have been an ancient Indian burial ground. It did play host to a number of paranormal events.

The young people living in the retreat reported strange things. They would be speaking to someone, glance aside, and see the person they were speaking to exit through a doorway. When they looked back, of course, the other person was still present. Some residents, including Nancy Guesman, reported hearing people talk when no one else was around. "I've seen my dogs chase things in my house when there seems to be nothing there," she told investigative reporter Arthur Myers. "They'll be running full tilt and then suddenly stop, dumbfounded." Men who hunted in the area rarely visited again, reportedly feeling "uncomfortable" on Mills' land. Conversely, people of Native American descent felt a "need" for the place, and emotionally troubled people felt more at peace on the land.

Susie Mills herself believed she was being visited by her late grandmother, especially in times of stress. She would smell her grandmother's distinctive perfume at night. "Horses born here often have blue eyes. They are invariably paint or Appaloosa, despite the breeding," Ms. Mills claimed. Even dogs born in the area often have one blue eye. The most intriguing manifestation at the retreat, however, is a long, lanky "dragon."

The dragon first showed up in 1984. Sometimes it appeared on a huge scale, up in the sky, its body formed from clouds, but at other times a smaller version would materialize on the ground. One evening, Ms. Mills took a photo of her tenants as they sat around the back yard. The picture showed a wispy arc with a curving "tail" over the young people, although none of them were smoking. Perhaps it was the dragon.

The creature, fortunately, exudes an aura of friendliness. "It's something that comes near us in time of trouble," as Susie Mills said. Ms. Guesman claimed to have seen it three or four times, once in its monstrous "cloud" form, sailing north to south high in the sky.

A Chinese friend of Susie Mills identified the entity as a "Ming" dragon, bringer of good fortune. Mills thought it more resembled the dragon on the Welsh flag, so she called it Argynr. Sometimes people split the difference and called it Argynr/Ming.

There was evidence of old Native American rituals found on a cliff overlooking the commune, but no one can say how that would relate to a dragon, Chinese or Welsh. The phenomena—and the dragon—were still manifesting themselves at the time of Myers' visit in late 1985.

This charming account puts me in mind of a short story by John Wyndham called "Chinese Puzzle" in which a Chinese dragon, brought to Wales as an egg, ends up being courted by a Welsh dragon. Perhaps Angynr/Ming was their offspring.

Dragons should be found in ancient myths and fairy-tales, not in Texas, or so one would think. There *are* modern dragon reports, but the credibility factor suppresses them, even in works on the paranormal. In 1966, parapsychologist Raymond Bayless visited the home of "Mrs. N." and her family (which included three children). They reported phantasmal footsteps, spontaneous fires, a doll that flew off a shelf by itself, and other typical poltergeist events. While he and the whole family were seated in the living room, Bayless himself heard dishes and pans being rattled and banged in the kitchen, which was an open area within his view.

Bayless interviewed family members, including the second oldest child. "He discussed these events logically and apparently factually," the investigator wrote in *Animal Ghosts*, "but at the end of his story he detailed a fantastic scene which was purely imaginary. He said that after one outburst of phenomena he saw the tail of a mysterious dragonlike beast drag across the floor." Bayless could accept poltergeists but not dragons, it seems.

SOURCES:

Bayless, Raymond. *Animal Ghosts* (New York: University Books, 1970).

Myers, Arthur. *Ghostly Register* (New York: McGraw-Hill, 1986).

TWICE TOLD TALES

The force of nature could no farther go;
To make a third she join'd the former two.

— John Dryden, "Lines Under a Portrait of Milton"

Thomas E. Barden included an odd tale in his *Virginia Folk Legends* (1991) called "The Haunted Woods." In that paper-trail fashion adopted by serious folklorists, we learn that the story came from "Mrs. R. V. Brayhill, interviewed by John W. Garrett in Hopewell, no date given."

"My grandfather Pernell had a large farm and in those days the farms all had to be fenced and the cattle run outside [the fence]." A strip of pine forest lay between this farm and one owned by the Crysel family, and people often heard and saw strange things there. Mrs. Brayhill's mother and her Aunt Bittish, while hiking between the properties, sometimes heard a "most pitiful cry," then a huge, black, bearlike animal would brush by them.

One night, rather suspiciously, the fence around the Pernell farm caught fire. "Aunt Bitty" spotted the fire first and ran for the house where Mrs. Brayhill's father and brothers lived. "And as she was coming through the pine forest there was something that looked like two men came running behind her," continued Mrs. Brayhill, "and as they passed her they suddenly disappeared. Bitty said she was scared almost to death, but it was closer to my father's than it was back home, and she was through the haunted woods. So she came running to my father's for help." The Pernell family left the farm not long thereafter. [Barden, p. 92]

Folklore professor W. K. McNeil of Indiana University collected dozens of folktales for his 1985 compendium, *Ghost Stories from the American South*. In the following account, we find echoed the "strange beast/two men" motif of "The Haunted Woods." McNeil added that this narrative was "Collected by Henry Wacaster Perry in 1938 from Mart Rankins, a white resident of Carter County, Tennessee." [McNeil p. 162]

"Batchin'" [unmarried] at the time, Rankins was out riding his horse along a rural Virginia lane, his little dog ranging along behind. He noticed two men off in a field, hiking toward the road as if to intercept him. "They was walkin' together purty fast, keepin' step."

Mr. Rankins' dog started after a rabbit. Rankins glanced toward it for just a second. "That quick they disappeared or turned into somethin', one. They was a black thing about the size of a sheep thrashed around an' took up through the field, tearin' up brush heaps where there wasn't no brush heaps an' makin' a lot of noise. It didn't look like nothin' I'd ever seen. Don't know what it was, but they had turned into it." [p. 126]

McNeil provided another interesting tale in *Ghost Stories from the American South*. The story came from an unnamed black male in 1974, an inhabitant of Rowland, North Carolina. The events were witnessed by the informant's father.

Many years ago, the McCormick family owned an extensive plot of land in the area. However, the McCormicks slowly went extinct. When the last family members—two sisters—died, a rumor went around that they had buried a large amount of money under the foundation of their mansion. The informant's father and several other local men decided to search for it.

Drawing upon backwoods magic and folk medicine, the treasure hunters first poured a vast circle of salt around the mansion. "You see, the evil spirit couldn't cross over that ring." [McNeil, p. 83] Then a man positioned himself at every corner of the house and started digging.

After a few minutes, the men heard something thrashing through a nearby cotton field. The informant's father said that "there was something that looked like a great big hog coming down through there! It was coming right at them, so they ran into the house."

The hoglike thing assaulted the mansion itself "and just shook that whole house like a tornado had hit it!" Eventually, the treasure hunters escaped their predicament and fled.

They were not yet beaten, however. Some of them contacted a man in McColl, South Carolina, "a man that could talk to spirits." The ghost whisperer ventured out to the mansion with the treasure hunters. Eventually, instead of a hog monster, two female ghosts appeared. The informant's father recognized them as the last two McCormick sisters. After some discussion with the medium, the spirits agreed to leave the money to the living. The fortune hunters finally dug up the treasure.

It's nice to read occasionally of a happy ending for our witnesses, but what intrigues me is the implication that the hog-thing might have been one—or maybe both—of the McCormick sisters.

A human being turning into a shaggy beast is a familiar motif we call lycanthropy—or therianthropy, if you want to be more generic. But what do you call it when *two* people become *one* bizarre creature? The nearest thing to an explanation comes from Katherine Briggs' marvelous volume, *An Encyclopedia of Fairies*, under "Bullbeggar." It seems that a Bullbeggar (a somewhat ill-defined entity) lurked near Creech Hill, near Bruton, Somerset:

> In the 1880s two crossed bodies were dug up in quarrying operations, and crumbled to dust when they were exposed to the air . . . after this finding, Creech Hill had a bad name and was supposed to be haunted by following footsteps and a black uncanny shape. A farmer coming home late one night saw a figure lying on the road and went to its help. It suddenly shot up to an uncanny height and chased him to his own threshold. His family ran to his rescue and saw it bounding away with wild laughter . . . This bullbeggar was considered a bogy or bogey-beast rather than a ghost because two bodies were found. [Briggs, p. 52]

Were these "crossed bodies" sacrifices in some ancient ritual? Did their life forces combine to create a single entity—the Bullbeggar? The first two folktales outlined above supposedly happened in Virginia. Is there a Bullbeggar tradition in that state? Could some backwoods *Hexenmeister* have created his own dual monstrosity from two unsuspecting victims?

I keep thinking of "The Pantomime Horse is a Secret Agent" skit from *Monty Python's Flying Circus*. While it's true that two men in a costume form a rather dashing Pantomime Horse, I personally hope I'm never drawn into a "dual creature" ritual.

With my luck, I'd end up as the Bullbeggar's behind.

SOURCES:

Barden, Thomas E. *Virginia Folk Legends* (Charlottesville, VA: University Press of Virginia, 1991).

Briggs, Katherine M. *Encyclopedia of Fairies* (New York, NY: Pantheon Books, 1976).

McNeil, W. K. *Ghost Stories from the American South* (New York, NY: Dell Publishing, 1985).

VICTORY THROUGH WERE-POWER!

Even a man who's pure in heart
And says his prayers by night,
May become a wolf when the wolfbane blooms
And the autumn moon is bright.

I made up that ditty when I wrote **The Wolf Man** *for Universal Pictures in 1941 . . . Now film historians believe that my four-liner was taken from German folklore and that Larry Talbot's name also is part of European horror history.*

—Curt Siodmak, "The Wolf Man: By Way of Introduction," in *Classic Movie Monsters* by Donald F. Glut

Werewolves and other were-animals are like onions. They stink. No! They make you cry. No—because they have layers. They are surrounded by layers of beliefs determined by the general population's knowledge—or lack thereof—of lycanthropic lore.

The average movie viewer knows that a person bitten by a werewolf becomes a werewolf—a hairy and wolflike, but still bipedal and semi-human, monster—under the light of the next full moon. This cursed individual will seek out and kill human beings, beginning with family and loved ones, who will be marked by pentagrams in the palms of their hands. They will never be free of this curse until they are finally shot down by a silver bullet.

Certainly that's how many an old movie plot runs, but it has little to do with actual folklore or legend. Most of the details listed above came from German-born writer Curt Siodmak, author of the classic science-fiction novel *Donovan's Brain* and screenwriter for many horror/sf films, including *Son of Dracula*, *The Invisible Woman*, *I Walked with a Zombie*, and, of course, *The Wolf-Man*.[1]

A second layer of "knowledge" comes from people who have read something about werewolves in myth and legend. Such people poohpooh the Siodmak additions and point out that most werewolves of folklore resembled normal (if overlarge) wolves; that they had no dependence on the light of the moon, full or otherwise; and that they had no particular fear of silver. Also, as often as not, lycanthropes took on their dual lives willingly in order to wreak havoc among their neighbors.

Then there seems to be yet another layer of were-lore in which the brave traveler finds—well, some strange and unlikely abilities among these shifty shapeshifters.

THE MAGIC CIRCLE

One of the oldest werewolf stories comes from *The Satyricon* of Petronius, written in the first century C.E. A Greek slave named Niceros tells how he accompanied a soldier on the road. The soldier turned out to be a werewolf. "The next thing I knew he was pissing around his clothes. . . . I went to get his clothes and discovered they'd been changed into stones." [Petronius, p. 68] A common theme in legend is that a werewolf will be trapped in wolf form if he or she cannot retrieve his/her clothes, so it makes sense that one would surround them with a magic circle (even if it is a circle of urine). What else might a werewolf turn to stone? Perhaps, to be on the safe side, you should not allow anyone or anything to make a circle of urine around you (redundant advice for most people).

---

[1] Or from Universal Pictures, at least; in *Werewolf of London* (1935), the title character (played by Henry Hull) is infected by a werewolf bite.

HAILSTORM

Librarian and publisher Frank Hamel wrote in her book *Human Animals*:

> In July, 1603, in the district of Douvres and Jeurre a great storm of hail fell and damaged all the fruit trees, and three mysterious wolves were seen. They had no tails, and they passed harmlessly through a herd of cows and goats, touching none of them except one kid, which one of the wolves carried to a distance without in any way injuring it. This unnatural conduct made it fairly evident that these were not real wolves, but sorcerers who had brought about the hail-storm and wished to visit the scene of the disaster. [Hamel, p. 52]

This passage suggests that werewolves might be able to control the weather and bring storms.

SHEEP'S CLOTHING

There is another power implied in Ms. Hamel's quote that I am tempted to call "Wolf in Sheep's Clothing": that is, the ability to pass through a herd of ungulates without alarming them. Something like this has been echoed in modern reports of phantom panthers, those mysterious panther-like beasts that appear and vanish mysteriously all over North America. In February 1970, for instance, Illinois was inundated by reports of black panthers, African lions, and even "strange ape-like creatures" (weres in a half-human form?). According to Loren Coleman and Jerome Clark, "Mrs. Donald Miller of Jasper County [Illinois] saw a black panther strolling less than 150 yards from her house. What startled her as much or more was that her German shepherd watched the strange animal but didn't even bark!" [Coleman and Clark 1972, p. 100]

Suppose lycanthropes have the ability to cloud animals' minds, *à la* the Shadow, so that the animals effectively do not sense them? They could raid herds of cows without the cows making an outcry and escape undetected, leaving death and confusion behind.

Dogs would be useless guardians against such a hypnotic power. And suppose it worked on humans? Imagine a werewolf padding right down the middle of a street, people looking at it but not perceiving it!

HEAVINESS

Folklorist Henry W. Shoemaker wrote:

> There was twenty-four-hour hauling of lumber through the gap and at night what seemed to be gigantic dogs or wolves came off Hundsrick Mountain and got on the loaded sledges; they were of such weight that they bogged down the horses, making hauling an almost impossible task. Others put their front paws on the back of the sleds, holding them down as if they were made of iron. [Shoemaker, p. 133]

This power seems to have cross-pollinated to werewolves from the "black dog" archetype, as these bogey-beasts sometimes leap on horses or carts and weigh then down so heavily they cannot move. Or perhaps it is an ability common to supernaturals, as certain versions of the Phantom Hitchhiker, from horse-and-buggy days, describe a similar phenomenon. Could this "heaviness" stop a motor vehicle? Sink a yacht or speedboat? Perhaps a were could climb to the top of a building and become heavy enough to punch a hole in the roof?

CAJUN WEREWOLVES

Robert Tallant, Lyle Saxon, and Edward Dreyer's *Gumbo Ya-Ya* carries several unique tidbits of lycanthropic lore. For instance, the Cajuns say that "Loup-garous have bats as big as airplanes to carry them where they want to go. They make these bats drop them down your chimney." An interesting relationship with another unusual species.

The Cajuns have also found new defenses against werewolves. "If you see one [*Gumbo Ya-Ya*]," said one Louisianan, "you just get yourself one nice frog and throw him at them things. They sure gon' run then. They scared of frogs. That's the only way to chase a loup-garou away from you. Bullets go right through him." Other defenses mentioned were: "Is a good idea to hang a new sifter outside from your house, yes. Then they got to stop and count every hole in that sifter, and you catch them and sprinkle them with salt. That sets them on fire." [Tallant, et al., p.191]

Bats, frogs, sifters, salt. If lycanthropes visit Louisiana, they may be in for a surprise.

BEARWALKS

Richard M. Dorson's *Bloodstoppers & Bearwalkers* quoted Alec Philemon, a Winnebego Indian, about the Bearwalk (a wizard who can take the form of an animal, usually a bear):

> We saw a flash, coming from behind us. The older fellow said, "It's a bearwalk, let's get it. I'll stand on the other side of the road (it was just wagon ruts) and you stand on this side." We stood there and waited. . . . It looked like a bear, but every time he breathe you could see a fire gust. My chum he fall over in a faint. That brave feller on the other side, he faint. When the bear walk, all the ground wave, like when you walk on soft mud or on moss. [Dorson, p. 30]

The bearwalk exhibits a number of strange powers, including the ability to create a will-o'-wisp-like flash of light, minor earthquakes ("all the ground wave"), and emit a draconian fiery breath.

FOX-FIRE AND HALOES

Documentary filmmaker Douchan Gersi's *Faces in the Smoke* mentions an odd light in relation with werewolves. [see "Sneaky Werewolves"] "Three different villagers saw a strange creature the size of a man and walking upright on his hind feet. He was covered with long, black hair and had a long tail. Above his head, which was that of a huge dog, there was a weak but glowing light." [Gersi, p. 189]

You may recall that the mayor, police chief, and army commander of

Saint-Marc mistook the werewolf for a food peddler: there was a light above its head that looked like the glow of the hot coals of the charcoal pan that food merchants carried on their heads. [Gersi, p. 192]

A tiny flicker of flame could traditionally be found hovering over the were-foxes of Japan and China. This fox-fire—or *Kitsune-bi* in Japanese—could be sent to persecute hapless humans. [Mitchell and Rickard, p. 33]

Fire and light are usually thought of as defenses against lycanthropes, at least in the Western tradition of weres as creatures of darkness. Accused werewolves were often burned at the stake in the Middle Ages. And what self-respecting mob doesn't carry plenty of torches when chasing a werewolf or other monster? But perhaps certain shapeshifters can turn the tables.

THE CALL OF THE WILD

You'll recall that Dr. Anne Ross, an expert on ancient Celtic culture, obtained the two small, spherical, carved figures known as the Hexham Heads and soon suffered a curious visitation. She woke one night feeling cold and frightened, and she saw a strange figure at her bedroom door, as she described to BBC reporter Luke Casey:

> The upper part, I would have said, was a wolf, and the lower part was human and, I would have again said, that it was covered with a kind of black, very dark fur. It went out and I just saw it clearly, and then it disappeared, and something made me run after it, a thing I wouldn't normally have done, but I felt compelled to run after it. I got out of bed and I ran, and I could hear it going down the stairs, then it disappeared toward the back of the house.

A few days later, while Dr. Ross made a trip to London, her teenaged daughter came home from school. She opened the front door in broad daylight and "saw a huge black creature, like a werewolf, on the stairs. The creature jumped over the banister, landed with a soft thud in the hall and then ran on padded animal feet towards the back of the house." The most intriguing part: "The girl, like her mother, felt compelled to follow the creature." [McEwan, pp. 161–165]

This compulsion might be used by weres to draw prey to their doom, but nothing untoward happened to the Rosses beyond a good scare. Perhaps this attraction was a less sinister desire to run with the were into the forest primeval: a Call of the Wild, as it were.

SUPERHUMAN (OR -LUPINE) SPEED

Loren Coleman and Jerome Clark wrote in *Creatures from the Outer Edge*:

> In January 1970 four Gallup, New Mexico, youths—Clifford Heronemus, Robert Davis, Carl Martinez and David Chiaramonte—claimed to have seen a "werewolf" near Whitewater. They saw a "hairy thing with two legs" pacing their car, which was going about 45 miles per hour. [Coleman and Clark, 1978, pp. 110–111]

Witness Heronemus added: "I started driving faster, about sixty . . . I know it couldn't be a person because people cannot move that fast." Clark and Coleman further paraphrase William Morgan's famous paper, *Human-Wolves Among the Navaho*: "Four decades ago anthropologist William Morgan talked of the human-wolves with a Navaho named Hahago, who said, 'They go very fast.' 'How fast?' Morgan asked. 'They can go to A. in an hour and a half,' Hahago replied. Morgan noted, 'It takes four hours by automobile.'" Modern Dogman reports tell of the canine entities running 50, 60, even 100 miles per hour!

WEREWOLF EYEBROWS?

Edward B. Tylor (1832-1917) was the world's first real anthropologist. His major work on the subject was the two-volume *Primitive Culture* (1873). In Vol. 1 he gives an interesting overview of the subject of lycanthropy and therianthropy, but one line made me look twice: "The Danes still know a man who is a werewolf by his eyebrows meeting, and thus resembling a butterfly, the familiar type of the soul, ready to fly off and enter some other body." (p. 313)

I'd heard of the connecting eyebrows as a sign of a werewolf since I was a little child. I thought it might have been something made up for the movies like the pentagram in the palm bit, but apparently it's an authentic piece of were-lore.

The idea of the soul appearing as a moth or butterfly is a motif one comes across occasionally—in "The Devil and Daniel Webster," the short-story by Stephen Vincent Benet, for instance. It's also mentioned in the 2002 movie *The Mothman Prophecies*. The idea that the soul can leave the body as a tiny creature was common in ancient and medieval times, the form chosen usually being a mouse or small snake (*The German Legends of the Brothers Grimm* carries a few such tales). I would never have thought of mixing them all together, however.

But from now on, when I see flittering forms dancing over flowers or swirling around a streetlight, I'm going to say, "Look at all those werewolf eyebrows!"

(Especially those really ratty, dusty gray moths attracted to porch lights. Those have to be werewolf eyebrows!)

SOURCES:

Coleman, Loren, and Jerome Clark. *Creatures from the Outer Edge* (New York: Warner Books, 1978).

Ibid., "On the Trail of Pumas, Panthers, and ULAs (Unidentified Leaping Animals), Part II," *Fate* 25:7 (July 1972), pp. 93–102. Italics theirs.

Dorson, Richard. *Bloodstoppers & Bearwalkers: Folk Traditions of the Upper Peninsula* (Cambridge: Harvard University Press, 1952).

Gersi, Douchan. *Faces in the Smoke* (Los Angeles: Jeremy P. Tarcher, 1991).

Hamel, Frank. *Human Animals* (New Hyde Park, NY: University Books, 1969 [1915]).

McEwan, Graham J. *Mystery Animals of Britain and Ireland* (Robert Hale: London, 1986).

Mitchell, John, and Robert J. M. Rickard. *Phenomena: A Book of Wonders* (New York: Pantheon Books, 1977).

Petronius. *Satyricon*, trans. by William Arrowsmith (New York: New American Library, 1959).

Shoemaker, Henry W., "Werwolves in Pennsylvania Wilds, Once More," *New York Folklore Quarterly* 8:2 (Summer 1952), p. 133.

Tallant, Robert, Lyle Saxon, and Edward Dreyer. *Gumbo Ya-Ya: A Collection of Louisiana Folk Tales* (New York: Bonanza Books, 1984 [1945]).

Tylor, Edward B. *Primitive Culture*, Vol. I (New York: Harper and Brothers Publishers, 1958 [1873]).

WHAT COLOR IS YOUR YETI?

Sometimes it seems that self-proclaimed cryptozoologists know little about their own profession. I can't count how many times I've read in a book or article or heard on a podcast how the Yeti, or Abominable Snowman, a large, unknown humanoid found in the Himalaya Mountains of Tibet and Nepal, is covered in shaggy white hair. Many mammals dwelling in areas of much snow cover evolve pelts or at least winter coats of white to blend into their environment, so it would make sense the elusive Snowmen would bear such natural camouflage.

The reality is, however, that white is not the common Yeti shade. As a matter of fact, I don't believe the classic Yeti of the high Tibetan plateau has ever been described as white.

I decided to check several Yeti sightings just to make sure. Not a large number, but after a century of serious exploration in the Himalayan range, it seems that actual sightings of this famous cryptid are few and far between. Most evidence for the existence of the Yeti has come in the form of its huge, manlike footprints, found in areas no humans should be traveling—especially barefoot.

A SAMPLE OF YETI SIGHTINGS

[Italicized words are my own.]

The early 1900s—"Before I was born my father had met one face to face."

Tenzing Norgay was a Nepalese Sherpa who gained worldwide fame by accompanying several expeditions to Mount Everest. He was one of the first two people to set foot on the summit of Everest, the other being the New Zealand explorer Sir Edmond Hillary.

Tenzing came across Yeti tracks twice in his life, but his father, Ghang La Mingma, ran into the thing itself sometime before 1914, the probable birth year of the future mountaineer. *"The color was grayish,* and a noticeable thing was that the hair grew in two directions—from above the waist upward and from below the waist downward." [Norgay and Ullman, p. 74]

Before 1910—"Shortly before the last Tibetan war," apparently referring to the Qing Dynasty (China) invasion of Tibet in 1910, during which the Dalai Lama was temporarily deposed.

William Hugh Knight, a member of the Royal Societies Club, was traveling from Gnatong towards Gantok on the way out of Tibet, accompanied by Claude White, another European, Tibetan guide Tenzin Wagdi and 40 or 50 porters. The porters refused to pass through a leech-infested area, so the party marched along a longer and steeper approach to Gantok. For reasons unstated, Knight (on horseback) dropped about half a mile behind the main expedition.

Just before sunset, Knight stopped to let his horse rest. He heard a noise and spotted a strange humanlike figure "some 15 or 20 paces away" that he realized, years later, must have been one of the Howard-Bury Expedition's "Abominable Snowmen."

The creature "was a little under 6 ft. high, almost stark naked in that bitter cold—it was the month of November. *He was a kind of pale yellow all over."* ["Abominable Snowmen," p. 11]

Knight observed the creature for five or six minutes. It in turn seemed to be watching something out of sight down the slope, perhaps potential prey. "His muscular development in the arms, thighs, legs, back, and chest was terrific." Finally, the Snowman charged off down the hill, and the explorer saw it no more.

What Color Is Your Yeti?

1915—Forestry officer J. R. O. Gant sent a letter to the *Proceedings of the Zoological Society of London* about a strange monkey- or apelike creature that appeared in "the forest below Phalut." The locals called it "Jungle Admi" or "Sogpa." It normally lived in the snow at high elevations. Its fur was the *"ordinary yellowish-brown colour* of the Bengal monkey." Eminent explorer and botanist Henry J. Elwes, who read the letter before the august society, claimed to have seen a Sogpa himself in the Himalayas in 1906. [Sanderson, p. 8-9]

1921—The Himalayan reconnaissance expedition of Lt. Colonel C. K. Howard-Bury was underway, exploring the terrain around Mount Everest before tackling the mountain itself. At about 17,000 feet up the Lhapka-La pass on the north face of Everest, they spotted through binoculars "a number of *dark forms*" above. When they reached this area, they found footprints three times the size of a normal human's. The sherpas called the creatures "Metoh-Kangmi," which Henry Newman of the *Calcutta Statesman* translated as "Abominable Snowman." [Sanderson, pp. 9–12]

1925—N. A. Tombazi, an English traveler in Sikkim (identified as an Italian in some accounts) was climbing the mountain Kangchenjunga, accompanied by a number of porters. About nine miles from Zemu glacier, the porters pointed out an upright figure walking along two to three hundred yards downslope that paused occasionally to uproot bushes.

"It showed up *dark against the snow*, and, as far as I could make out, wore no clothes." [Heuvelmans, p.131]

1949—During the Himalayan Expedition of 1953, Sir John Hunt discussed the Yeti with lamas at the Thyangbochi monastery fifteen miles southwest of Everest. The Senior Abbott told him how a Snowman had approached to within 200 yards of the monastery in November 1949 "and played for some time in the snow." The monks made loud noises with trumpets and cymbals, and the creature finally left. It was "covered with *grayish-brown hair*." [Heuvelmans, p. 138]

Before 1953—late in that year, Tibetan monk Chemed Rigdzin Dorje Lopu announced to the world that he had studied the mummified corpses of two Yetis, one in the monastery at Riwoche, the other at the monastery of Sakya between Katmandu and Shigatse. They looked like monkeys but would have stood eight feet tall in life. "Their bodies were covered with *dark brown hair* about 1 inch to 1 ½ inches long." [Heuvelmans, p. 139]

1955—The porters of the Argentine Himalayan Expedition came upon a yeti in Nepal and killed it in a barrage of gunfire. They hauled the corpse away before any scientists on the expedition could examine it, perhaps fearing that the learned explorers' poking and prodding would anger its ghost or other Yetis in the area. "It was also described as ten feet high, *covered with reddish fur*, and it walked on its hind legs." [Keel, p. 195]

1955—Long before he started chasing UFOs and Mothman, writer John Keel hiked thousands of miles across the Middle East and Asia. At the monastery of Dubdi in northwest Sikkim, not far from the Tibetan border, he heard a strange, shrill cry in the night like that of a seagull. The lamas spilled out of their cells and began banging drums and blowing their ceremonial horns after informing Keel that a Yeti was approaching.

The next day, the American adventurer started for the mountain Kangchenjunga, 25 miles away. The high lama assigned a young monk, Norbhu, to accompany him. Every monk, farmer, and villager they met said the Yeti had passed by not long before them. The travelers spent the night in a shack by a *chorten* [hilltop shrine] only to hear the Yeti's scream again. Keel wrote in his diary: "July 29, 1955. 3:35 A.M. Sound of Yeti in darkness. Exact position unknown. Roughly, lat. 28 degrees, long. 88 degrees." The next day, they found a trail of footprints in the mud, and, after following them for a while, they discovered another set of tracks that approached and joined the first.

Norbhu eventually turned back, but most of the population of a village called Lachen led Keel "through the torturous passes to a marsh."

What Color Is Your Yeti?

Eventually, the entourage reached a lake full of dead trees. Something moved along the opposite shore:

> Something was out there, across the lake. Something big, breathtakingly big, and *brown*, and moving swiftly, splashing through the shallow, icy waters toward a pile of boulders. As it neared them, another *brown* blur moved out to meet it and together they disappeared beyond the debris of a landfall.

The creatures scaled a cliff that neither bear nor ape could climb and disappeared, their seagull-cries echoing down to the American traveler. [Keel, pp. 226-234]

1974—A 19-year-old Nepalese woman named Lakpa Sherpani was watching over a herd of yaks in a pasture not far from Mount Everest when a hairy humanoid creature appeared. Though standing only four to five feet tall, the monster killed five of the shaggy bovines by seizing their horns and using them as handles as it twisted their heads to the breaking point. The creature knocked Lakpa unconscious, but thankfully she received no further injuries. This Yeti had "*thick black hair* below the waist and *brown* hair above." [Bord, p. 147]

I could continue, but I think the reports speak for themselves: Yetis aren't white. (Curiously enough, I have come across several North American Bigfoot reports concerning man-beasts of an ivory shade.) How do researchers make such a basic mistake?

The earliest reference to the Yeti having white hair was, I believe, in Rupert T. Gould's 1929 book *Enigmas*. He mentioned the "'Migues,' or 'abominable snow-men'" in a chapter called "There Were Giants in Those Days" because of their supposed stature of 10 to 12 feet. "They are also said to be white, hairy, and extremely fond of honey—points which naturally suggest that they are really snow-bears." [Polar bears are not native to the Himalayas.] As if to cover himself, he added, "They have never been seen by a white man, although the Mount Everest expeditions heard some vague rumors about them." [Gould, p. 23]

Commander Rupert T. Gould was a meticulous researcher, a true Renaissance man. Jonathan Betts' 2006 biography of the fellow, *Time Restored*, is subtitled "the man who knew (almost) everything." If *he* could miscolor a Yeti, I suppose we can forgive a few modern cryptozoologists.

SOURCES:

"'Abominable Snowmen': A Traveller's Experience" [letter], London *Times*, November 3, 1921, p.11.

Bord, Colin and Janet. *Alien Animals* (Harrisburg, PA: Stackpole Books, 1981).

Gould, Rupert T. *Enigmas* (New York: Bell Publishing, 1980 [1929]).

Heuvelmans, Bernard. *On the Track of Unknown Animals* (New York: Hill and Wang, 1959).

Keel, John A. *Jadoo* (New York: Julian Messner, Inc., 1957).

Norgay, Tenzing, and James Ramsey Ullman. *Tiger of the Snows* (New York: G. P. Putnam's Sons, 1955).

Sanderson, Ivan Terence. *Abominable Snowmen: Legend Come to Life* (New York: Chilton Book Company, 1961).

WHO ARE YOU CALLING IMAGINARY?

Michael J. Hallowell is a journalist from South Tyneside, United Kingdom, who specializes in the paranormal. In the late 1950s, when he was about three years old, his family lived in Park Road, Hebburn, and one fine morning a young girl appeared at the house. "She was small, elfin-faced—almost urchin-like. Her blonde-cum-chestnut hair was unkempt, and I remember little about her clothes other than that they were plain and unassuming." [Hallowell 2007, p. 2]

The girl, Maureen, remained in the house from then on, Michael's mischievous live-in playmate. Then one day the family moved to South Shields, and Michael never saw her again.

However, another girl, Elizabeth, appeared in the new house. Unlike the naughty Maureen, Elizabeth acted mature, "cultured like Lewis Carroll's Alice." The family moved again when Michael was eight, and like Maureen, Elizabeth vanished, never to be seen again.

Hallowell forgot his imaginary companions until adulthood, when he started writing "Bizarre," a column in the *Shields Gazette*. In March 2000 a retired tailor named John Tatters wrote in. It seems that in the 1940s Mr. Tatters' son had an imaginary friend named Stephen. One day he came upon his son tossing a ball around the yard. The child called "Here, Stephen—catch!" and threw the ball toward a rhododendron bush. Then:

I swear down that the ball seemed to stop in mid-air by the bush and then sail back across the garden towards my son, as if thrown by and invisible pair of hands. [Hallowell 2007, p. 8]

Recalling his own invisible friends, Hallowell requested his readers to send in accounts of imaginary playmates. He received tales from all over the world, and he attempted to classify them.

Hallowell disliked the term "imaginary playmate." He used the phrase "Quasi-Corporeal Companions" and divided them into four broad categories.

Type One, "invizikids," look and act like ordinary children, except other people can't see them.

Type Two QCCs are "Elementals," which resemble elves, gnomes, and other fairy beings. It has been suggested such creatures actually are fairies or nature spirits.

Type Three, "Animals," usually look like normal animals, except, of course, they can talk. "Intriguingly, although Type 3s usually only appear to the primary experient, they are often heard by others in the vicinity." [Hallowell 2007, p. 54] Everything from dogs and cats to lions and elephants have appeared as Type Threes.

Type Fours, the "Wackies," he splits into "Sages" and "Animates." "Sages" are always adults and often appear in some clichéd ethnic guise, such as a Chinese Mandarin, a Native American warrior, or an Inuit hunter in a parka. They usually dispense worldly advice or speak out against a child's bad behavior, like a conscience made visible. For some reason, many Sages only appear from the waist up, as if they are embedded halfway through the floor.

"Animates" also give advice of a wise and adult nature, but they are absolutely cartoonish in that they are inanimate objects that suddenly grow arms and/or legs (rarely heads) and start to speak. "Animate QCCs have included miniature human skeletons, yoghurt cartons, banana skins, pokers, cardboard toilet tissue rolls, a Barry Manilow CD and even a sanitary towel." [Hallowell 2009, p. 32]

The statistics derived from QCC cases do not mesh well with psychological theories. Orphans, only children, and other lonely youngsters don't develop imaginary playmates any more than other children. Neither do middle or younger siblings, who are often characterized as desiring more attention. Nor do QCCs vanish when new babies join families.

It was hypothesized that "lonely" toddlers invent QCCs, but once they start school they have no more need of them. "In fact," according to the book *Invizikids*, "the statistics give the lie to this idea completely; a greater percentage of school-age kids have QCCs than pre-school children!" [2007, p. 35]

The fact that details of actual QCC cases refuse to conform to psychologists' ideas suggests a real phenomenon existing independently of children's circumstances and personalities.

This discussion of imaginary playmates is a prelude to one of the most popular accounts from "Obiwan's UFO-Free Paranormal Page," an archive of some 1,700 supposedly true tales of the paranormal that was once known as GHOSTS.ORG. "Mr. Kangaroo" was posted by someone calling himself "Markets" (though he signs as "Randy") on March 10, 1999. It seems that when Randy/Markets was five, he had a friend he called Mr. Kangaroo for obvious reasons. "He had a tail that was rather thick, but not too long . . . His head had a snout and a large mouth, filled with teeth, though they didn't frighten me. His ears were long and hung to his middle back. He had fur that was short and light mottled brown." ["Markets"]

Mr. Kangaroo first showed up when Randy's family moved into a new house. He only appeared in the boy's bedroom or in the hall near his door. His appearance did not frighten Randy—quite the opposite. The two talked for hours, and the marsupial played with Randy's toys. And if something upset Randy . . .

A kid named Jerry called one day and made fun of the boy because he owned many *Star Wars* figures and Randy didn't. Even as they spoke, "a voice came over the phone telling him to shut up or he would get hurt." Then the line went dead. Despite this incident, Jerry came a week later to stay overnight. Jerry had no sooner climbed into the upper section of Randy's bunk bed than he flopped down to the floor. He accused Randy of pushing him out. Randy denied it.

Then one day Randy's sister wanted to play in his room. Randy was none too keen on this idea, but their mother told him to allow her in. Soon enough, the sister broke a toy car. The boy did nothing, but the girl ran screaming for Mom, saying "the monster was going to eat her." Evidently a "monster" had appeared behind Randy "and opened its mouth and licked its teeth, then pointed at her." Randy explained about Mr. Kangaroo, but despite his sister's testimony, he was put in a corner for lying.

At age seven, Randy contracted a severe case of chicken pox. He could not even set his feet on the floor. "I pushed myself on a big yellow truck to get around," he wrote, but most of the time he was too weak even for that. He asked Mr. Kangaroo to bring him things, and despite his fear of the outside world the imaginary playmate from Down Under would go for them. Once Randy was caught with a bottle of soda pop and scolded by his mother for fetching it in his condition. Randy claimed, "I didn't even have the strength to hold it hardly, much less push myself out on my truck" to retrieve it.

As an adult, Randy stuck to his guns. "He was not a figment of my imagination, he was an actual entity." Even his disbelieving mother thought she saw "something" in his room on occasion, but it did not bother her. "I always felt that you were safe in your room, like someone was watching over you."

Randy's mother's observation underlines a factor about "imaginary" companions I find heartening. Over the past 30 years it seems that more and more phantasms, cryptids, and other strange entities have been reported, each more frightening than the one before. Chupacabras, the Bray Road Beast and other "Dogmen," Black-Eyed Kids, Shadow People, gargoyles—the list is long and terrifying. Even the familiar old Sasquatch has been accused of molestations and attacks unknown (or at least unreported) a few decades ago.

QCCs are the exception to this trend. "To date, I have not come across a single instance of a QCC intentionally causing harm or distress to an experient," Hallowell stated plainly in *Invizikids* (p. 54).

SOURCES:

Hallowell, Michael J. *Invizikids* (Wymeswold, Loughborough, UK: Heart of Albion Press, 2007).

Ibid. "Jok Zottle and the Invizikids," *Fortean Times* no. 250 (Special edition 2009), pp. 30-35.

"Markets," "Mr. Kangaroo," on "Obiwan's UFO-Free Paranormal Page," uploaded March 10, 1999: http://ufofreeparanormal.com/stories/viewstory.php?sid=658

WISCONSIN WEREWOLF—AND ODD THINGS ABOUT ELKS

In the early 1990s, I wrote a werewolf novel. I love to sprinkle my stories with references to actual paranormal cases, so I wanted the protagonists to mention genuine werewolf tales during the narrative. The problem was, I couldn't find any.

There were plenty of legends during the middle ages, of course, but after the "Beast of Gevaudan" in the eighteenth century, the were-well ran dry. There was the "Bray Road Beast" in Wisconsin in 1991; a Mrs. Delburt Gregg of Greggton, Texas, claimed to have awakened one night in March 1960 to find that "a huge, shaggy, wolf-like creature was clawing at the screen and glaring at me with baleful, glowing, slitted eyes" [Gregg, p. 222] A few ambiguous "Bigfoot" reports told of shaggy beasts with clawed fingers, long fangs and/or pointed ears. Sasquatch hunter John Green dismissed such details as newspapers trying to spice up Bigfoot accounts, and what was good enough for Green was good enough for me. There hardly seemed to be any modern werewolf reports.

In the years since, however, the subject of "Dogmen" (huge bipedal canines that resemble Hollywood werewolves) has grown exponentially. Unidentified canids, most able to walk and run on their hind legs, have been reported in Wisconsin, Michigan, New York, Maine, Alabama, Tennessee, Oklahoma, Georgia, and many other states, as well as England and Australia. There have been many books on the subject, several written by Wisconsin journalist Linda S. Godfrey, and there is at least one podcast devoted entirely to Dogmen (Vic Cundiff's *Dogman Encounters*, which is close to its six hundredth episode at this writing).

Why the upsurge of unknown canid reports in the past quarter century? Have they been living in our wilderness areas all this time, or are they arriving from somewhere else? A bizarre Dogman report from Wisconsin implies that the creatures might be able to distort the three dimensions we usually assume to be immutable.

The aforementioned Linda Godfrey received a report concerning a 35-year-old man and his son. Late in 2004, the witnesses were driving from Eau Claire to Mondovi, Wisconsin, when they found State Route 37 blocked by snowdrifts. They were forced to take a small dirt road through the woods.

The father worked his Ford Contour through the forest, although the engine kept dying every few hundred feet. Finally, the two reached a point they recognized: Clairemont Avenue, a major thoroughfare in the area.

Now the first of several strange events occurred: The father and son decided to eat at a Blimpie's restaurant on Garfield Avenue, but when they turned from Clairemont onto Garfield– they found themselves on the narrow country road again!

More than a little confused, the father rolled on—and again the engine kept dying. Then an enormous elk jumped into the road.

"It towered over the Ford Contour sedan," reported Linda Godfrey, adding, "It looked in at the father and son and snorted so hard that steam came from its nostrils."

Five other monstrous elk joined it, and they ran across the road and back into the woods. They possessed very long antlers with few points and otherwise did not look normal. The father called them "cartoonish," whatever that might mean.

The witnesses finally reached another road and drove back toward SR 37. Incredibly, when they turned onto the highway, they found themselves on the dirt road in the woods again with their motor still periodically stalling out.

The weirdness factor continued to climb. After rounding a sharp corner, the father noticed something entering the road about 90 feet behind them. It was a gigantic canine of some sort that walked with a "swagger." The creature rose up on its hind legs—then the Ford died again. As if taking advantage of the humans' distress, it dropped to all fours and charged them.

The motor turned over just in time, and the Contour lurched away. The beast followed, running sometimes on four legs and sometimes on

Wisconsin Werewolf—And Odd Things about Elks

two. Eventually, it gave up and melted back into the forest. The terrified witnesses once again found a street they recognized, and this time they made it all the way home. [Godfrey, pp. 169–171]

The woods around Eau Claire seem to qualify as a small Window Area. A few weeks before this nightmare trip, the man and his son, with the wife along this time, were driving along Route 10 when a black triangular UFO "as long as a football field" passed over them. Strange lights also followed the vehicle occasionally. Other Dogman creatures have been reported in the area.

As for the huge elks, David Paulides of *Missing 411* has always noted strange coincidences in missing people cases: similar names of victims, people hundreds of miles apart disappearing within days of one another, terrible storms arising within hours of a person vanishing, etc. In some of his later books, Paulides noticed a new detail: a lot of rural disappearances of human beings involved *elks* in one way or another.

1. Arthur Dillon Jordan traveled to Seely Lake, Montana, in October 1959 to hunt elk. He phoned his wife frequently during hunting trips, and when he stopped calling in early November she reported him missing. After two weeks of searching by dozens of volunteers, Jordan's pickup and camp were found. Wherever Jordan had gone, he had left behind his .30-06 rifle, his hunting jacket, and most of his clothing. The *Daily Interlake* newspaper reported, "Thirty-four searchers tracked through the snow-covered Seely Lake country. They found remains of an elk with one quarter missing." Did whoever or whatever take Jordan also take the elk quarter? Why only a quarter? [Paulides, pp. 146–147]

2. In September 1982, James Schroeder, 23, and two companions, David Benesh and Dan Cummings, all from Wisconsin, drove out to a wilderness camp northeast of Grangeville, Idaho, to hunt elk. After two days of hunting and camping, James rose at 6:00 A.M. and announced he was going after an elk alone. He took only his 7mm rifle and 13 rounds. "The two hunting partners reported that they told James to take a hat, matches, food, and other supplies. He refused." [Paulides, p. 62] The young hunter marched off into the woods and was never seen again. Why on Earth had he refused to take even the most basic survival items with him?

3. In the autumn of 1951, Roy Agee, a 63-year-old attorney, went elk hunting with a friend seven miles east of Elk City (!), Idaho. On the afternoon of October 1, Agee waited on a high point as his companion hiked across the valley and drove elk toward him. The partner returned to their camp afterwards, expecting to find Agee there. Agee never returned. He was never seen again. "Sev-

eral hunters have gone missing from this general area, which is associated with elk hunting," remarked Paulides [p. 49]

4. William R. "Russ" Lyons was a Vietnam and Korean War veteran trained in survival techniques. On October 9, 1986, Lyons met up with his brother-in-law Tom Bechard and his friend Fred Taskar in Durango, Colorado. They drove to the San Juan National Forest, 20 miles north, to go elk hunting. On the 11th the men split up, each out on their own to bag a wapiti (elk). Fred and Tom eventually returned to camp. The well-trained veteran Lyons never came back. Search and rescue operations lasted only three days due to extreme weather: 30 inches of wet snow that fell during the search (which triggered several avalanches) and temperatures as low as eight degrees Fahrenheit. The only possible clue to Lyons' fate turned out to be a false lead. A military helicopter flying over Sliderock Mountain passed a line of footprints. The crew followed the trail, hoping it would lead them to Lyons. It did not. The would-be rescuers had been led astray by an elk. [p. 33]

SOURCES:

Godfrey, Linda S. *Michigan Dogman* (Eau Claire, WI: Unexplained Research Publishing Company, 2010).

Gregg, Delburt, "Werewolf of Greggton," in Kenner, Corrine, and Craig Miller, *Strange But True* (Woodbury, MN: Llewellyn Publications, 1997).

Paulides, David. *Missing 411: Hunters* (North Charleston, SC: CreateSpace, 2016).

EPILOGUE:
THE UNCLASSIFIED RESIDUUM

The late physicist and editor William R. Corliss called it "the Unclassified Residuum," the body of reports made by competent and careful observers of events that do not fit into reality the way the edicts of logic and science wish them to. We have touched upon many such observations in this volume, and at the end this author admits to leaving a residue of this residue behind on his metaphoric desk.

Still, on the most basic level we cannot truly define what a ghost is, or a Sasquatch, so we cannot with confidence wall anomalous phenomena off into air-tight categories.

Besides, how does one categorize, for instance, a penguin that wants you to eat your bread crusts?

When Mr. Anthony Purcell of Chelmsford, Essex, was about six years old (approximately in 1958), he often slept in his parents' bed, one parental unit stretched out like a protective barrier to either side. Down beyond the foot of the bed stood the elder Purcells' wardrobe.

One night (after awakening, Anthony assures us), the boy watched a circle of light appear on the wardrobe door and expand until it was a yard in diameter. The face of an ordinary man coalesced in the circle and began giving some sort of news report, the subject of which Purcell forgot over the years (or perhaps it was just beyond the understanding of a six-year-old).

Eventually, the newscaster finished his report and announced, "The moment you've been waiting for has arrived!" Whereupon he introduced "the Penguin."

Then a penguin as large as a grown human being wriggled out of the circular "TV screen" and waddled around to Mrs. Purcell's side of the bed. It bent over the sleeping form of Anthony's mother, then "it poked its beak in my face and told me that if I didn't start eating my crusts (something my mother had constantly nagged me to do) it would return and eat me!"

The penguin waddled back to the circle of light and slid in. Absurdly, there came a fanfare-like burst of music and the light faded.

Predictably, young Anthony woke his parents and told them of the horrific event. Equally predictably, they dismissed the threatening Antarctic avian as a dream. The boy insisted there was an uninterrupted flow of waking reality before, during, and after "the Penguin."

> I accepted the incident as real for probably more than 20 years; had someone asked me if I had really been visited by a nocturnal flightless bird with an interest in my eating bread crusts, I would unhesitatingly have said yes. [Purcell, pp.154–155]

That staid old British publication *The Fortean Times* printed well-meaning letters from its readers who calmly explained that Mr. Purcell was misremembering the "Penguin on the Telly" sketch from *Monty Python's Flying Circus*. Mr. Purcell responded that his experience occurred over a decade before that seminal British comedy hit the airwaves. (I would add that his age is an important factor in this chronology; in my memory, my life at age six is eons away and light-years different from life at age 17.) The paranormal TV show also stood out because it was in color, years before any ordinary family owned a color set.

So how would we treat this? Call it a dream anyway? A hypnopompic illusion? A not-so-friendly imaginary playmate? Entities from space or another dimension playing a joke?

Some accounts of zooform beings are irritatingly abrupt. In 1992, Stanley Shoop of Elstree, Hertfordshire, sent a brief note to the omnipresent *Fortean Times*. When he was five or six—"almost 60 years ago," so probably

Epilogue: The Unclassified Residuum

the mid-1930s—Stanley and this twin brother visited their grandparents' creepy habitation. "My grandparents lived in an old house with a very dark basement reached by a steep flight of steps behind a door." This architectural arrangement was deemed so dangerous the Shoop boys were forbidden even to open the basement door.

So, that was just what young Stanley did one fine day. Something stood there right at the top of the stairs that was large enough to fill the doorframe. "It gave me the fright of my life. I was looking at Mickey Mouse!" [Shoop, p. 147].[1]

Did young Master Shoop slam the door? Flee the house? Refuse to visit his grandparents ever again? He just ends with: "When I was not much older and wiser, I knew that I couldn't possibly have seen a fictional character, but at that time—and to this day—the figure was very real." A penguin—or any other creature—seen in the middle of the night from bed could be a dream or hypnopompic vision, however real it seems. But what about a larger-than-life Mickey Mouse appearing right in your face? Assuming Mr. Shoop wrote the truth, logic and sanity suggest a trick played on the boy. A poster hanging down in the dark staircase? A huge dummy balanced there? We will never know.

Over 30 years ago, I wrote a long, rambling, scatterbrained paper entitled "Multiple Murder in Conjunction with Fortean Events." It was so muddled and overwritten I made it a joke in my own fiction, the author of that thesis feeling embarrassed whenever a new character admits to having read it.

I don't learn from my mistakes, apparently, because I started kicking around the idea of cryptids and supernatural animals being attracted to serial killers or vice-versa.

The December 1964 issue of *Fate Magazine* presented a newspaper clipping the editors had received from a reader. They printed it even though it was undated and unattributed, and it has popped up in books on the unexplained ever since. The clipping tells of two young people camping on the

---

[1] To add to the horror, it was probably that silent-era "Rickey Rat" version of the character.

slopes of Mount Tamalpais in Marin County, California, who were "disturbed" on three separate occasions by two bipedal, lion-like humanoids. (To be accurate, they saw only one lion-person, but it "chittered" back and forth with a second that stayed out of sight in the woods.) One witness, Paul Conant, described the visible one as standing about five feet tall and weighing possibly 200 pounds. "Its head was close to its body and below the shoulders it was very muscular. No ears could be seen."

Mount Tamalpais was haunted from 1979 onward by the "Trailside Killer," a serial murderer documented by Robert Graysmith, author of *Zodiac*. John Kane, elderly husband of first victim Edda Kane, searched the mountain trails after Edda went missing on August 19, 1979. Perhaps some odd critter still roamed Mount Tam: "Suddenly there was a noise in the brush. John stepped quickly back. Something, some animal, appeared in the path ahead of him. The only impression the distraught man had was one of fierceness—man and unknown beast observing each other. Whatever animal it was plunged into the thicket and was gone." [Graysmith 1990, p. 52]

Or perhaps zooforms and murderers are drawn to certain areas, both feeling a power of place, *à la* ley lines. If so, Mount Diablo, California, is such a place.

First of all, writers such as Loren Coleman and David Paulides point out the correlation between "devil"-related place names and strange occurrences. The implication is that paranormal and/or disastrous events have occurred in such areas for generations, and people in olden times accordingly named them for His Satanic Majesty.

Second, the uncaught serial killer "Zodiac" chose Mt. Diablo as the center of his "co-ordinates," his killings occurring along lines running out from radians (an angular measure approximately equal to 57.3 degrees) measured around that mountain. "Did he stand like a king on top of the double-peaked mountain at night, the Bay Area spread beneath his feet, surrounded by a sky filled with all the actual symbols of astrology?" asked Robert Graysmith in the aforementioned *Zodiac* (1986).

Third, a phantom panther has been reported on the mountain and in nearby Devil's Hole (!) in Las Trampas Regional Park. "Well, ordinary mountain lions dwell in California," the voice of logic says. Witnesses describe the Mt. Diablo cat as a black panther, however, and black panthers, of course, are not a species unto themselves.

Beyond these examples, however, correlations seemed to peter out. David Berkowitz, the New York gunman better known as Son of Sam, reputedly took his orders to kill from a neighbor's black dog—a whole book could be devoted to the black dog phenomenon; perhaps in a future volume. Cary Stayner, the Yosemite Killer, claimed to be obsessed with Bigfoot, but I don't think he claimed to have actually *seen* a Sasquatch while stalking his victims in that national park. I believe I will leave killers and cryptids as a "stub" for now, as they say on Wikipedia.

Here is a story old enough to be safe from investigation. On July 31, 1899, the *Virginia Evening News* reprinted "A Tale from the Mysterious East" from the *Times of Burma:*

> A few months ago near Shwebo the villagers heard a strange and mysterious voice in the jungle uttering in Burmese these words, "I am going to lay," which were repeated frequently several times a day for many days. Eventually the egg was laid [by what?] and its size is said to exceed that of ten large paddy baskets. Nobody will go near this egg, from which now come the words, "I am going to hatch," also repeated many times every day.

This is certainly a bizarre tidbit from long ago and far away. The implication is that this egg had actually been seen somewhere in the rain forest, though people feared to go near it. Did it hatch, releasing a Roc out of the Arabian nights?

Perhaps this odd newspaper anecdote can be tied to another brief but weird account: In early June 1985, "Four huge depressions, eight feet long, five wide and 16 feet across were found in a maize field outside Milan [Italy]," announced the *Fortean Times*. The ground markings were discovered by a farmer named Gianpiero Baizi, who quickly alerted the police, and within days they became a tourist attraction.

"They were the exact shape of a chicken's footprint, but enormous," Baizi said, "as if some gigantic bird had swooped down, landed, and taken off again."

The farmer admitted he was terrified. My advice: Keep watching the skies!

Back in the 1980s, Trivial Pursuit was the hottest board game around, and no one had smart phones to look up the answers. One Saturday night, yours truly and the guys I wasted time with played this new trivia game instead of Dungeons & Dragons or Star Fleet Battles. We were all reasonably intelligent, the cream of the crop of Bixby [OK] High School—faint praise though that may be.

One fellow—who I'll call "Gerald"—got a question that read something like "Name a class of animals with six legs." He was utterly bemused and gave up. The answer was "Insects." At this revelation, Gerald suffered an emotional meltdown.

"Insects aren't animals!" he yelled. "This has got to be a misprint! A mistake! I've been cheated!"

I was genuinely puzzled.

"If insects aren't animals, then what are they?" I asked.

"They're—insects!" Gerald shot back.

"Look, pal," I said, "we've got the animal kingdom and the plant kingdom. And a couple of weird kingdoms created for some primitive microorganisms. But basically living entities are divided into animals and plants."

No amount of argument would assuage my friend. He complained all night about the Trivial Pursuit question. I thought his Quixotic stubbornness strange at the time, but over the years I've met other people who refuse to admit that insects—or spiders, fish, lizards or birds—are "animals."

I've covered mammals, birds, reptiles, and even fish in this book, but not insects. I think this final anecdote from Frank Hamel's *Human Animals* will rectify that oversight.

Hamel's story about a nasty supernatural insect was translated from a volume called *Superstitions et Survivances* (1896) by someone named Berenger-Feraud. In a house near Toulon, France, a woman had been sitting up with her father, who was very old and sick. Several neighbors visited to help out and allow the daughter some much needed rest. As she talked to them in the kitchen, the old man cried out in pain and fear. Everyone ran to the bedroom and found "a huge stinging-fly which hovered round and round him, buzzing in a horrible manner."

The insect was so huge and aggressive that the visitors were loath to get near it. It landed on the old man again and again, causing him to scream in pain. "Those who were near him could see large black blisters rising at the spots where the stinging-fly attacked him." Finally, one of the men knocked the monster insect to the floor with his hat, picked it up with a pair of tongs, and threw it outside.

To everyone's horror, "they could plainly hear the buzz of the insect outside. The noise was so loud that the windows positively rattled. Then a howl arose outside, a cry so strange that no one present ever heard the like." Silence followed, but now the visitors asked to stay the night because no one wanted to go outside with the giant fly! The old man could only say that he woke to the insect's buzz and that it started attacking him.

The next morning, the people in the cottage finally ventured out. The insect lay dead on the ground. It did not appear to be a real insect, "but merely its outer shell or covering, just like the skin sloughed by a grasshopper and left behind." The general consensus was that it was the creation of a sorcerer, and the "howl" was the evil magician's cry of anger at being thwarted. [Hamel, p. 248]

SOURCES:

"Food of the Gods?," *Fortean Times* no. 46 (Spring 1986), p. 29, quoting London *Sunday Express*, June 9, 1985.

Graysmith, Robert. *Sleeping Lady* (New York: Dutton, 1990).

———. *Zodiac* (New York: Berkeley Publishing, 1986).

Hamel, Frank. *Human Animals* (New York: University books, 1969 [1915]).

Muirhead, Richard, "I Am Going to Hatch [letter]," *Fortean Times* no. 358 (October 2017), p. 74.

Purcell, Anthony, "Listen to the Penguin," in Sieveking, Paul, and Jen Ogilvie, *It Happened to Me* Vol. 1 (London: Dennis Publishing, 2008).

Shoop, Stanley, "Disneyfication of Terror," in Sieveking and Ogilvie, *op cit.*

www.ingramcontent.com/pod-product-compliance
Lightning Source LLC
Chambersburg PA
CBHW060454030426
42337CB00015B/1580